SHE SLEEPS WITH DOGS

HANNAH STEVENS

Verde Press

Also by Hannah Stevens

The President's Wife

Madam POTUS

To Lily and Sophie, my best friends
And all of the dogs that have passed through my life

Chapter 1
A New Year

It was mid-January and the hangover from holiday celebrations had long worn off. Although, last year, there were few celebrations. It was a year of loss for Jasmine. She'd lost her job in October and her best friend, her big red Doberman, just the month before. Losing her job was devastating; she could always get another job, she thought. Her dog could not be replaced.

But now Jasmine was finding that losing a job in a time of recession was more serious than she had first thought. In prior years, when she had been laid off, she was always able to find another job within a couple of months. IT professionals, computer programmers, were always in demand. She knew this time would be different. So now the game was to scramble and figure out how she could stay solvent with little or no income. Her company had given her two weeks severance pay and another two weeks vacation pay that she was due, and that had carried her through December. Now she would be living on Unemployment Insurance which amounted to a grand total of $1000 a month, and anyone knows that, in today's economy, that amount of money will not cover the bills.

The first thing Jasmine did the day she was laid off was sit down at her kitchen table and make out a budget, but no matter how hard she tried she couldn't make the money stretch until the end of the month. Single and living alone, Jasmine didn't require a huge amount to live on, but everything was expensive these days. She allocated seventy-five dollars a week for food. Could she cut that to fifty dollars if she ate meatless meals three days out of the week? Jasmine started collecting store coupons and watching the Wednesday food market ads to find the best deals of the week, something she had never done before; — hadn't had the time and didn't need to. Now she had enough time, but little money. Fortunately, her house was paid for and she had some savings from her 401K. When she had bought the small ranch style home in North Central Phoenix, banks were hesitant to grant mortgages to women and since Jasmine had a lump sum settlement, along with short term alimony from Richard, her ex husband, she just paid cash for her home. At the time she thought that this would be her haven and she could weather any recession or layoffs. Little did she know that she would need that haven so soon.

Even though she had no house payment, she did have a student loan. And there were utilities; low in January in Arizona, but air conditioning in the summer months in the 100 degree-plus heat is expensive. And property taxes, telephone and automobile cost, insurance, and on and on..... she was overwhelmed. She stopped the newspaper, canceled her land line phone, and looked at every other cost to see where she could pare down. When she did, she found that she had already been living in austerity and there wasn't much else she could cut. She wouldn't be eating out or going to movies — and definitely would not be going to Europe this year.

Jasmine thought back to the fateful day her boss called her into his office. She was busily writing code to finish up a project and she thought he was going to review her work. Frank was half her age, balding and overweight, but he was an okay boss, fair and even most of the time. And Jasmine always made sure that her work was of a high quality and done on time.

Frank motioned for her to sit in the chair opposite him. She noticed that he was frowning and knew that was a bad sign. He heaved a sigh and then said, "Jasmine, I am sorry to say that I'm going to have to lay you off." He paused. "This wasn't my decision and it isn't because you're doing a bad job. We're having what you call a reduction of our workforce, and others in the company are being laid off today as well."

The tears rolled down her cheeks. "Could I work part time?" Jasmine asked. No, he said, that wouldn't be possible. "I'll take a cut in pay," Jasmine pleaded. "I'm sorry, Jasmine," Frank repeated as he told her to pack up her things and be out of the office as soon as possible and without talking to anyone.

Jasmine went back to her desk and just sat there for a few minutes, not believing this was happening to her. Carol the receptionist came by her cubicle. "It's happened to you too?" she said. "I don't know what I'm going to do. I'll lose my health insurance and that can't happen right now." Carol was the only one in the office who was older than Jasmine. She had cancer and was on chemotherapy. The ravages of the treatment were showing in how thin she was.

Jasmine didn't know what to say. "I'm so sorry, Carol, but it wasn't your fault," she finally said, hoping that her words would be of some comfort to Carol — but knowing otherwise.

Jasmine found a box in the storage room and put the pictures of her daughter and her dogs, her calendar and other personal belongings into it. As she cleaned out her file drawers, she got angrier by the minute. Why was she being laid off? She worked hard, was always on time or even early, put in more hours every week than was required. Why her and not the others? She cleaned all of her files off of her computer and all evidence of her Internet activity in temp files. Maybe she should just delete all of the work she'd done that week. That would show them. But no, that wouldn't help her get her job back. If she ever wanted to work there again, sabotaging her work now would not help in any way.

Gathering up her boxes and loading them into her car, she drove the twenty-one miles to her home in North Central Phoenix in a fog. What a miserable day, she thought. The worst day of my life.

But when she got home, she flew into action. Sitting down and feeling sorry for herself would not be helpful, she thought.

The next order of business was to contact her recruiter and register with on-line employment sites. She also joined LinkedIn, hoping to connect with people there who were looking for programmers or who knew someone who was. And then she applied for unemployment benefits. She marveled how easy it was these days to do everything on line. Hurrah for the Internet, her best friend.

How long would it take for her to be back in the grind again, she wondered? Would she never find another job in her field again?

After her divorce ten years ago from Richard, her husband of fifteen years, Jasmine, a stay-home mom, had gone back to school and learned computer skills and how to be a computer programmer. Jobs were plentiful in this field at the time and the pay was good. Richard was skeptical that she could do this; he'd always thought of Jasmine as being a scatter brain, a bit ditzy. But she would show him. She did well in school and soon found an entry-level position with the state that paid better than any other job she had ever had.

That was ten years ago, although it seemed like a century. So here she was again looking to find a way to support herself and unsure as to how she could do that. She searched for jobs every day, sending out resumes and hoping to hear back from at least one of these companies. This is not the '90's, she thought. When Jasmine lost a job in '99, she sent out a resume and had three interviews and as many offers in a week's time. But now it was different. America was suffering from the largest recession since the 1930's. Millions of people were looking for work, and they were all competing for the very few jobs available. Surely she could find something; IT, Information Technology was at the core of every business — most companies could not function without it.

As she continued her job search, she was fast becoming a recluse. After years of going to an office where she'd interacted with co-workers, she now got up in the morning, turned on the morning news on the tele and then turned on her computer. Still in her pajamas, she played computer games for an hour before sending out more resumes.

Jasmine felt like a rudderless ship at sea. There was no structure to her life. And she was beginning to feel worthless. No one wanted her. But then she would give herself a lecture; it wasn't her fault. And she was a valuable person. Her job didn't define who she was as a person. Even if she didn't get another job, she was still a person of worth. What is it in this country she thought, that you are judged by the work you do? I am generous and loving, she thought. And I have many talents. Doesn't that count for something?

She walked or jogged every day and went to the grocery store and did other errands, trying to stay positive. Every Friday she went to the nearby Costco at noon to buy food at a discount and then partake of the food demos of the day. There were mini-hamburgers, pizza, and cereal fruit cookie bars and fruit juices. Free food for the taking and a carnival atmosphere to go with it. She enjoyed mingling with the families with small children, teens to seniors. The diversity was wonderful; the rainbow of skin colors a delight to see.

But for the most part she stayed at home . . . alone. Most of her friends were from work, and fortunately for them, most were working and had little time to spend with Jasmine. And she missed her dogs terribly.

After a month of this routine she knew she had to do something. As she was having her morning coffee she put together a plan. I know what I'll do, she thought to herself. I'll go to the Humane Society and volunteer. That way I can be with dogs and I'll meet people and maybe make new friends. "And who knows, maybe I'll even find a dog that will want to come home and live with me," she said out loud.

That very Wednesday, Jasmine put on a pair of jeans, a t-shirt and her sneakers and drove the five miles from her home to the closest Humane Society facility on West Hatcher Road. When she arrived in the parking lot, she saw that there were two entrances, one for Intake and one for Adoption. She entered the Intake area first. She saw a young couple standing at the counter with a medium-sized, brown mixed-breed dog on a leash. They were obviously relinquishing this sweet little animal. She overheard the man saying that they were moving out of their house and couldn't keep the dog in an apartment. How sad for that dog, she thought. But then better to bring the dog here than to dump it in the desert which is what some people do. She turned around and went out the door and into the adoption area, approached a man at the front desk and asked about volunteering.

"Go through that door over there," he said pointing his finger, "and then go to the next door on your left and that is the volunteer office."

"Thank you," she said as she passed an older couple filling out forms, hopefully to adopt a pet. Maybe they'll take home the little dog that those other people were bringing in. Jasmine never understood how people could give up their pets so easily. Her dogs were like her children; when she took on a new pet, it was for life, regardless of whether she was moving or having a baby. That pet was part of the family. And you just don't get rid of family.

Jasmine went through the door she was directed to and found the volunteer office. She walked inside and saw two women, both past middle age and matronly, sorting papers..

"I would like to volunteer," she blurted out. "I have experience with dogs and cats too, for that matter."

"Well, before you volunteer, you have to sign up for our Orientation class, and they're probably full right now," said the heavier woman with short gray hair at the far desk.

"Must be a lot of people volunteering these days with so many out of work," Jasmine said and both women chuckled. She asked where she could sign up, and when the woman asked if she had a computer at home she said yes.

"Go home, get on line, go to our web site and you can sign up there," the other woman told her.

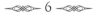

Feeling dejected, she left the building to go back to her small house in her north Phoenix neighborhood, a house she had lived in for more than ten years now. Can't get a job. Can't even get a volunteer job, she thought. What to do now? Well, I'll just see when I can get into that class, she said to herself. But maybe there is another way that I can volunteer in the meantime.

Chapter 2
A New Life

Jasmine Martinez Jorgenson was born in a small town in Southern Minnesota. Her mother, Carlotta Martinez, the daughter of a migrant worker brought to the area from Southern California to work in the Birds Eye processing plant one summer, met and married the son of the local mayor, creating a scandal for years. As she grew up in this nearly all-white community, Jasmine, named by her mother after the exotic fragrant flower, always felt inferior to her peers. Her skin, the color of mocha coffee, her hair and eyes mahogany brown, she stood out amongst her blond haired, blue eyed friends of Nordic and Swedish heritage. Carlotta always told her that she was special and that she should never feel second-rate to anyone. "I gave you my last name as part of your name, Jasmine. I don't want you to ever forget where you came from. We are a proud, hard-working people."

But if Jasmine felt uncomfortable with her friends, she shouldn't have. They called her JJ when she went to high school, and her best friend Carol told her one day that all of the other girls were envious of her Latin looks. And she had many admiring young male friends by the time she'd reached eighth grade. This of course created another problem for Carlotta who told her unequivocally that she would not be allowed to date until she was sixteen. In Mexico Jasmine would have had the celebration of quinceañera, a coming-of-age party for young Latinas upon their fifteenth birthday, but her father Dale, would not allow it. So both her mother and her father told her that her grades were the most important thing in her life right now and boys could come later. Jasmine knew that she, along with most of her friends, was college-bound and she had better keep her grades up. And she did. Through many evenings of math and English tutoring from her father, Jasmine pleased her parents by bringing home mostly A's and some B's. She was a beautiful young woman, but she was also very bright and upon graduation from high school, she had been accepted at three prestigious universities, Stanford and Berkeley on the West Coast and Columbia University in New York City. Jasmine chose Berkeley. She felt that she would fit in with the other students. She knew she didn't want go to New York and she felt that Stanford was out of her league.

Jasmine moved to Phoenix for a job opportunity after divorcing her husband of fourteen years, Richard Bailey. The marriage had never been strong, and friends and family predicted they would break up long before they did.

Five years into the marriage, Jasmine discovered that Richard was dallying with his secretary and after some research found that this wasn't the first time. They had marriage counseling for a year, but Richard wasn't about to change. From all appearances he preferred other women to Jasmine and that was hurtful to her. But she understood. Richard was Ivy League, a graduate of Dartmouth College with a master's degree in business. His field was hospital administration and he went on to become one of the top administrators in the country. He was a working machine; driven, precise and controlling. And Jasmine, diametrically the opposite, was an artist and a writer, graduating from U.C. Berkeley with degrees in Humanities and Art History. After her marriage, she took up landscape painting and played with writing and even had a poem published in the Oakland Tribune.

Richard never placed much value on her pursuits. He kept telling her that artists didn't make much money, and that is what counted for him. Therefore Jasmine always felt diminished as a person in his eyes. And she needed to change that.

One might wonder how these two very different people came to be married at all. They must have had a commonality at some time, and certainly they did. Jasmine and Richard met while skiing at Lake Tahoe early one December. Jasmine was staying with four of her college friends in a small cabin they had rented for the weekend on the North Shore. They were part of a larger group from various colleges across the country, all friends and acquaintances who met for this ski weekend every year at this time. The snow was good and the prices were low. The group of half a dozen or more, which varied from year to year, skied together and partied together. Jasmine and Richard might never have met, had they not literally run into each other at the bottom of the bunny hill of the Homewood Ski Area on Jasmine's first day of skiing.

"Why didn't you get out of the way," shouted Jasmine.

"You skied right into me," Richard returned. "You were just bombing down that hill, not watching where you were going. You're out of control, girl."

"Don't call me 'girl'," Jasmine blurted out, anger flashing in her dark eyes. Richard laid his head back down on the snow and she thought he might be injured. "Are you okay?"

"Yes, of course I'm okay. I'm a tough guy. It takes more than a little girl like you to knock me out."

Jasmine was fuming now.

"And *you're* supposed to be watching out for *me*," continued Richard, who was a beginner skier.

Jasmine got up, brushed the snow off her ski pants, and pulled her ski hat over her long brunette hair. Then she looked at Richard and started to laugh. It was contagious, and Richard started laughing as well.

"I'm sorry. I just hate this part of the hill. It's so dangerous for everyone," said Jasmine.

Richard looked at Jasmine's olive skin and her lithe little body tucked into tight ski pants. "You could make it up to me by having a drink with me," Richard said.

This guy was being very forward, Jasmine thought and she was caught off guard. Then she took another look at him. He was good looking. His face had high cheek bones with a strong nose, piercing blue eyes, along with an athletic body; a turn on for her. "Yes, well …. okay."

And a drink led to dinner and dinner led to another date the next night and the next. On their last night together they fell into bed. When Jasmine took off her tie-dyed t-shirt and ragged jeans, Richard saw the body he had always dreamed of. Their lovemaking was the most exciting of his life. Jasmine gave Richard her phone number but never expected to hear from him again.

The phone rang the day she arrived back at her apartment in Berkeley. It was Richard calling from Reno, where he was living and working as an assistant hospital administrator. He asked when he could see her again. And that was the beginning of their long and torturous relationship.

Richard drove to Oakland every weekend and the long drive was getting to him so he started to look for work closer to where Jasmine lived. After several months he secured the assistant hospital administrator job with Highland Hospital in East Oakland, and they were married a year later. They bought a lovely home in the Oakland hills, overlooking the Bay and Jasmine brought home a black Labrador puppy, hoping that Richard liked dogs as well as she did. Fortunately for the puppy and for Jasmine, he did. They named the male puppy Jackson after Michael Jackson and settled into marital bliss. It was a happy time for both of them.

Baby Celeste, the image of her mother, arrived a year after that, and Jasmine was a stay-at-home mom for the next four years of her married life. But then she became restless and thought it was time for her to launch her career. Celeste was in pre-school part of the day, leaving Jasmine the time to have at least a part-time job. Richard was against it. He told her that she could not be a good mother and have a job too. He was the breadwinner in the family and made enough for Jasmine to stay home and play the housewife/mother role full time. But Jasmine knew that she would in fact be a better mother if she had a career of her own.

She gravitated to the Berkeley Art Museum where she had been volunteering for over a year, hoping that one day they would hire her. This was her first love. And she painted every day in water colors and was showing and selling some of her work from local art galleries along the waterfront.

That seemed so long ago, but the memories were sweet. And now here she was, without a job, not even a volunteer job. Jasmine decided if she couldn't get into the Orientation class, she might help out in some other way. She went to the web site for the rescue group and saw that they had a foster program. This is perfect, she thought. She could take in a foster dog. She wanted a dog and there were so many dogs needing homes, even if it was a temporary home, especially with people losing jobs and many times their homes as well. She had a home with a yard and a big heart with lots of love to give. As luck would have it, she was able to register for a foster care orientation the next weekend. And that was how she found Chance.

The Orientation lasted all of a Saturday morning, teaching potential pet foster parents how to care for sick or injured pets; how to give medications, change bandages and put dressings on wounds, and how to feed a sick or injured animal if they were off their food for some reason. These were often special animals that had survived trauma of one kind or another, some physically abused or abandoned.

Later that week they called from the shelter to tell Jasmine that they had a dog for her to foster. Driving to the shelter, she was apprehensive about whether she could handle this. What if the dog was surly and didn't like her? What if it wouldn't eat? What if it messed in the house? She had all of these worries.

She was met by Jason, a heavy-set young man in his early thirties, who would give her the background on the dog that she was about to take home.

"We have a chocolate lab mix for you today. I don't think this dog has been abused, but he was abandoned and hasn't had regular meals for awhile. So you'll want to fatten him up. He seems to be a sweet dog. I don't think he'll bite. And he gets along with other dogs, so if you have another dog at home he should be okay with that."

Jasmine took her written instructions on feeding, a leash, and a collar that the shelter provided and walked to the room where she would meet her new foster dog.

When she entered the room all of her fears melted away. He sat in the corner, his ribs showing and his eyes full of matter. When Jasmine walked over to him, he lay down in submission with his tail between his legs. "I know just how you feel, buddy. I was abandoned too. It's humiliating isn't it?" she said as she reached down and scratched his ears and rubbed the fur on his back.

He rolled over on his back. "Hey, you know I'm going to take care of you for awhile," Jasmine said in a soft voice as she stroked his belly. She figured he was about two years old and had been neutered. When he stood up she commanded him to sit, and he sat. He's had some obedience training, she thought. Jasmine brought her hand down on top of his head and he didn't flinch. She felt that this was a good way to find out if a dog has been hit or physically abused. "Come on fellow, we're going home."

Jasmine had to lift him into the back of her Subaru Outback, and she tied him in to prevent him from disrupting her driving. As she was driving she glanced back at him and saw that he had a concerned look on his face. "It's okay, buddy, we'll be home soon."

When they arrived at Jasmine's house, she untied him, took him out of the car and into the house and immediately into the back yard. "This is your play area. I hope you like it," said Jasmine of the small grassy area in the back yard that she had planted just for her dogs. The rest of the yard had desert landscape to save water. She let him off the lead and he rolled over on his back, then got up and sniffed around in all of the corners. "What a lucky chance for me to find you," Jasmine said as she watched him romp around the yard. "That's what I'll call you. Chance. Do you like that name?" And he came over to her and licked her as if to say yes, he did. And for Chance to have Jasmine was a good thing as well. He could not have found a better, more loving home.

He then ran to the back door which was still open and into the house with Jasmine following. She watched in dismay as he went around the living room lifting his leg on her couch, her antique chair, her writing desk. "Chance," she yelled at him. But he didn't really know this name yet. She promptly dragged him outside by the collar as she shouted, "No, no, no. You can't do that in my house." As she went back into the house to clean up, she thought this is not a good start. But these are strange surroundings for him and he just wants to make it his own.

Fortunately, as the days passed, Chance didn't repeat the marking event and he soon fit into Jasmine's routine, especially the eating part. At first, she had to hand feed him with rice and ground turkey, adding kibble in small amounts. But after a couple of days he ate his kibble ravenously from his dish twice a day. He was beginning to put on some weight and his eyes were brighter. He was a friendly enough dog, wagging his tail in anticipation every time Jasmine opened the back door to go out and check on him or pick up after him. She kept him outside most of the time, as again she didn't want to become too attached to him and then have to give him up. She did bring him in every evening while she read or watched TV. But he slept outside for now, in the big old dog house by the back door that she had used for all of her dogs.

It was now the later part of March, going into April, and Jasmine continued her search for work almost every day. There were jobs, but there were also twenty people in line to take them. Was it time for her to make another career change? With the unemployment insurance she had the cushion to do so. She thought about starting to paint again and selling her paintings to the galleries in Scottsdale and Phoenix. But getting established in the art world would take time, and Jasmine didn't know if she had enough time or the money. Jasmine thought she could also write articles for magazines. She had friends who were freelance writers and they made good money. And that would leave her time to paint as well.

She knew one thing to be true; the longer she was out of work the more she didn't want to go back. The thought of going back to the daily grind of a forty or fifty hour work week made her shiver. She could be her own boss and do things on her own terms. She might be poor for awhile, but she had confidence in her painting and along with the writing, she could do this. She might even open her own gallery. Phoenix was a resort area, the ideal place for this; thousands of people traveled to Arizona in the winter to escape the cold of the northern states. They came from around the world as well. And the desert landscape and evening sunsets were magnificent subjects.

Chance was gaining strength every day now. His chocolate brown coat was becoming full and shiny and his amber eyes were bright and clear. He was getting back the energy that she knew he once had, and they were communicating. When Jasmine talked to him, he seemed to know just what she was saying. His ears stood up and he cocked his head to one side and then the other, all the while focusing his eyes on her. He was beginning to understand her words – "outside," "walk," "dinner." Jasmine bathed him and he, being a water dog, loved it. He loved the attention, too. She cleaned out his ears, clipped his nails, and brushed his teeth. Chance was in dog heaven.

Chance still had some bad habits. He jumped on people and licked them when he greeted them, almost knocking them to the ground. He was just so happy to see everyone. She had to break him of that. No one wants to be jumped on by a sixty-five-pound dog. Jasmine didn't mind the licking, but most other people were a little wary of dog germs. And Chance took Jasmine for a walk instead of the other way around; constantly pulling hard on the leash, which strained her arms.

She worked with him on the jumping and licking, and he was learning. The leash pulling was another matter; he was so exuberant to be out for a walk and wanted to explore everything. This would take some time. Jasmine took him with her on her daily walks and her Saturday four-mile jog because she enjoyed his company. And even though she knew that he was up for adoption, she was becoming attached to him and hoped no one would claim him.

Jasmine was in contact with the shelter almost weekly, and she found out that Chance had been abandoned; they had found him at his home where he had been left by his family weeks before. His food dish had been empty for quite some time, and he was drinking water from the slimy, green swimming pool. His tags had been removed so no one knew his name. Because his former owners were long gone, there was no way they could bring charges.

But people were desperate. When a home is foreclosed, people will find an apartment if they have a job and money or, if not, go to a shelter or to live with relatives. Those were the fortunate ones. Or they could be living on the street, under freeways and in tent cities, as many were these days. Not knowing any other way to find a safe haven for their pets, they simply left them behind hoping that someone would find and take care of them. This might be better than just throwing them out on the street where they would wander for days and then be run over by a car. Some were merely dumped in the desert to fend for themselves, and slowly starve to death or be attacked by rattle snakes or coyotes. The people who were foreclosed on probably hoped that once the bank took over the property, it would be given to a realtor to be put on the market and someone would inspect the property and find the abandoned animal. But this sometimes took weeks, and animals died. Of course, some people were more responsible and either tried to find another home for their pets or took them to the already overflowing shelters.

In any case, Jasmine was glad that she had taken in Chance. He was turning out to be a wonderful pet and companion. He made her laugh and, in these tough times, that was what she needed.

Chapter 3
Chance

I knew something was up when my family started packing everything in the house and loading the trailer in the driveway. Oh good, I thought, we're going to the mountains again. They'd taken me there before on a camping trip and they loaded the car up then with camping gear and food. We had a wonderful time. I ran my legs off in a green meadow and almost caught a rabbit and I swam in a lake and shook all over Bill and Kathy, my humans. I helped the kids with their fishing, picking up the fish for them as they landed on the shore.

But then they filled a bucket with water and opened a bag of my food and put it in the back yard. This is different, I thought. They closed the back door and I heard a truck drive away and then the car. "Hey, didn't you forget somebody?" I barked as they were leaving.

I ate as much food as I could that night and I drank most of my water. They surely are coming back for me. But no, I spent the night alone in my old dog house. The next morning I put another good dent in the food until I was sick. And that night I was alone again. This is sure strange. The next day passed and then the next. The food and water were all gone now. I had to drink out of the pool where we swam in the summer, and it was turning green.

I heard people passing by. "Hey, I'm in here," I barked. "Come and get me." More days went by. I was so hungry, my sides were coming together and I would have eaten anything. I was tired and lonely. I paced along the back fence for hours, but nobody came. I couldn't sleep at night because I thought I had to guard the house and one night I heard people inside making a lot of noise, pounding and ripping on things.

I kept wondering why my family would do this to me. I had held up my part of the bargain, been a clean dog in the house. I guarded the house from intruders, and they were always there waiting to break in and take stuff. I had been happy and playful. I sat when they said sit and came to them when they called; and for that they leave me. What did I do wrong?

Then, and I don't know how many days went by, I heard a key in the lock. Two people walked into the house and looked out the sliding glass window. "Hey, look at this, there's a dog out here. Poor thing, he looks like he's starving. I wonder how long he's been here like this," the man named Stan said to the lady who was with him. The woman, dressed in a light blue suit with a white blouse, started to open the door, but then Stan stopped her. "Better call the pound. He might bite you."

She got on her cell phone and punched a number, talked to someone and then closed the phone. "You're right, Stan. I called the office and had them call the Humane Society and tell them it's an emergency. I just don't get it. Why would people do this to their trusted friend?"

The people left. They didn't rescue me. I would have cried if I could. Hours went by. I was beyond being hungry. I stepped down on the pool steps and lapped at the awful green, smelly, slimy water. I could barely walk now and I was afraid I would fall in and never get out. Then, hours later, I heard the key in the lock again. "Out here," I heard someone say. Then two men in brown uniforms opened the door and stepped out into the yard. They were carrying a long stick with a noose at the end. "I don't think you'll need that," the taller one said.

I walked over to them and barked as best I could. But then I lay down on the ground in front of them. Together they lifted me up and put me in a little compartment in the back of a truck. Now I was really worried. Where were they taking me? But an hour later, they opened the compartment and carried me inside a big building where I heard a lot of other dogs barking and some cats meowing and screeching as well. They put me in a cage, gave me fresh water, and then awhile later they took me to a room where they lay me on a cold, steel table.

"Well, I think we can bring this one back. He's pretty malnourished, but with some good food and some lovin, we can find a good home for him," said the young man in a white coat with a funny thing hanging around his neck. They put a needle attached to a bag hanging from a wire rack in my front leg and then they put me back in the cage. I was too tired to protest.

Later in the day they brought me a dish filled with some mushy food, not like I was used to, and I went over to the dish and sniffed and then went back lay down again. I was so hungry but I couldn't eat. Then later on another girl came by my cage and looked in. "This one's not eating," she said. "Hey big boy, you've got to start eating." And then she opened the cage and took some of the food in her fingers and held it up to my mouth. I turned away. Then she took my head in her hands and opened my mouth and stuffed some of the food in. It tasted pretty good. "Come on fella, dig in. We know you're hungry." I looked at her and then looked at the food and then I took a lick and it tasted pretty good. I then took a big bite and swallowed and then another. "That's it fellow, keep on eating," she said. And, for the first time in a long time, I was not hungry.

Some days later, they took me to a room and in a little while a woman opened the door and came in. She had a soft voice and she petted me on my back and scratched my ears. I liked that so I rolled over for her and she scratched my belly. Then she took me out of the room and put me in her car and we rode for a while. When we stopped, she took me out of the car and into a house and we went out into a back yard where there was green grass. I was in heaven. I hadn't seen grass in a long time — not since the dog park. I rolled over and then got up and went into the house and did what any normal male dog would do; I claimed this space as my own. I don't think she like it, because she called me a funny name and yelled at me and dragged me outside by my collar. I guess I won't do that again.

Chapter 4
Chance Has a Home

Dogs are uncannily like humans in their social development and ability to learn and communicate. This is possibly due to the long relationship canines have had with humans throughout the centuries. It is a widely held belief that the dog is a long distant relative of the Grey Wolf family, *Canis lupus familiaris* and has been a partner with humans for at least 15,000 years. In the beginning, in Central Asia, they were most likely helpers with their humans in finding and bringing down prey for gathering food. As time went on dogs were bred for very specific purposes; herding, guarding, as exterminators in the barn to protect the stored wheat and corn from rats, and most recently as companion animals. They are a pack animal and thrive in a family unit where one member is the leader with subordinates. Dogs need social interaction with the pack, and if that pack is of the human type, then one or more persons in the family will have to assume the leadership role. Otherwise the dog will become the leader and this can be very undesirable.

Most people think of the seasons in Phoenix as hot and hotter and as the days passed and winter turned to spring, the weather started heating up. Jasmine and Chance settled into a daily routine, up at five in the morning. This was mostly at Chance's insistence that it was time to eat and Jasmine was afraid that his barking would wake the neighbors and so she acquiesced.

She spent the next couple of hours searching for work always hopeful that she might find something that would fit her skills and where she had a chance at being hired.

These were extraordinary times in Phoenix and across the nation. The recession appeared to be deepening, banks and businesses closing, more people losing their jobs and their homes. Jasmine had noticed when she had been driving to work before her layoff, how several of the large car dealerships along McDowell Road had closed their doors. They had been there for years and suddenly they were gone. With tax revenue diminishing from both businesses and individuals this was filtering down to the state level where the budget deficit was causing the governor to look for ways to cut government and in doing so was cutting many services, education, and health care for the poor. The city had threatened to close libraries in Phoenix until the people protested so loudly that they came up with a compromise of limited hours of operation. Jasmine thought about how most of these services were originally designed to help the poor in this very competitive world and now they were going away and who was affected the most? The poor and the middle class. And then the state started raising taxes; a food tax was added, again affecting the poor and the middle class more than anyone. She then thought about those CEO's salaries and benefits, people making 400 times what the workers were making.

Jasmine sent out resume after resume. She seldom heard anything back. These companies were receiving hundreds of resumes. She was experienced in her field, but she was past middle age. She couldn't compete with the younger workers who were willing to work for far less money. This of course was very good for employers; they could set the wages lower and they had a huge bank of potential employees to choose from.

Jasmine was demoralized that her career as a software design engineer might be over and she would have to move on to something else. She had worked so hard for so many years. But she would have to face that possibility soon.

"You know, Chance, we are both rejects in a way," Jasmine said as they stepped out the door for their daily walk. He still pulled her along and, as many times as she corrected him, he wouldn't stop. She had more or less given up on this one.

They were becoming more of a team, though, and she was thankful to have that big bark in the back yard again; there had been several break-ins in the neighborhood and Jasmine always felt safe when she had a big dog. She had a sign in the front window as a reminder to anyone who might try to enter uninvited: BEWARE OF DOG. She really didn't know if her dog would protect her, but when anyone was even walking across the street, Chance would bark, and if they looked in the back yard, his fur was up on his back and, with teeth bared, he looked like he could do damage. Any thief or potential intruder would move on to another house where it would be easier to gain entry.

When she had first moved into her house and before she had a dog, Jasmine recalled how she came home early one afternoon from a shopping trip. It had been raining and as she was opening her front door she noticed large footprints on her front walkway leading off to the alley on the north. She went inside, not thinking there might be danger lurking, and went from room to room. Nothing had been disturbed. She then went outside and saw the same footprints on her back patio trailing off to the block wall. Wow, she thought, I must have come home just as he was getting ready to break in. She shivered at the thought. She decided right then and there to get a dog and to put in an alarm system.

She found a wonderful big red Doberman and named him Kona. She never feared for her safety after that. But then she thought about how Kona had died in her arms on her patio one sunny September afternoon last fall. She had been telecommuting that day. At noon she had gone outside to check on him and saw that he was vomiting. Thinking nothing of it, as he had done this before, she went back to her work. When she checked on him again an hour later, he was down on the patio in obvious distress. Jasmine called her vet and they told her to bring him right in. There was only one problem, he couldn't walk and she couldn't lift a seventy-five pound dog. She called her friend Ralph, but by the time he got there, Kona was gone.

When they brought his limp body into the vet's office, the vet examined him and said, "It was bloat."

"What is that?" Jasmine asked, with tears streaming down her face. And the vet told her that it was torsion, a twisting of the stomach. It was very common in large, barrel-chested dogs like Kona. "What should I have done?" she asked. He told her there wasn't much she could have done. If she had gotten him into the office in time, they could have done surgery, but it was likely that it could happen again. She kissed Kona and carefully removed his collar and went home to grieve. She would miss him terribly.

Soon after she lost Kona, she knew that she was vulnerable without her big dog. She had visited the Spy Store in the strip mall near her home to see what she might buy to help secure her home. She looked at a small device that emitted the sound of a large barking dog whenever it was activated by someone trying to open a door or window. "This is really neat," she thought. "I could have the big bark without the hassle of taking care of a dog; the cleaning up, the cost of food and vet expenses. This could be a solution." But the more she thought about it the more she realized that her big dog was much more to her than just a big bark. Her dog was her friend and companion. You couldn't pet a bark in a box. No, this wasn't for her.

Jasmine thought about how she'd found Kona. She'd answered an ad in the newspaper five years before; *Red Doberman, Male, Five Years Old*. When she went to see him that Sunday, he walked up and lay down in front of her to have his belly scratched and she knew then that she would take him home. The person who owned Kona, Scott, was a Native American and he told her that he couldn't keep Kona because he was divorcing and moving to an apartment. He asked if she were frightened of him and she said, no of course not. She brought Kona home that day and they bonded immediately.

As much as Jasmine tried to prevent it, she was becoming attached to Chance. They were bonding more and more every day. In the evening Chance would come into the house and jump on the couch where she was reading or watching TV and lean on her until she noticed him and then she would stroke his ears and he would let out a sigh of pleasure. When she was working on the computer, Chance would often come up behind her and bump her gently with his nose and when she looked at him, she could see that he wanted something. She asked him if he wanted to go out, and if he did he would whimper and look to the door. Or if he just wanted attention he would lay his head in her lap and look up at her with his expressive eyes. Then she would stroke him and after a few minutes he would lie down next to her desk.

She kept hoping no one would adopt him. But then it occurred to her that if she felt this way, she should adopt him. She had really wanted a puppy but Chance was a great dog and he was long past that naughty puppy behavior she so disliked. She recalled the days of a backyard that looked like a moonscape and teeth marks in everything that was chewable and then of course the house breaking, cleaning up the puddles and making sure the puppy went outdoors. It would be much better to adopt an older dog like Chance. That was it; that's what she would do.

She called and then drove to the Humane Society, to the adoption area and talked with a woman there who was ecstatic when she told her that she wanted to adopt Chance. "This is wonderful. Do you know how many animals we're getting with this recession?" the young woman asked. Jasmine shrugged her shoulders. She didn't know. "Thousands.

With people losing homes, and jobs, some can't keep their pets because they can't afford to feed them or provide veterinary care."

"I'm so sorry to hear that. I've lost my job as well, but I can get by for awhile. And your organization is a great help in providing low cost veterinary services, I know. I've had a dog spayed here and it cost a fraction of what my vet was charging."

She acknowledged Jasmine's remark and then helped her fill out the papers. "He's yours. And now do you want to take another foster dog?"

"Not right now. I want to get used to having Chance first before I take on another one," said Jasmine.

She went home and Chance greeted her at the back door. "Chance, this is your home now, forever. How do you like that?" she said as she lifted his front paws and they danced around the patio. "You are my dog now and I'll love you forever," said Jasmine as she hugged him and ran her hands over his silky coat. Chance seemed to know what she was saying. He burrowed his head in her lap and then licked her as if he was saying thank you. Dogs do know more than we think, thought Jasmine.

Chapter 5
Chance

I've been here many days now, and I've tried to mind my manners. I keep thinking that this human might take me back to the cage in the big building with lots of other dogs and cats again. She seems to be a caring human and gives me good food twice a day and fresh water. I'm trying to please her so she won't yell at me again. Now I know that I need to pee outdoors and do my other business out there as well. I did throw up one day, but I couldn't help that and she didn't seem to mind. And I'm trying to do an extraordinary job of guarding the house when strangers come around. I think she's pleased with me for that. She did tell me not to bark when people are walking across the street, only when they get very close to the yard. But I can't help it; I have to bark.

She was keeping me outdoors at night until recently. She came home one afternoon, all smiley and happy, and we danced and she gave me special treats. I wonder if that means that I'm home to stay. I hope so. I like her and I want to stay here with her. I am allowed on the place where she sits and where she sleeps when I'm inside the house. My other family didn't let me do that. She even gives me rawhide bones and biscuits.

Tomorrow I'll take extra care to make sure the yard is secure before I take my mid-morning nap. I'll check the gates first, then sniff the air for any strange people or animals, and then I'll listen. If I hear something outside the gate I'll bark until they're gone. No one will enter my yard without my permission. And that includes cats. It seems there are a couple of cats in the neighborhood that love to tease me by walking on the top of the fence and, try as I may, I cannot get to them. I jump up and bark and make like I am a big and mean dog, but they just don't get it.

And then there is the bird bath. The other day, I was walking on the patio and I looked over there and saw this big black bird. I slowly, stealthily crawled up to it and then snatched it right out of the water. I crunched down once and it was dead. The other birds were squawking and dive bombing me. My human opened the door and I ran inside with the bird in my mouth. I don't think she was too happy with my killing the bird. But that's what I do. I kill lizards too.

My life is good. I hope it continues this way. But in life you just never know. Things can take downturn at any time. As long as I have regular food, water, and my human friend, I'll be happy.

Chapter 6
Time to Socialize

Dogs are social animals. What they saying to one another when they meet for the first time appears at first to be a mystery, but by watching how they behave you can usually decipher the dog talk that is happening between the animals. The etiquette is to sniff, nose to nose, then nose to rear end, and determine what the relationship will be. They are pack animals and there is a definite hierarchy even among those that are meeting for the first time. If one dog is dominate and another submissive, the dominate dog will stand tall with ears forward, maybe putting a paw on the other dog as if guarding the submissive dog, while the submissive dog will many times lie down, demonstrating passive behavior. Generally the male-female relationship will be dominate to submissive, but when two females meet they will also try to establish who is going to be in control. This is also done by one dog mounting another. A female dog will sometimes mount another dog albeit male or female to show dominance as well. If all is well, the tails wag and the bodies wiggle in a friendly manner and they will go into play mode with one or the other dog going down on its front legs. But sometimes, especially with two males, the meeting is not friendly and the fur goes up on the back, the teeth are bared with some growling and loud barking, and it may be time to intervene.

Some dogs are just by nature more aggressive. This can be due to how they have been treated by their owners, if they have been abused. Some small dogs like the Jack Russell Terrier, a small dog with a big attitude, oftentimes will be very confrontational with every dog they meet, including the larger breeds. And some of the larger breeds that have a reputation for being aggressive are really very passive and loving animals.

Memorial Day weekend was approaching and the temperature had been hovering around the 100-degree mark for days now. However, this was the norm for the Southwest desert and most people living here take it in their stride. Jasmine continued to look for work every day, checking the Internet and the newspaper and sending out resumes, with zero results. She had plenty to do. She painted every day and played with Chance, walking him every morning. Friends and neighbors came by occasionally, sometimes with their dogs and they would spend time on the patio watching the dogs play as they drank coffee and talked about the events of the world. Even so, she felt isolated; she needed more social time in her life, and so did Chance.

Her friends with dogs had been telling her about taking their dogs to the dog park. Jasmine had taken Kona once, but when she entered the park with him and let him off the leash he watched the other dogs with interest but stayed as close to her as he could. When she told him to go and run and play, he walked around her and then sat by her side, leaning his body against hers. Chance was younger and a more outgoing dog and Jasmine thought he would like to run and play and meet dog friends — and she could meet new friends as well. But before she could do that she had to know that Chance would come to her when called. For five days she worked with him, putting him in a "sit-stay" command, then walking away and calling him back. At first he would just look at her and do nothing, but then she held out her hand with a treat and when he came over to get the treat she made like it was a party. Soon he was coming to her without the treat, and it was then that she knew he was ready for the dog park.

Early one Monday morning, Jasmine put Chance's leash on him and gathered some dog biscuits. "We're going to the dog park, Chance," she said as she was loading him into the back of her car. She chose Monday, hoping that there would be fewer people and dogs on this day so as not to overwhelm Chance.

She opened the car door and told him to get in the back where she tethered him in with another leash so that he couldn't climb into her lap and distract her driving. He looked at her quizzically, cocked his head in a knowing way, with his tongue hanging out and his eyes focused intently on her.

The park was about seven miles from her home, and as they were driving, Chance hung over Jasmine's shoulder, panting and looking at her with questioning eyes. He seemed to be unsure as to where she was taking him.

"It's okay, pal. We're going to the dog park. I'm not taking you back to the shelter, I promise. You're *my* dog now," she said as she scratched his ears with her right hand while holding the steering wheel with the other and watching for traffic.

Turning into the dog park area, Jasmine could see dogs running and playing on the green grass and Chance began to get excited. He squealed and jumped up and down, as much as his tether would allow. Jasmine knew there were two areas, one for small dogs and one for larger dogs. She would of course take Chance to the large dog area.

She parked the car and took Chance out of the back. He strained at his leash and pulled her along, tongue hanging from the side of his mouth. Jasmine opened the first of the double gates designed to ensure that dogs would not escape the area on their own. She took off his leash; they went through the second gate and were out in the open. It was a large grassy area about the size of a football field, with trees in places along the edge where tables and chairs had been placed for people to sit and watch their dogs. There were two drinking faucets, one on either end of the park, with buckets for the dogs to drink from and dispensers and garbage cans to be used to pick up and dispose of dog poop spaced along the chain link fence.

As they entered the area, three dogs raced over to check out Chance. These were the greeters. They sniffed his rear, then touched noses and circled around him as if to say, "We need to approve you before you can come in here." Chance circled with the dogs, a Golden Retriever, a Pit Bull mix and a small terrier, sniffed them back, and then ran off with the dogs following in his wake. Jasmine, left standing alone in the middle of the park, watched the running dogs for awhile, so happy to see Chance racing over the grass, tongue hanging out and ears flapping. They ran to the far end of the chain link fence, turned and ran back, tumbled over each other, and then took off in another direction.

Well, Chance has made friends and I'll try to as well, thought Jasmine. She decided to walk over to the side and talk to a group of about six people sitting at a picnic table under a large umbrella-like tree. "Good morning," she said as she reached the table. A couple of people looked up and said "Hello." Not very friendly, Jasmine thought.

"That your dog?" asked an older man, thin with tan wrinkled skin and a cigarette hanging from his mouth.

"Yes, his name is Chance," Jasmine responded.

"Kinda skinny ain't he?" the same man said. He was wearing a blue workman's shirt with a Shell Oil emblem on the left chest pocket and navy blue pants. "Don't you ever feed him?"

Jasmine thought that one over for a minute. And before she could answer, the same man said, "But then you're kind of a skinny kid yourself."

Now she was feeling affronted. First he says her dog is too skinny, and then he insults her by calling her skinny and a kid? She hadn't been a kid since tenth grade. This is not a friendly crowd, she thought to herself. Then a very large woman who was overflowing her lawn chair spoke up, "Don't pay him no mind. He's always like that to new people. What's your name, missy?" she asked through two missing front teeth.

"Jasmine. What's yours?"

"Mary, and this here's my little girl, Putzy" she said introducing a small Pug sitting in front of her, waiting for her to throw a tennis ball.

"Glad to meet you Mary, and you too, Putzy," said Jasmine as she petted the little dog. "Chance is a little thin. He was a rescue dog. He'd been on his own for awhile." She didn't want to go into detail.

Her statement raised eyebrows, and the temperature in the group became noticeably warmer. "That was good of you. There are a lot of homeless dogs these days," said Mary. "And homeless people, too."

As she surveyed the group Jasmine figured that these were the regulars who probably brought their dogs to the park daily. They appeared to be retired, in their fifties and sixties and beyond, and this was likely the highlight of the day. And while she was sizing up the people, Chance was having his own problems. Two male dogs, a German Shepherd mix and an Alaskan Husky, were chasing him down and biting at him and he didn't like it at all.

"Hey," she called out. "Stop that, right now!" she said as she went over to if Chance was okay.

"Oh, don't worry, they're just playing," said an apple-faced man with a large belly.

"Playing kind of rough," Jasmine said. "I wouldn't call that 'playing.'"

"They always do that, especially with a new dog. Kind of trying him out, I guess. My name's Jim, by the way."

She acknowledged Jim while she checked out Chance to see if he had been hurt. He seemed okay. She picked up a tennis ball and threw it for him, thinking that these people were not friendly and the dogs were like their owners. But maybe that was pack mentality. The dogs had probably been playing together at this park for a long time, and they weren't going to accept a new dog without an initiation. That seemed to be true of the human pack as well.

She would give it another try. Jasmine walked over to a woman wearing Capri's and a t-shirt with a white cap on her head covering her long blond and gray hair tied in a pony tail. Her face was wrinkled, but she seemed to be in good physical shape. She was throwing a Frisbee for her dog, a Blue Heeler that she called Lightning. "Hi, your dog is really fast," Jasmine said as she approached.

"This breed is known for their agility and speed," the woman said. "My name's Sally. And don't let 'em give you a hard time. They always do that when a new person comes to the park. Kind of like they have to prove themselves as real dog people."

"It's okay. I keep saying that people are like dogs in that way."

"Would you like to sit down?" asked Sally as she motioned to a chair that Jasmine had noticed a male dog peeing on earlier.

"Thanks, but I'll stand. I sit most of the day."

Lightning ran over to Chance and sniffed his rear and then his face, and Chance did the same. They ran in circles for a couple of minutes and then were off running side by side. It looks like Chance has found at least one friend, Jasmine thought, and maybe she has too..

"How old is your dog?" asked Sally.

"I think he's about two, but I'm not sure. I took him in as a foster dog and I grew to like him so I adopted him just last week."

"That's really neat," Sally said. "What do you do for a living?"

"I'm unemployed right now. I was a software design engineer." Jasmine then thought that she sounded pompous and she wouldn't win any friends that way. "That's a fancy name for a computer programmer." Jasmine picked up a tennis ball and threw it for Chance. "What about you?" As Chance returned with the ball in his mouth, two mixed-breed dogs came running over and started tussling with Lightning, and Chance got into the fray as well.

"I'm a nurse at St. Joseph's Hospital. This is one of my days off. I work three twelve hour shifts and then have four days off."

"You must be exhausted, but you're lucky to have a job. Then I guess there's a demand for nurses." A small skirmish broke out in the far corner of the park, and two people went over to break it up.

"Yes, it's very tiring. But I love my job. I'm a surgical nurse, so I'm in the OR my entire shift. And yes, nurses are in demand and fewer are graduating from nursing school, so that makes it really difficult. We have to double up on our work for lack of people."

"It must be very rewarding to help people get well," said Jasmine. They were silent for a few minutes as they watched the dogs running and playing "Most of the people here seem to be retired."

"They're retired, unemployed or work weird shifts like me," Sally said as she threw a Frisbee for Lightning. They chatted for another few minutes, and then Jasmine took Chance into the middle to throw a tennis ball for him again. He was beginning to wear down a bit, and it was getting warmer.

"Should we call it a day here, Chance?" Jasmine said, and she attached the leash to his collar. She said her goodbyes, but few noticed. Three dogs, however, followed them to the gate, wanting to play with Chance.

"I think your acquaintances were friendlier than mine, Chance," Jasmine said as they were driving away from the park. She looked around at Chance, who was by now flopped out on the floor in the back of her car, nearly asleep. "We'll have to do that again. We need for you to run off some of your energy."

Chapter 7

Celeste

There are many similarities between the life cycle of a dog and that of a human. The big difference is, of course the life span; dogs often live only ten to fifteen years, depending on the size of the dog, and humans six times that and more. Puppies, like babies, early on have to be potty trained, but they actually learn much faster than human babies. It may be anywhere between two and three years before the baby's diaper can be dispensed with, while a puppy at six weeks can be completely housebroken in a day or two. As the puppies grow, they sometimes wreak havoc with almost any household, chewing and digging holes in the garden, just as toddlers may get into cupboards and other places where they shouldn't be. But a puppy will outgrow these bad habits, usually between the ages of one and two years, whereas a human can remain a child well into his or her late twenties and beyond.

When Jasmine and Richard divorced, there was a huge custody battle over custody of Celeste, who was thirteen at the time. All of her young life, Celeste, who was the mirror image of Jasmine, had been torn between her two parents. Both her mother and her father adored her.

While her father constantly showered her with compliments and gifts, partially due to his guilt of being a father in absentia, it was her mother who took on the daily duties of raising her, and it was her mother that Celeste spent most of her time with as she was growing up. And so too, most of the discipline fell to her mother; Jasmine was always on her daughter's case about something. When Celeste was little, it was mind your manners at the table, drink your milk and eat your vegetables, no cookies before dinner, always say please and thank you. Don't do this and always do that — a constant barrage of corrections.

As Celeste entered her teen years, whenever she wanted to do anything her mother constantly told her she was too young. She wasn't allowed to wear makeup until she was fifteen; her mother seldom wore it. She wasn't allowed to date until she was sixteen. That had been the rule in Jasmine's house when she was growing up as well.

Her mother told her it was because she loved her and wanted to keep her safe, but in Celeste's eyes her mother was preventing her from living life.

If she wanted to stay overnight at a friend's house, Mother had to know who the parents were and if they were going to be home. And Jasmine had to vet each one of her daughter's friends. Celeste thought she could live without all the loving. But on other hand, her father was a soft sell. When Mother refused to allow her to go to a party across town, she would ask Dad for permission if he was there, and he almost always said yes, causing a battle between her parents. It was the same, time after time.

To compensate, Celeste went underground. She decided that if her mother was going to nix everything in her life, she just wouldn't tell her. While dressing conservatively each morning to please her mother, who was always there at the door when Celeste left for school, she would stuff revealing halter tops and too-short mini-skirts in her backpack, changing in the girl's bathroom at school. Celeste started not bringing her new hip friends home. She was running with a faster crowd these days, and she knew her mother would *not* approve. Her new friends were exciting, flamboyant with their wild hair of purple and orange and spikes and Mohawks. They wore groovy clothes, the boys' baggy jeans falling off their butts and the girls wore mini-skirts covering almost nothing and too-tight tank tops showing almost everything with pierced body parts, black mascara and eyeliner.

Celeste and her new friends were also into experimentation on all levels – cigarettes and alcohol, and then came the drugs — marijuana, ecstasy, cocaine — and, of course, sex. Jasmine's beloved daughter was tired of being labeled a saint, as her name implied. She wanted to experience life to the fullest, but with a name like Celeste, changing her image was not an easy task.

Celeste remembered the first time her new best friend, Sharon, gave her a Camel cigarette and showed her how to smoke it. She was thirteen at the time, and they were sitting in a booth at Tom's Hamburger shop on Cedar Street in Berkeley, where they migrated every afternoon after school to eat French fries and drink Cokes.

"Here, just put it in your mouth and I'll light it for you," Sharon said. "Then suck in on it." Celeste wasn't sure she wanted to do it, but three other friends were there and she didn't want to look like a nerd, as they called the geeks who always studied and never partied. Neither of Celeste's parents smoked. They hardly ever drank alcohol; Dad was too busy working and Mom was always volunteering, painting and doing her art work. Alcohol was just not part of their routine. In fact, there was seldom any in the house.

Following Sharon's instructions, Celeste sucked on the cigarette. As smoke engulfed her head and got into her eyes, she sputtered and coughed while tears rolled from her eyes.

They all laughed at her, and she felt foolish. "Come on, take another drag," said another friend, Brandy. "Like you're not gonna die."

Celeste another drag, just because she didn't want to disappoint her friends. She really didn't like this smoking business. Why do people do this, she wondered to herself?

"Okay, Celey, this time suck on it and inhale the smoke," Sharon coached. Her new friends called her Celey; they said that Celeste was just too long a name for them.

"I can't, I'll choke."

"Yes, you can! Like, just DO it," commanded Brandy.

So Celeste did it, pulled hard on the cigarette, and inhaled it deeply into her lungs. She felt the burning and she coughed, but then she experienced a kind of euphoria that she had never felt before, lightheaded and far away. She took another drag and another, and felt the euphoria, and she started liking it. Her friends cheered. And her worth rose in the eyes of her friends.

As she got older, in her later teen years, she stopped asking her mother and did as she pleased. Both of her parents were now working long hours and into their own lives, and she could get by with almost anything without their knowing. And when they weren't working, if they were together they were fighting, and the big "D" word was being tossed about often. Eventually, they separated and finally divorced. And then Celeste's world fell apart.

She didn't know what would happen to her. Would she have to leave her school, her friends? Who would she be living with? Would it be her dad, who gave her a long leash, or her mom, who watched her constantly? She was sad and confused. Although life had been intolerable with her parents fighting all of the time, she still wanted them to be together. She admitted to herself that it was for selfish reasons. She hated change and, with the divorce, her life was about to change.

After two years of haggling, when all was settled, Celeste was able to choose the parent she wanted to live with. She chose her father, thinking that he would be the more lenient parent; he was the soft touch.

But, as it turned out, it was her father who was more concerned about her education and her future. Dad made sure that she took calculus and the science courses and – because he wasn't always available — paid for a tutor when she needed it.. He was the hard task master, expecting her to get a B or better in every subject, telling her that if she didn't buckle down he would send her back to her mother. Celeste did not want that to happen.

It was her father who enforced a curfew and checked out her friends. It was her father who told her that she could no longer wear the heavy mascara, tight tops and short, short mini-skirts. "Dress like a young lady," he told her one afternoon when he picked her up school unexpectedly. "You don't want to look like a trollop."

"A *what*?" Celeste exclaimed.

"You heard me. I don't want my daughter dressing like this. I know you want to attract attention. But this isn't the way you should do it. You'll get more than you can handle, trust me."

Celeste was incensed. But she was listening.

Then late one Friday night, Richard was pacing the floor, waiting for Celeste to come home from a party. It was three o'clock in the morning, four hours past her curfew. Had she been in an accident? Should he call the police, the hospitals?

He sat in the dark, worrying.

The door opened, Richard turned on the light, and a very ragged Celeste walked in, mascara running down her face, her clothes half-hanging on her. Surprised to see her father sitting there, she burst out of the room and ran to the bathroom and threw up. Richard followed her, and when he sadly looked at his beautiful young daughter and he was nearly sick himself. "We'll talk in the morning," he said quietly. "Go to bed and sleep this off. You must feel terrible."

The next morning Richard got up early and made French toast with bacon and squeezed fresh orange juice. He called out to Celeste to come down and join him for breakfast. He poured a cup of coffee, sat down, and waited.

Celeste's head felt like a sledge hammer had hit it, and her stomach was still churning. After hearing him calling to her for a half hour or more she decided that she'd better get up and face him, as hard as this was going to be. Although he hadn't shown it last night she knew that he was infuriated with her. She put on her blue flannel robe with bunnies on it and went into her bathroom to splash water on her face, brush her teeth and comb her hair. When she looked in the mirror she barely recognized the face staring back at her.

"Here, sit down," Richard said as he pulled out her chair. He sat across the table from her and passed the food on a platter. He poured her juice and then poured some for himself. Celeste was waiting for him to blow up, but he seemed very calm.

At first she wasn't hungry at all, but then she took a bite of the French toast which she'd always loved. "Hey, Dad this is pretty good. Did you put cinnamon on it?"

"Yeah, you like it?"

They ate in silence. Richard drank his coffee and offered some to Celeste, and then he started talking. "You know Celeste, you have choices."

"I know, Dad, I know."

"You have two paths right now. The one you're on, drinking, doing drugs, dressing like a whore and out-of-control partying." That got her attention. He had never used that word before in her presence. Is that what he thought she looked like? "Or you can change to another path of studying hard and preparing for college."

"Dad, I can do both. And I'm not doing drugs."

"No you can't. The distractions are too great. Trust me, I know."

"But I don't want to change. I'm having too much fun."

"That looked like a lot of fun last night. Not!" he said looking straight into her eyes. He continued. "Now, everything has consequences. If you continue down the path you're on, you could end up a druggie and on the street. You could even end up dead."

"But you wouldn't let that happen, Dad. If I ended up on the street you would take me in."

"You think so? I won't 'enable.'" Richard picked up a piece of bacon and crunched on it and let Celeste think about these words for a few minutes.

Celeste looked down at her food. She'd lost her appetite. She drank some juice, thought over her dad's last words, and pictured herself living in a dirty apartment somewhere in South Oakland, with no money for food or clothing.

"But then if you take the other path . . ."

"I don't want to, Dad. I won't. Everybody'll laugh at me. Call me names. I won't have any friends . . ." Celeste got up from the table and stormed out of the kitchen crying.

Richard waited a few minutes and then went after her. Celeste's bedroom door was closed, and when he tried the knob it was locked. "Let me in, Celeste. We haven't finished our talk."

"Yes we have. Go away."

"No I won't go away. Open the door now or I'll break it in, do you hear me?"

Celeste got up from her single bed with the soft pink comforter and opened the door. She then went back to her bed, lay down and curled up, looking like a new fawn in the woods.

Richard sat down on her bed and stroked her hair. He looked around her room originally filled with dolls and teddy bears now being replaced with rock star posters. "I know how you must miss Mom."

Celeste didn't move.

"But you know, I'm responsible for you. And if something bad happens to you, they can take you away."

Celeste's brown eyes turned to him. "Is that for real? You wouldn't be shitting me, would you?"

Richard winced. "No, I wouldn't be . . . I'm telling you the truth."

And then he told her about the other path she could take. If she stopped the partying and worked on her grades he would send her to UC Berkley. She could get her degree and find meaningful work that would pay her well and she would have a feeling of accomplishment and a happier life.

"I'll think about it, Dad."

"You can start today. You can clean your room, get organized, and wash your clothes. Get rid of the sexy clothes, and I'll take you out to buy some new things. Tomorrow we'll go for a hike on Mt. Tamalpais and then have lunch in the city. And then on Monday you will go to all of your classes, and I want a report Monday night."

"I'm tired, Dad. Let me sleep for awhile."

"Okay, it's your choice," Richard said and he walked out of the room, hoping Celeste would do the right thing.

Celeste slept for an hour, and when she awoke she thought about everything her father had said. She knew that she didn't want to go and live with her Mom, in Arizona. How revolting. She got up off the bed and started picking up her clothes and hanging them in the closet.

Chapter 8
Celeste Comes Home

Parenting in the dog world is a brief affair. In the wild, the pup will remain with the pack for several years before striking out on its own. Domestic canine pups are often "adopted" into new human families at six to twelve weeks of age, and this is where the real training begins. By six months the pup will be house-broken, and by age two, fully trained if the new family takes the initiative to do so. No to train your puppy means that this cute little animal may rule over you and your household instead of you being in control. A trained puppy is a happy puppy.

Human parents, in contrast, often remain so for life. Humans too are very protective of their offspring; there are exceptions, of course. And there the similarity ends. The human baby may be "housebroken," out of diapers by age two. The "training" is almost a lifelong process, but to be sure, a human child is usually not ready for the world until at least eighteen years of age, and the learning goes on throughout his or her adult life. Being the parent of a human child never ends. They leave home comparatively late in life and often remain attached, sometimes coming back home again.

The phone call came late one warm summer evening in June. "Mom, I'm coming over to live with you — of course, if that's okay with you,"

Celeste said. "I'm out of money and about to be homeless. Can you help me out for awhile?"

Jasmine grimaced as she thought of the implications. She hadn't enough money to keep herself going, and now her grown daughter was coming to live with her. But then, how could she refuse?

"Of course, honey. I'd be happy to help you. But I haven't enough to live on myself. What about your father?"

"Oh, I called and asked him. He's always talking about personal responsibility and how I haven't done anything right, the way he wants me to."

"But he's working. He's got money. I'll call him and talk to him." Maybe she should ask Richard for money if Celeste came to live with her. No, I could never do that, she thought. He always said that I wouldn't make it on my own, and he would use this to prove it.

"No, don't do that. And besides, he's got those other kids to take care of," said Celeste. Richard had moved in with his girlfriend soon after Celeste went off to college, and Richard and Deborah were married a year later. Jasmine always thought he had been seeing Deborah while he was still married to Jasmine. Deborah came with two boys, Bart and Aaron, aged five and eight. Then a year after Richard and Deborah married, they had a child, a girl they named Cheryl.

"I know your Dad and Deborah have a houseful, but they live in a mansion. Couldn't they find one small room for you to move into?"

"Mom, what would I *do* in Oakland? I don't get along with Deborah at all. She hates me. Probably because I'm your daughter. And those bratty kids of hers are horrible . . . ."

"I guess . . . " Jasmine said, reluctantly.

"Look Mom, I'll be on the street, sleeping under a bridge if you don't help me. I've lost my apartment; they took away my car yesterday so I can't even sleep in that. A lot of people here are doing that, you know." Celeste had gone on to graduate from high school tenth in her class of 200 and then attended Stanford University, graduating with a degree in biology. After college she could have easily gotten a job in research but decided to go to Los Angeles to try to break into the movie business. She had been participating in college plays for two years before graduation and loved acting. And she was a beautiful young woman, tall and slim with olive skin, huge brown eyes, long eyelashes and long, dark brunette hair. She had picked up small bit parts now and then and she just knew she would make it big soon, but she couldn't live on the money. The jobs were sporadic, the pay was low and so she had to get a day job. Fortunately she found one with the Los Angeles County doing data entry of medical records and she could support herself on the wages she was paid while she waited for her big break. But then funding for the project that she was working on had been cut with the recession and she had been looking for work for nearly two months.

"Celeste, what have you been doing with your money for the last four years?"

"I *lived*, Mom, I lived. Spent it all on living. The rents are not cheap here, you know, and I wasn't making that much."

"When do you plan on coming over? And how're you going to get here without a car? You know, Phoenix is not easy to get around in without a car."

"Thanks Mom. I'll be there tomorrow. Ramon's giving me a ride."

"So, who's Ramon?" Jasmine asked. Her thoughts were racing. Where would she put Celeste? Her house was small, only 900 square feet — and it was full, every closet, every room and every cupboard. She'd lived alone in this house for ten years now and she had filled it up.

"I've been living with Ramon for a couple of weeks now. He kind of took me in when I ran out of money. But he's unemployed, too. He lost his accounting job last week, and he can't afford to support me."

"We'll see you tomorrow. Have a safe trip," said Jasmine. What was she going to do, refuse to give shelter to her only daughter when she needed it? She loved Celeste, she really did. But there was always this tension between them, like the spinnaker on a sail boat, if the wind changed so too did their relationship.

She also thought about how life was so unpredictable these days. Even people who were highly skilled with a good education were losing their jobs. One wondered if it was worth it to go to college anymore. College costs had skyrocketed in the last few years, and most students had to take out huge loans and then found themselves in debt when they graduated. Fortunately, Celeste had not had to do that. Her father had paid for almost all of her college costs, hoping that she would get a good job in bio-physics or something of that caliber, and he was devastated when she chose to go to L.A. He had told Celeste that it was a slap in the face and that she was turning out to be an airhead "just like your Mom," he'd said. When Jasmine heard that, she took offense. "Not everyone is a robot like you, Richard," she'd told him when she talked with him, which wasn't often. "She wants to experience life, and I understand that." But, as Richard predicted, it had not turned out well for Celeste. And now Celeste's career choice was having an impact on Jasmine's life as well. Or was it the recession? She really couldn't blame Celeste for this one.

As Jasmine was hanging up the phone, Chance came over and put his nose in her rear, as he had been trying to do quite often lately. "No, Chance, I'm not a dog. Even though you want to treat me as one of your own kind, you can't do that to me," Jasmine said, mildly disgusted. "We need to go to the dog park and think all of this over, Chance. We're going to have another person living here, and I don't quite know how this is all going to work out." Chance's ears perked up when Jasmine said the words "dog park."

When they arrived at the dog park there were very few dogs or people there. It was late, past ten in the morning, and most people had gone home as it was getting hot. Chance didn't mind. He took off as soon as Jasmine released him and ran to other end of the fenced-in area, ears flopping, tongue hanging out and joy in his heart. One happy dog, to be sure. This is what dogs love to do the most, just run until they can't run anymore. Jasmine often thought that it was sad that most dogs that were bred for working on ranches, herding sheep or cattle or some other important activity, had to be confined to a small yard and could never really run off the excess pent-up energy. And, of course, that is one reason why dogs chew up furniture and act out. They need a job to do, and lying around the yard looking cute is not the one they have in mind.

Jasmine lost sight of Chance for a few minutes, but then she saw him rolling in a puddle of mud underneath a tree at the far end. "Oh, Chance, no. Don't do that." Chance ran back to greet her and proceeded to shake muddied water all over her. "Guess we'll be giving you a bath when we get home," she said as she led him to the water faucet to rinse him off.

Chapter 9
Richard

He hated turning his daughter away when she came to him for help. It wasn't as if they didn't have room in their five-bedroom, four-bathroom, 5000-square-foot home in the Oakland Hills. And it wasn't that he didn't have the money; he made a salary in the high six figures — not including perks and benefits. It was his wife, Deborah. He knew she would not want Celeste in their home, *her* home. Deborah called the shots.

But maybe Deborah was his excuse. He didn't want to admit his anger toward Celeste. Anger because she had gone to Los Angeles to become an actor after he had invested over 200 thousand dollars in her education and, she threw it away. Anger because she was hanging with people below her station in life. Ramon was Mexican-American. He wondered why she was attracted to people like him.

Richard Adams Bailey III, son of Charlotte and Richard Bailey, Sr., was born into wealth and a long lineage of prominent people. His father's brother, Kenneth Bailey, had been a United States Senator, and his grandfather, Percy Adams, a judge on the Massachusetts Supreme Court. Their ancestry had been traced back to President John Adams.

Richard Sr. had high hopes for his only son: first Harvard Law ˉhool, then join his prominent Boston law firm, Bailey, McClain ˙Peckham, and get into politics and maybe even run for president ˙y.

But Richard Junior had other ideas. He was interested in medicine and had at first wanted to be a doctor. It was in his second year of pre-med at Dartmouth that he decided he was more interested in the business side of medicine, namely hospital administration. Running a hospital was medicine on steroids. You were there where the action was, but you didn't have to get down into the nitty-gritty of it. Although keeping a hospital profitable was a tremendous challenge these days, this was what he knew he could do well, and he had heard that it was very lucrative. Graduating with honors, he was immediately hired away to Reno, Nevada, to become the Assistant Administrator of Tahoe Pacific Hospitals in the region, specializing in critical care services for medically complex patients. It was the perfect first job for him. This was the area of medicine he enjoyed the most, as an avid skier, he loved this region of the country.

His parents didn't see it that way. Not only was he leaving the family business, he was moving to the West Coast, for God's sake, unheard of in the 200-year history of the family and a snub to his parents, especially his father. But Richard felt that it was *his* life and he needed to live it on his terms, not his parents'. Screw his father and his great - great - great grandfather.

And then when he brought home a young half-Hispanic woman, Richard's parents and family were dismayed. How could Richard do that to them? He hadn't even asked them. Richard and Jasmine had eloped; they got married at the edge of Turtle Lake in the high Sierra at sunrise. He showed them photos of the wedding party: Jasmine in a long white peasant dress with a wreath of wild flowers on her head; Randal a colleague, his Best Man; and Sheryl, Jasmine's friend from college, her Maid of Honor. Richard wore a light blue Hawaiian shirt and his Best Man a colorful pink, blue and green Hawaiian shirt. The maid of honor wore a peasant dress similar to Jasmine's, in light green. And they were all barefoot.

"Looks like a hippie wedding to me," Richard's father had said when he saw the photos.

His father's words were hurtful, and his mother wouldn't speak to him. Richard took his new wife Jasmine to a hotel that night and they left for the West Coast the next day.

Sitting at his desk looking over the Bay from his corner office, he thought back to the day of his marriage. He had felt so free. He was marrying the woman he had dreamed of. She was beautiful and smart and they had fun together, hiking and skiing and running. And then there was the sex. He didn't think anyone had it as good as he did. She was always there, ready for him. One evening, in the early days of their marriage, when he came home opened the front door Jasmine popped out from behind the door wearing nothing but an apron, her long brunette hair brushing across her breasts. Another time, in the winter, when he walked into the house, he looked into the living room. In front of a roaring fire in the fireplace lay Jasmine on a white sheepskin rug, sans clothes, reading a novel and waiting for him to join her. He was the luckiest man in the world.

But then he was promoted, given a raise and more responsibilities, and that meant more hours at work. And then, Jasmine became pregnant. He was coming home later now, and when he walked in the door, he would find Jasmine in the bathroom throwing up; the morning sickness was relentless. It became so severe that she was hospitalized for a week because she was dehydrated and unable to keep any food down.

Four months into the pregnancy, Jasmine's morning sickness disappeared completely, but she was still so very tired, sleeping twelve hours a day. When Richard even mentioned sex, she waved him off, saying, tomorrow, maybe tomorrow she would feel better and feel like having sex. But there were few tomorrows. Okay, he could wait until after the baby came. He could do that. He loved her. He was pleased that they were having a child.

As the birth was drawing near, Richard remembered, they argued about everything. What color to paint the nursery? Jasmine wanted to paint it a hot pink and he wanted a pale yellow. Jasmine got her way. They argued about the name of the baby. He wanted to name their little girl Chelsea, a good old English name, and Jasmine wanted her name to be Celeste. She was sure this baby was sent straight from heaven. Jasmine won.

The more they argued, the more Richard stayed at the office.

And then the baby was born. He remembered how he was on Cloud Nine for weeks afterward. She looked just like her mother and had the same temperament — cried all night long for the first month. No sleep. No sex.

Now, when he came home from the office, there were dirty diapers in a bucket in the hallway waiting for the diaper service. The house was a mess, dirty dishes in the sink, baby blankets and toys all over the living room. He had to tangle with a baby jump-up in the doorway to the kitchen, and a playpen had become a permanent fixture in the living room in front of the fireplace where they used to make love. It wasn't fair, he thought. He deserved better.

Richard told Jasmine to hire a housekeeper to take care of the house and a nanny for the baby. She agreed on the housekeeper but refused to hire a nanny. She was home all day. Taking care of this baby was her job and no one else's. She wasn't going to miss the first smile, the first laugh, and those first wobbly steps.

Jasmine nursed Celeste until she was a year old. And Jasmine was the one who got up at night to feed the baby, change her diaper. Richard begged off, saying he had to work the next day; he was the breadwinner. He had to be alert. And he had a good excuse: he couldn't feed Celeste anyway — only Jasmine had the milk.

And then there were his parents. Since their marriage, he had had little contact with them. When the baby was born, he sent them a baby announcement with pictures. He heard nothing back from them for a year. And then, the following Christmas, they received gifts from his parents: A silver spoon and bowl for Celeste, a beautiful ivory-colored wool shawl for Jasmine and gold cuff links for him. What was this about, he wondered? He soon found out. His father called him in January, and they talked for an hour. Richard, Sr. said he was coming to the Coast the next month on business, and he wanted to spend some time.

Richard's father pulled up to the house on February thirteenth, the day before Valentine's Day, in a silver gray Mercedes Benz rental car. Jasmine had told the housekeeper to prepare the guest room. When Jasmine opened the door she welcomed him as she would her own father. Richard thought, "The family rift is over!"

But it wasn't to be. Richard recalled the lunch they had at the Oakland Hills tennis club.

"Richard, I have to say that I am pleased with the way your career is going. You'll be top administrator in no time. And it looks like you're making good money at this," said Richard, Sr., as he sipped his scotch on the rocks. "And California is not a bad place. I'd just never spent much time here and you hear about all the crazies in California, you know."

"Crazies? Dad, what're you talking about? People are people, no matter where they live."

"Well, you know what I mean. We have a certain decorum, a respectability, on the Eastern Seaboard. Upper crust, whatever you want to call it, we're more civilized. It seems so wild out here. And all those gays in San Francisco. I don't even want to go there."

"Dad, your bigotry is showing. San Francisco is one of the most beautiful cities in the country, maybe the world. Just because it's not New York. California is the eighth-largest economy in the world, and most of our innovative new ideas come from this area of the country. There's a freedom, an openness to think creatively. And people are friendly and open-minded."

"And how are you and Jasmine doing? She's certainly a beautiful young woman. Even after having a baby," said Richard, Sr., changing the subject.

"Oh, um … all right, I guess."

And there it was. His father had found the chink in his armor. And he took that back with him. From that point on, Richard heard from his family regularly. His mother called on the phone every week. Sometimes she would call his office and ask how things were going. And Richard obliged. He was ready to tell his family that maybe he had made a mistake.

As he sat in his grand executive office, he thought about Celeste. Wasn't Celeste doing the same as he had done as a young man? She wasn't following the career he had chosen for her. She was selecting her friends and her boyfriend on her terms, not his. Did he have the right to interfere, he wondered? It was her life and she had to live it.

There were times when he was sorry that he had divorced Jasmine. He still loved her. And trading her for a new wife from a family with connections hadn't worked out the way he had thought it would. Deborah was bitchy and never willing to compromise. And now they had another child, more responsibility. The kids were always getting in the way when he was home.

As in the past, he started to spend more time at the office. It was more peaceful there.

Chapter 10
Three Is Too Many

Monday morning arrived like any other. Jasmine got up, let the dog out, made the coffee, let the dog in and fed him, poured herself a bowl of Shredded Wheat, and sat down to read the newspaper, which she had re-subscribed to so that she could read the want-ads. Only this was not like every other morning. Her daughter, Celeste, would be arriving with her boyfriend today, and Jasmine had no idea how she would fit her wayward adult daughter into her house and her life. Celeste wasn't that wayward, come to think of it. Just a little off track right now. She was young and therefore allowed to make mistakes. "I must not be so judgmental," Jasmine said to herself.

Jasmine poured a second cup of coffee and opened the newspaper to the business section: *"Number of foreclosed homes in Phoenix rises"* and another article, *"Businesses still shedding jobs, unemployment reaching an all-time high of 9.4%."* With the economy still on the skids — what kind of a job — if any could Celeste get in Phoenix, Jasmine wondered? She knew one thing for sure: Celeste would have to get a job, any kind of a job, even if it was flipping hamburgers. She would have to contribute something to the household.

"Hey, Chance, want to go for a walk?" Chance, ears perked and tongue hanging out in anticipation, pranced over to the closet where his leash hung. "Yeah, let's go for a short walk and get this problem worked out."

The sun, looking like a ball of fire, was high in the sky by now, rays beating down on Phoenix, radiating heat to the earth with a vengeance. Jasmine looked up at the endless blue sky. "It's going to be hot today, Chance. We'd better keep you inside this afternoon." They walked two blocks to the canal that ran near Jasmine's home and then onto the path beside the water until they came to Central Avenue. Turning onto Murphy's Bridal Path, named after W. J. Murphy, one of the early developers in Phoenix, on Central, they walked beneath the ash trees along the avenue where the temperature was cooler. A couple of women were jogging, and they passed an older man with his black Scottish Terrier. Chance tried to nose the dog, but Jasmine pulled him along and said no, this was not the dog park. Then, coming to where the canal met the street, they walked back to Jasmine's house and went inside. "Chance, that was a good walk," Jasmine said as she scratched his ears and took off his leash. "Now we have to get busy."

And just as she said that, the doorbell rang. Jasmine looked up. "They can't be here already. I'm not ready."

"Hey, Mom this is Ramon. Remember, I told you about him on the phone?" Celeste blurted as Jasmine opened the front door.

"Come in," Jasmine said and she shook Ramon's hand. "Please sit down. Can I get you some iced tea?"

"Mom, forget the Emily Post stuff; we're family. We left really early this morning to beat the heat. I hope that's okay. It was a long drive over the desert and the AC in Ramon's car doesn't work," Celeste kept running on. She looked at Ramon and grabbed his hand.

Jasmine looked at her daughter, dressed in faded, ragged blue jeans with holes in the knees, a tank top that revealed a small rose tattoo peaking from her right breast, and oversized silver hoop earrings larger than her ears. Her long dark hair was pulled back in a pony tail tied with a red ribbon. Then she thought, like mother, like daughter. But by the time she was Celeste's age she was married and had a child.

The three of them sat and looked at one another in awkward silence. Then Ramon said, "Iced tea sounds pretty good right now. That was a long, *hot* drive."

Jasmine went into the kitchen and brought back two glasses and handed one to Ramon and one to Celeste. Ramon said thank you. Jasmine looked at Ramon, his baggy tattered jeans and oversized white t-shirt hanging on his tall, lanky body. He had dark brown skin and black, curly, short hair. He had a thoughtful look about him, Jasmine thought. She wondered how involved they were. But she guessed that he was here to stay with Celeste as well. They were a package deal.

"I'll get your room ready. You can help. I'll have to put some stuff in storage. We'll move the TV into the living room and you can have that room. All I have is a sofa bed in there."

Jasmine went to open the back door to let Chance in and he bounded into the living room and jumped into Celeste's lap and started licking her face all over. "Wow, I didn't know you had a dog, Mom. Where'd you get him?" Celeste asked as she scratched Chance's ears and neck. "He's really friendly."

"He's a rescue. I got him from the Humane Society. Now let's get your things in from the car and get you settled." Celeste followed her mother's instructions and went out to the car and came back bringing in two bags, with Ramon's help and Chance following, wagging his tail. Chance loved new visitors; in fact, Chance loved people in general.

They hauled two black duffle bags into the TV room and put them in the middle of the floor. "Mom, can Ramon stay the night? He's too tired to drive back to L.A. and he can't afford a hotel room."

"One night is okay," Jasmine said, thinking that she had to draw the line. She was prepared for Ramon to stay a night or two, but having Celeste's boyfriend living with her was too much to ask.

"Yeah, one night and then I'll be out of here. It's too hot over here anyway," Ramon said as he wiped the sweat from his forehead. "I don't know how you can live here."

"You get used to it, Ramon," murmured Jasmine.

With Ramon's help, Jasmine pulled the TV into the small living room. She cleared most of her clothes out of the closet in that room. Since coming to live in her little house, she had accumulated clothes and hated getting rid of anything, always thinking she might need it some day. She had clothes from the '80's that were out of style and didn't even fit her anymore, and consequently every closet in her house was stuffed. "I really need to sort through this stuff and give some of these things away," she said as she was trying to jam more clothes into her bedroom closet.

"Sell it, Mom. Go on E-Bay and sell your clothes and make some money. Oh my god, you've only got one bathroom in this house," Celeste exclaimed as she was walking through the house.

"Hey, babe, I told you, you'd be better off with your dad." Jasmine was half-teasing and half-serious. In a sense, she took offense that her small 900-square foot house was inadequate. It had worked for her all of these years. But then, she'd never had anyone living with her before. Oh, she'd had "offers," like the self-employed commercial artist she'd once dated who called her one night and asked to see her. He drove over and parked his car in her driveway. She could see that the back seat was loaded with clothes and other various items. Jasmine cooked dinner and then Arnie turned to her and asked if he could stay the night. His current girlfriend, whom he had been living with, had thrown him and his belongings out of her apartment. Jasmine looked him straight in the eye and told him to call one of his male friends. "My house is too small," she'd told him that night.

They settled Celeste and Ramon in, and Jasmine went to the grocery store to buy extra food; she had very little on hand, as she was trying to live on a strict budget and not spend her savings. When she returned, she prepared a meal of salmon with broccoli and fresh bread. They ate in silence. Jasmine wanted to talk with Celeste, set some boundaries for the household and rules for her behavior, but throughout the day Ramon was always there and Jasmine didn't want to include him in this family discussion.

After watching TV, they retired for the night, Jasmine and Chance to her bedroom and Celeste and Ramon to what had become the guest room. As Jasmine turned down the light blanket on the bed and crawled in, Chance jumped up and settled in next to her body. She knew he wouldn't stay long. It was too warm, and he would soon crawl off the bed and settle into the dog bed she had placed for him beside her bed.

Sleep didn't come easy. So many thoughts were running through her brain like a movie. How would she cope with having another person to take care of? How would she find a job? Could she support herself with her painting? Should she start her own company? She could hear the slight whir of the overhead fan as Chance shifted to his bed on the floor. Undoubtedly it was cooler there. The air conditioner came on again. It would be a hot night, not dipping much below ninety degrees. Jasmine was finally drifting off to sleep as the air conditioner turned off, but then she heard Ramon in the next room, grunting and groaning as he was having sex with her daughter.

The sun blasted through the curtains in her bedroom. It was 5:30. Better get up, she thought, and face the day. Chance jumped onto the bed and licked her face until she relented and went to open the door and let him outside. She noticed that the guest room door was shut. Still sleeping. Well, she had to admit it was pretty early in the morning. Oh, to be young without a care in the world.

After making her morning coffee, Jasmine went into her office, turned on the computer, and began the daily search for jobs. Within and hour she'd found two that she was qualified for and submitted her resume. She knew, however, that there would be at least 100 other people going for those tow jobs, and the likelihood that she would even be considered was remote. But she went through the motions every day, hoping that one day someone might want her skills and expertise. It was demoralizing.

"Hey, Chance, let's take a walk." Getting out of doors, walking with Chance, always lifted her spirits, and they were pretty low right now. No work, very little money coming in, and now having her daughter come to live with her.

They walked the neighborhood. Chance saw some pigeons walking on the grass across the street and strained against his leash to run and chase them. They took off and he looked up at the sky, longing to get one in his mouth. Then he saw another dog with its owner and pulled Jasmine to say hello. The woman smiled and asked, "Is he friendly?" Jasmine nodded yes and they brought the two dogs together starting the usual dog greeting ritual. "Greyhound?" asked Jasmine. "Yes," said the woman. "A rescue?" asked Jasmine. The woman nodded. Jasmine asked the age of the woman's dog, and she said it was four years old. "Is that when they retire these dogs from racing?" asked Jasmine. "They retire them when they're no longer winning, when they are no longer in the top four winners. And then if they aren't adopted, they put them down. Fortunately, there are groups that take these beautiful dogs and find homes for them. They make wonderful pets."

Jasmine agreed. The woman's dog was a beautiful animal, in its prime with many years left. She thought how people exploit these dogs, all for money and greed. The same was true with pit bulls, although dog-fighting had recently been outlawed in Arizona. Jasmine remembered reading an article in the *Arizona Republic* about dog fighting and how they used bait dogs, usually more submissive animals, to train and test a dogs fighting instinct. The snouts of the bait animal were wrapped in duct tape so as not to injure the dog being trained, and the bait dogs are often severely injured and sometimes killed.

Jasmine praised the woman for adopting her dog. She and Chance then walked farther down the street and through an office park near her home. It was heating up by now, and Chance was panting heavily.

"Hey, Chance! Let's go over to the water fountain so you can take a drink." They walked over to the magnificent three-tiered fountain, with four pineapple fountains around the edge, surrounded by a large circular pool. Jasmine thought it was cooling just to look at it. "Be careful, Chance," Jasmine told him as he tried to maneuver the prickly cactus around the pool. He put his front legs on the ledge of the pool and then pulled himself up to get a drink. Putting his front feet in the pool he lapped the water with his very long, pink tongue, but then he lowered his back feet in and started splashing, reveling in the coolness. Jasmine looked around her to see if anyone was watching. "Chance, I don't think you're supposed to do that," Jasmine said laughingly. "This is not a dog swimming pool." Chance kept on diving and playing in the water until Jasmine pulled him out, and then he shook all over her — which she rather enjoyed on this hot July day.

Chapter 11
Love Is Blooming

Female dogs become sexually mature between six to nine months of age, the larger breeds later. If they have not been spayed by that time, they will come into estrus, or heat, as it is normally called. The genitals of the female become swollen, there will be bleeding, and she may lick herself often. If the bitch is to be bred, it is advisable to wait until the second or even third heat, to allow the dog to mature enough physically and emotionally to handle motherhood. And if the animal is not going to be bred, it is important to spay her before she comes into heat. Once she is in estrus, the surgery is more difficult and more costly. It is a given that when she is in estrus, she will attract every male dog within five miles, risking the possibility of the female dog breeding and becoming pregnant.

Male dogs mature at about the same time — and this becomes obvious when the testicles drop and are visible. Neutering had been controversial up until the 1970's, when it was borne out that neutering the dog, unless you are breeding him, is the better way to go. It reduces aggression and roaming; females in heat give off pheromones that are airborne and can travel for many miles, attracting every intact male in the neighborhood. And there are medical benefits as well, including eliminating testicular tumors and cancer, fewer prostate problems and hernias.

Humans, much like dogs, become sexually mature at a very young age as well, long before they would be ready to take on the responsibility of parenthood in our culture. And the age of sexual maturity is becoming increasingly younger. Some scientists attribute these phenomena to everything from growth hormones in our food, childhood obesity—fat cells produce estrogen, to warming of the climate. Whatever the cause, an eight-year-old girl in modern society is not prepared to take on the job of raising a child. She, herself, is still a child.

If there was one lesson that Celeste took from her mother, it was probably the most important one of becoming a young woman. That was to prevent pregnancy and protect herself from STDs; take her birth-control pills, and always use a condom.

Jasmine spent quality time with Celeste as she was maturing and was aware of the changes in Celeste's body from year to year. Jasmine noticed when Celeste was eleven, she had started developing small breasts. She noticed hair growing on her daughter's body and an increase in body odor. And, as any helpful mother of a preteen girl might do, she provided her with the guidance that Celeste needed along the way. But Jasmine did something else. She took every opportunity to have dialogue and provide teachable moments in an appropriate way for Celeste from a very young age. When Celeste was eight years old she had brought home a stray cat and it just happened to be pregnant. As the baby kittens were being born in Celeste's closet, she talked to her about how that cat became pregnant and that caring for young was a huge responsibility.

And then just before Jasmine thought Celeste might be starting to have her period, she gave her a very informative book that explained in language young girls could understand all about her body and what was happening to her. If only her own mother had done that for her. Jasmine remembered when she was eleven, she started "bleeding between her legs" and thought she was injured. She was so frightened. When Jasmine went to tell her mother, he mother gave her this terrible look, as though she had done something wrong. She recalled her mother saying something about Jasmine being too young, and then her mother told Jasmine that she was having "the curse." She gave her some sanitary pads, and that was that. Jasmine then went to her friends, and that was where she learned about sex. Jasmine vowed she would not let that happen to her daughter.

As Celeste grew into womanhood, Jasmine tried to keep the lines of communication about sexuality open. She told Celeste she should wait to have sex until she was sure that she was mature enough to have and take care of children. But if she wasn't willing to wait, she should come to her and she would see that Celeste had birth control to prevent pregnancy. Or she could go to Planned Parenthood and they would help her. As Celeste became a teenager, many of her friends were engaging in sex, and several became pregnant. Celeste saw what a hardship it was on them. Some dropped out of school, not able to take care of the baby and work and go to school, too, putting their futures in jeopardy. She decided that wasn't for her.

Not only that, but there weren't any boys she was attracted to. The boys her age were mostly short and had pimples, body odor and bad breath, and she wasn't about to hook up with older boys. There was even a time that Celeste thought she might be lesbian. Her friends talked about gays often, and Celeste was beginning to wonder about herself. But then, in her senior year, she met the boy of her dreams, tall, dark and … well, everything a young teenage girl would want in a boyfriend. And on prom night that year, they did it. Fortunately, Celeste was prepared. And she had her mother to thank for that.

Throughout her college years, Celeste dated occasionally but concentrated on her studies and, upon graduation, getting her career going. But now there was Ramon. She'd met him two years ago in a bar in L.A. They went to dinner two nights later and ended up in bed. After dating for a year, she moved in with Ramon.

Celeste enjoyed being with Ramon, but did she want to marry him and spend the rest of her life with him? He was smart, stable, and seemed to have his life in control. And that was attractive to her. He reminded her of her Dad. She had met so many men who thought that life owed them something. They were into drugs and alcohol. They didn't want to work too hard and wouldn't have to because Daddy paid their way and there was the family business that they could step into when they finished college.

Ramon took nothing for granted. He had told her how his grandparents were refugees from the Dominican Republic, a country with a long, troubled history of foreign occupation and unrest. How they had to flee from the country during the 1965 uprising when the US sent 23,000 troops to crush a popular revolt aimed at returning Juan Bosch to power. He explained that Juan Bosch, a leftist reformer, had been elected president in the Dominican Republic's first democratic elections in nearly four decades, defeating the heir of former President Rafael Leonidas Trujillo Molina, Joaquin Balaguer.

His grandparents, Ada and Miguel Alvarez, first came on a fishing boat to Florida, asking asylum, and then traveled across the country by train to Los Angeles where they had relatives who had immigrated ten years before. They had been small farmers in their native land and knew how to work the land. But Ramon told her how, even though his grandparents had enough money, they were not allowed to buy property in America and had to work as common laborers in the fields of Southern California. It was backbreaking work, and when their two children were born they encouraged them to get an education. They didn't want to see them become common laborers.

And so Ramon's father, Henry, graduated with a degree in business from UCLA. But there was a recession when he finished school, so he took a job at a fine Mexican restaurant in Santa Monica as a waiter. He soon moved into the kitchen as a prep cook and then got the job as sous chef when the person who held that job left to start his own restaurant. It was at this point that Henry decided that food was his life. He loved everything about cooking; he equated it with giving love and making people happy.

After a year in this job, Henry decided that he wanted his own business as well. When he researched what it would cost to start his own restaurant, he found that his finances, even though he had been saving all that he could, fell way short of what he needed. But there was another way. He bought a food cart and placed it in downtown Santa Monica, offering Caribbean cuisine. He worked sixteen-hour days, and it was such a success that he bought another food cart, hired a person to work it in Beverly Hills, and then set up a third cart on Melrose Avenue.

Henry's Caribbean Cuisine now had a name, and he was making enough money to bankroll his own restaurant. He opened The Islands restaurant a year later. Ramon told Celeste that his father now had five restaurants in Los Angeles and two in San Francisco and was planning on opening another in Austin, Texas. Ramon and his sister Marie worked in their father's restaurants until they graduated from college.

When Celeste heard this story, she was very impressed by Ramon's father's entrepreneurial spirit, and she could see that Ramon had this same drive as his father. That was attractive to her. And he was good-looking; there was no doubt about that, with curly dark brown hair framing a face with prominent cheekbones and dark amber eyes below thick dark eyebrows that nearly came together at the center and the body of a Greek athlete. But there was just something about the relationship that was missing. And she couldn't quite place what that was.

However, Ramon was in deeply in love with Celeste. There was no doubt about that. He would do anything for her. He had helped her out when she was in need by having her move into his apartment with him, and maybe she felt that she owed him something. Once she left L.A., she thought this would give her, both of them, time to find out if this relationship was genuine or not.

They awoke around ten the next morning, drenched in sweat. Ramon looked up at the whirling ceiling fan above the hide-a-bed. "My god, it's hot in this house. Doesn't your mother run the air conditioner?"

"I think she's trying to save money. I don't know. I'll ask her," said Celeste as she pulled on a t-shirt and some shorts. "Anyway, you're going back today, so what do you care?"

"I might stay around a little longer. Maybe I could get a job over here. There are a lot of neat restaurants around here, I've noticed."

Celeste looked earnestly at Ramon. "I don't know how Mom's going to take that. She's not happy having *me* here, and if you're staying, that might be too much for her."

"Just a couple of days. Until I find out if there's anything happening here."

Celeste heard her mother come into the house. She opened the guest-room door and saw her taking the leash off Chance.

"Morning. There's breakfast material in the kitchen. Help yourself. Orange juice, bread, cereal, milk in the fridge. I've got to get on-line and check the jobs," Jasmine said as she put Chance outside and then went into her office.

The next few days were a blur to Jasmine. Although she tried to treat her life as if nothing had changed, the burden of having Celeste and Ramon in her home was becoming more apparent as the days went by. She sensed that they were trying to stay out of the way. They woke up late every morning and left the house to go somewhere all day, Jasmine knew not where. And then they returned at various hours of the day or night, she could never predict. When they came back late, like one or two in the morning, Jasmine worried.

"You know, Celeste, you need to let me know when you're going to be out late. I worry about you. This is a dangerous city." And Celeste agreed but still didn't let her mother know their whereabouts. She was an adult and she felt she didn't have to do that.

A couple of evenings later they showed up just as Jasmine was sitting down for dinner. "Hey, Mom, is there enough for us?" Celeste asked. "We're starved." Fortunately, managed to pull a couple of hot dogs out of the freezer and made a meal for them. "You know, Celeste, I'll be happy to cook for you any time; just let me know," implored Jasmine, not mincing words.

Some days, when they came back early in the afternoon, Jasmine didn't know what to do with them. They hung around in the living room watching TV. They played with Chance in the back yard. They went for walks along the nearby canal.

From what Jasmine could see, they weren't looking for work and Ramon was still there. She'd said when they came that Ramon could stay the night. He had stayed seven so far.

Late on night, more than a week after Celeste and Ramon had arrived to stay with her, Jasmine decided to phone Richard. She hadn't talked with him since Celeste had arrived. Celeste and Ramon were out somewhere, probably at one of the bars in downtown Phoenix. The phone rang and rang, and Richard's wife answered. "Is Richard there?" asked Jasmine.

"What do you want with him?" Deborah's unfriendly voice inquired.

"Deborah, I just need to talk to him about our daughter," said Jasmine.

Minutes passed and then Richard came on the line. "Jasmine. What's going on?"

"Don't give me that. You know what's going on. Celeste and her boyfriend are here with me, and I don't know what I'm going to do with them."

"Well, throw them out. They're adults, and they shouldn't be coming to you for help."

"Same old compassionate guy. I'd thought that since you'd married again and had another child you would be more caring," said Jasmine. "But I would be wrong." She paused. "If I throw them out, they'll have no place to go. Neither of them has a job. They'd have to live in their car, on the street... I don't know where. Is that okay for your daughter?"

"No it's not okay. But I can't have Celeste come up here, if that's what you're thinking. It would be a problem. And I don't want her boyfriend hanging around here. So if you could help her out for a couple of months, help her get a job, go back to school, something . . . ."

"Look, Richard, there aren't any jobs. Not in this town for someone like Celeste. If she had some salable skill, but she doesn't."

"She should go back to school and learn something useful, like accounting. She has a degree in biology, but she didn't want to do that. I don't know what to say."

"I guess that means you're not going to help us."

"I can't right now."

Jasmine slammed down the receiver of the mobile phone, almost breaking it. He could but he won't, she thought. And Jasmine was too proud to ask him for money. He wouldn't help them financially, if he wouldn't help them in any other way. There was one sure thing here. Ramon had to go. And then she would deal with Celeste, help her get a job or go back to school. Jasmine had heard about government grants for education. Maybe Celeste could get some of that money and learn a trade or skill where she could support herself.

Chapter 12
To the Dog Park

Monsoon was anticipated in Arizona any day. The air hung heavy with humidity in the 110-degree heat. Dust storms, called haboobs, raged nearly every evening, rolling a cloud of dust into the city and beyond, and lightning flashed across the distant sky. The elusive rain, however, would not arrive until it was ready. Average rainfall in Arizona desert is a little over seven inches, and half of that falls during the summer rainy season. But then most of the southern half of Arizona is taken up by the Sonoran Desert.

Jasmine went to the dog park every day for the next week, sometimes twice a day, in the early morning and later in the evening around eight o'clock after the sun went down. Chance was in his second puppyhood and thoroughly enjoyed the outings.

After checking out the jobs on-line, Jasmine would put on her jeans shorts with a t-shirt, her blue Teva sandals, and a white cap. She had a special pair of sandals for the dog park because she knew that in walking around the park, it was easy to step in dog excrement. Even though people were told to pick up after their dogs, some never did, and some dogs pooped on the sly while their owners weren't watching. She took the sandals off as soon as she stepped in the front door so that she wouldn't spread bacteria in her house.

Chance watched her intently and knew that when she put these shoes on and these shorts and that hat, it meant they were going to the dog park. He would start turning round and round, squealing with joy. She even wrote a dog park song that she sang to Chance as they were driving to the park. Sung to the tune of the Ball Park song, it went like this:

> Let's all go to the dog park;
> Let's all go where they bark.
> With poodles and pit bulls and dogs named Jack,
> I don't care if I never get back.
> Let's all run with the greyhounds;
> Frisbees, tennis balls fly!
> Oh, it's great fun, all dogs agree,
> At the old dog park.

Chance loved it when she sang to him, and he would raise his voice in song as well, seeming to mouth the words.

For Jasmine, going to the dog park was a way to escape. She felt comfortable there now. She had met many people who were dog lovers like herself and they were her new friends and support group. They talked about dogs mostly, but sometimes they would talk about personal matters.

If there were a lot of people at the park, they gathered in small groups around the table and trees with their dogs, and Jasmine began to notice that those with big, aggressive dogs tended to hang out together, and fights would periodically break out. The dog owners would pull the dogs apart and reprimand them until they did it again. This sometimes was due to a still-intact alpha male dog attempting to dominate a female or other males. Jasmine stayed away from this group. Chance was a very sweet, submissive dog, and on another day he had been attacked by a pit-bull-sharpei mix that bit him on the face. Jasmine was so concerned and upset with the owner of the dog that they almost came to fisticuffs. It seemed to her that the aggressive dogs sometimes emulated the behavior of their owners. One woman, owner of a pit-bull mix, in her late fifties and grossly overweight, packed a gun on her hip. What was that all about, wondered Jasmine? She didn't want to find out, so she tried to find the groups of "nice" dogs and "nice" people.

By Thursday of that week, some of her friends were beginning to notice that Jasmine and Chance practically lived at the dog park. One of her new friends, Kaylee, the owner of a Golden Retriever named Maggie, approached Jasmine. "You're spending a lot of time here these days," she said.

"Yeah, I guess I am. Gets my mind off problems at home."

Kaylee was thoughtful for a few minutes, and then she said, "Do you want to talk about it? I'm a good listener." Kaylee, a third-grade teacher, whose lines on her face showed her middle age, had flowing dishwater-blond hair and blue eyes that bore into her listener when she talked. She told Jasmine she was single and was dedicated to her cause of teaching young children. She seemed to be very perceptive.

"Sure. Can't hurt. To start with, my twenty-five-year-old daughter came to Phoenix last week to live with me. She's out of work and out of money too, I would guess."

"How long have you lived alone?" Kaylee asked.

"Over ten years. Yeah, you get it, adjusting to having another person in my home is ..." she cleared her throat, "difficult even if that person is my daughter. But it's not just one person; her boyfriend is with her, and they asked if he could stay. I said one night and, well he's still there and it's been more than a week. I don't know what to do. I'm afraid if I ask him to leave, she'll go with him. And I want Celeste to stay. I need to help her get some traction in her life."

"What's the relationship between Celeste and her boyfriend?"

"I'm not sure. She's known him a couple of years. They lived together in his flat for, I guess, six months until they were evicted. He's unemployed, too."

"Oh, boy. Well what do you want to do? I see the problem, but you have to know what you want."

Chance came up to Jasmine with a tennis ball, daring her to throw it, and when she did, both Maggie and Chance ran as fast as they could to catch it.

"Yes, thanks for pointing that out. I'm sure I'd have gotten there, but I'm too stunned to think straight these days. Being unemployed myself . . . ."

"That's understandable."

As Jasmine talked with Kaylee, she began to think this problem through in a logical way. She wanted Celeste's boyfriend to move out. She wanted Celeste to go back to school and get a skill that would provide a decent living. She would help her do that.

"I think what I need to do is take my daughter aside and tell her that Ramon has to go and she has to take steps to becoming independent again. That's what I have to do," Jasmine said with resolve.

"See, that was easy."

"Easy thinking up solutions, hard to implement them," said Jasmine. But was she afraid of her daughter? She didn't think that was it. Maybe she was afraid of alienating Celeste. They'd had such a difficult relationship in the past, and Jasmine wanted to make amends. She wanted to be close to Celeste, now that her daughter was an adult. Could she achieve that if she threw her daughter's boyfriend out of her house when he, too, was basically homeless? But Ramon could take care of himself; Jasmine was sure of that.

Jasmine continued to visit the dog park twice a day, and one Saturday she arrived later than usual in the evening, around nine o'clock. The dog park closed at ten. There were very few people and dogs at this hour, but it was cooler and certainly less hectic than during the daytime. Chance loved it, too. He could run and chase the ball without competition and investigate different areas of the park without other dogs interrupting, sniffing him, and challenging him in some way. And the drinking water was clean without all the slobbering from the other dogs. Chance was very particular about his drinking water and wouldn't drink if it had been standing awhile and was warm. He must have developed this little quirk since she had gotten him. No doubt he had had plenty of stale, warm water in his lifetime, Jasmine thought.

Jasmine saw a flash of lightning in the distance over South Mountain. It wouldn't rain tonight, but it was trying, she thought. Then the lights dimmed as a reminder that it was time to leave. She called Chance, who was chasing bugs around a mud hole, and put his leash on him. As she was walking out of the park an older fellow asked her if the dog in the far corner that looked like a Poodle-Cocker mix was hers. "No," she said. I thought I saw its owner earlier. Is the dog alone?" she asked.

"It was here yesterday," said the man who by now was walking his beagle out the gate.

"Do you think someone dumped the dog here?" Jasmine said.

"Looks that way. Poor thing. Someone should take her home. It must be pretty hungry after being here a couple of days," said the man. And then after a pause he said, "Why don't you?"

"You think I should taker her home?" Jasmine thought about this for a few minutes. Another dog? Why not. And, who would help this little dog if she didn't. She tied Chance near the gate so as not to frighten the buff-colored dog hiding in the corner of the field. She saw a park ranger coming to lock up and she said, "I'm going to check on the little dog over there. I think his owner left him." She took a treat out of her fanny pack and slowly approached the animal. It started to run but then saw the food in her hand and changed its mind. She held out the treat and the little dog came over and gingerly took it from her hand. She offered another one and as the dog grabbed for it, she held on to its collar. Hm, the dog has a collar but no ID. Sounds familiar, doesn't it, she thought. She looked at the dog's belly and saw that it

HANNAH STEVENS

was a young female. The dog wasn't in bad shape and appeared to have been eating regularly until recently. "What do you say, little girl? Do you want to come home with Chance and me? I think we might have room for another dog at our house." And she picked it up and carried it out the gate, leading Chance, who by now was beside himself with excitement as his person carried another dog. She put them both in the back of her car and drove home. On the way home she glanced in the back to see if everyone was getting along. Chance licking the new dog's ears, and it was cuddling up to him. Yes, I think they'll get along okay, she thought. But then she's a girl and he's a boy. Makes it easier.

Chapter 13
Chance

Changes are happening fast at my house. Yes, I do think this is my house now, as my owner has made it clear to me that I'm her buddy and here to stay. But, a couple of days ago, I don't know how many now, two more people showed up at the door and my owner let them in, and in fact kissed and hugged the young woman. She just shook the hand of the other person. I don't know who these people are, but the girl, I'll call her that because she looks young, looks kind of like my person. Well, anyway, things are a little mixed up here now. They sometimes sleep until noon in the TV room, but it's not the TV room anymore, and I can't get in there to my bed where I used to go hide sometimes. And for awhile we weren't going for walks or to the dog park at all, and I felt like my person had forgotten that I was even here. Oh, she fed me, gave me fresh water, and made sure that I went outside to do my business. But that was all. The boy and the girl, though, took me out in the back yard and played ball with me. I think they like me and I do like them. But I want life to get back to normal. I sense there is a lot of tension in the house now. I can't put my paw on it, but something is wrong.

Then, as if that wasn't weird enough, we start going to the dog park every day, twice a day. I'm lovin' it. I get to see my friends. I even got into a fight with this big burly male with balls hanging from his

rear. That was really exciting, except he did get the better of me and bit my face. My person ran over to us and pulled me away and kicked the dog because he would not stop fighting. And then she got into an argument with the male dog's owner, who was a big, burly man. Well, we just walked away and I guess we'll stay away from that dog from now on. And the owner too.

But there's more. The night before last, I think, when we were just leaving the dog park, there was this little mutt hanging out by herself. Well, my owner went over to her and offered her a treat, and wouldn't you know, she picked her up and put her in the back with me and we took her home. I'm ecstatic. She's the cutest thing I've seen in a long time. She has curly blond hair and big brown eyes that just melt me. I wish I could still have my way with her, but that's been over since I was seven months old or there-about.

We get along so well. I now have a playmate, and we run and chase in the backyard and fight over toys and have the greatest time. I do get a little jealous when my person pays more attention to her than to me. But I just butt my head right in to make sure that I get noticed. I hope she's here to stay. It would be really lonely if she didn't, because my person has these other people and pays more attention to them than to me these days.

Chapter 14
Reality Check

"**M**om, you got another dog? You can barely afford to pay for Chance. How can you get another one?"

"I rescued another dog. There was nothing else for me to do. I didn't even think twice about it. She'd been at the dog park for at least a couple of days. What'd you expect me to do, leave her there to starve another day? Somebody dumped her there, and she needs a home. We'll find a way to pay for her. Look, Celey, I took you in, didn't I? Should I not have done that?"

"Oh, Mom, that's different. At least I hope it is. I'm your *daughter*."

There was silence as Celeste glared at her mother from one end of the living-room couch while the dogs tugged at a rope toy in front of them.

"You're always complaining about not having enough money for utilities. Why would you want to take on this responsibility?"

"I have to level with you, Celey. Part of limiting the use of the air conditioner is to save energy for the environment. And the same with water; we're in a drought. It just makes sense to use as little water as possible."

"Well, how about the local environment in this house?" shouted Celeste.

"Look, until you're contributing around here, I control the air conditioner. And it won't hurt you to be a little warm. Take off some clothes. Go to the mall. Get a job!"

Jasmine didn't want to fight with Celeste. She wanted to be her friend and help her, but tensions were high and Celeste was probably right about one thing: getting another dog would put an extra burden on her budget. within three weeks time she'd added two extra house guests and now another animal to feed and care for. This young dog was not spayed and would need shots, and it would be costly.

"Look, honey, I love you. Let's not fight. Let's take the dogs for a walk, just the two of us. I need to talk with you alone, without Ramon hanging around." While Celeste and Jasmine were having this heated conversation, Ramon was out back drinking coffee on the patio and enjoying the early morning. He seemed to be oblivious to all that was happening in the household. Jasmine thought he was either socially inept or he didn't care.

And they did just that. They told Ramon they would be back in half an hour at the most. They put the dog's leashes on and out the door they went. It was only nine o'clock, but the sun beat down on the earth and it already felt like being in a pizza oven.

"I wonder when it's going to rain." Jasmine posed as she looked up at the cloudless sky, trying to make small talk to diffuse the anger they'd had moments before.

"What difference would it make? Hot is hot and I'm thinking that Phoenix in the summer is a bad idea."

"When it rains, it does cool down a little. The temperature will go down to the low 100s."

"Whoopee. Down to a hundred. I can't wait. How do you stand it?"

"I rather like it here. The desert is beautiful, and it's only really hot between July and October. That's three months out of the year. June is so dry that you don't notice how hot it is, and it cools off at night. And you've been here at Christmas when it was seventy-five degrees. You liked it then."

"I did," Celeste murmured. "But it was 115 yesterday. You don't want to do anything, especially outside."

They walked several blocks, crossed Twentieth Street, and came to a park. Chance and the new dog walked out in front, the new dog pulling hard on her leash, investigating the ground for things to eat, bird feathers, anything she could get in her mouth. A bird flew close by and Chance strained to give chase but was reined in by Jasmine.

"We need to name her. What do you think we should call her?" Jasmine asked thoughtfully.

"I don't know. I'm not good at that." Then Celeste thought for a few minutes. "Sally, Sadie…. Sarah…. Fluffy, that's it. Fluffy's a good name."

"We could call her Blondie. She has blond hair," offered Jasmine.

"I like that. That's a great name for a dog."

And so it was decided that the new puppy would be named Blondie.

"Blondie and Chance. Sounds like Las Vegas," quipped Celeste.

"Life is like Las Vegas, it's a crap shoot." They sat down at one of the picnic tables with the dogs crawling under the table for shade. "Celey, are you and Ramon a couple?"

"What do you mean?"

"I mean, are you committed to each other?"

"No, not really. We're friends, have been for a couple of years." Celeste hesitated and then said, "I love him in a way. He took me in when I had no place to go. But I don't think I want to marry him if, that's what you mean."

"Does he have other friends back in L.A.?"

"Yeah, sure." Silence, then, "I know where you're going with this; you're saying he has to go. That's what you're saying, isn't it?"

"I'm afraid so, honey. I would love to take in every homeless person and every homeless dog too, but I can't. I can take you in for awhile and that's all I can do. You do understand, don't you?"

"I get it, Mom. I get it. I'll tell him today that he has to leave and go back to California." Then she thought for moment and looked at her mother and said, "Do you not like Ramon, Mom?"

"I hardly know him. He seems okay. And like you say, he offered you shelter when you needed it. He can't be all bad."

"What I mean to say is, would you like him better if he was white like Dad?"

Jasmine looked at Celeste in amazement. "Sweetheart, I'm half Mexican. Why would you think that?"

"Because when I took Ramon to meet Dad, he wasn't friendly to Ramon at all. Is Dad prejudiced?"

"He married me, didn't he? I doubt it. But I never knew what was going on in your dad's head anyway, and his parents never treated me like one of the family. They were against the marriage from the start."

"There is something I've always wanted to know about our family. Was Grandma Jorgenson an illegal alien when she married Grandpa? She never wanted to talk about that time in her life, and I've always wondered."

"Yes, she was. She came across the California border with her family in the late '40's. They came to work the citrus orchards in Southern California. Grandma never talked about it with me, either, but when I was in college I did some research. It was my family background, after all."

"So was she worried about being deported?"

"No, I don't think so. After she married Dad, she was able to get her citizenship. And in those days the immigration laws were almost non-existent. It wasn't until 1952 that a comprehensive immigration law was passed, I think they called it the Immigration and Nationality Act of 1952. And then in 1965 Congress passed another law that gave preference to immigrants with skills needed in the United States and to close relatives of U.S. citizens."

Jasmine played with Chance's ears and looked like she had gone back to another place and time. "The farmers wanted the cheap labor to get the crops picked, and Mexicans wanted to come to America because they had no work in their home country," she continued.

"I bet they didn't make very much money."

"You're right. They paid as little as they could, a dollar an hour, but that was more than they could make back in Mexico. They had to work from sunrise to sunset, sometimes they had no bathrooms, no water to drink and they were exposed to lethal pesticides every day."

"Didn't they have unions protecting them?" asked Celeste. "I thought there was a farm workers union for these people."

"You must be thinking about Caesar Chavez, who founded the United Farm Workers. But that didn't happen until the '60's. In the early days the workers were afraid to complain or organize because they feared being deported."

"So how did Grandma get to Minnesota? That's a long way from Southern California."

"They were recruited. In the summer there wasn't much work in Southern California; most of the crops were picked in the winter in the mild climate, and it was just the opposite in Minnesota. So this company promised them work in the north, offered more money, and bussed them up there. They even provided modest housing for families. They lived in barrack-like buildings, sort of like a concentration camp."

"How did Grandpa ever meet his wife? They were as far apart in social strata as they could be."

"They were far apart, all right. But Grandpa had always been a young rebel. He went to the Waseca County Fair one Saturday night and there she was, in all her Latina loveliness — the dark hair, dark eyes, voluptuous young figure — and she captured his heart the minute he saw her. He kept seeing her secretly for a couple of months, and he fell in love with her.

Carlotta's, Grandma's, family was getting ready to go back to Southern California and Grandpa was about to lose the love of his life, so they eloped to Iowa. By the time his family found out, it was all done. Grandpa's dad tried to have the marriage annulled, but Grandpa prevailed and the marriage stuck. Grandma's family wasn't too happy about the marriage, either, but there wasn't much they could do about it, so they went back to Southern California without her."

"So did Grandma's family get deported? We never had contact with them. I never knew my maternal great-grandparents."

"No. They went back to California and continued to do the field work, I guess. I think there was a huge rift between my mother and her family that was never repaired. And I think my mother was always trying to be as white as she could; she wanted to be an American. And yet a part of her cherished her heritage."

Jasmine thought about how, when she had been a young girl, she was ashamed of her mother because she was so different from the other mothers. Now she knew that she had been wrong. But she was only a child. And when Jasmine became an adult, she became closer to her parents. She wrote to her mother and went to visit as often as she could. She loved her mother and embraced her Mexican culture.

"What a story. Why didn't you tell me about that before?" asked Celeste.

"You never asked," said Jasmine.

Celeste reached down to pet Blondie on her head and the dog licked her hand.

"Then in 1986 all of these hundreds of thousands of undocumented workers that had come across the Mexican border over the years to do the low-paying, backbreaking work that Americans didn't want to do were given amnesty," Jasmine continued with the story. "They had to have been continuously working and living in the country since 1982. President Reagan was in office at the time. And then a 1990 law continued these preferences under President George H.W. Bush. Aliens must be admitted as legal immigrants to get U.S. citizenship."

"Mom, you seem to know a lot about this. I had no idea. And there is so much controversy now about people coming over the border. And to think that part of my own family came here illegally. It blows my mind."

They slowly walked back to the house, talking about living in Phoenix and about the neighborhood, making small talk.

Celeste had realized that her mom would be asking Ramon to leave. She knew she needed to get her life together and be her own person, so it was probably for the best. And Jasmine was relieved that Celeste didn't object. She'd wanted Celeste to tell him. She didn't want to be the person with the bad news and have both Celeste and Ramon angry with her. Until this talk with her daughter she'd no idea what the relationship was between her daughter and Ramon. She had to admit she was relieved to find out that it wasn't as serious a relationship as she had thought. Going forward, the conversation would be about Celeste and her future. But that would come later.

Celeste told Ramon that night that he should leave and go back to California.

"I know this has been a burden on your mother," Ramon said. "Are you going to be okay?"

"Yeah, I'll be fine. But where will you go?" Celeste asked, worrying that he would have no place to live.

"I have friends. I could even go and live with Dad for awhile. I'm sure he would love to have another cook in his kitchen. I just hate having to depend on my parents, but I guess that's what I'll have to do. Anyway, it's too hot in Arizona, and I haven't found any new opportunities."

Celeste knew that he had looked hard, in the newspaper and on-line, and he even went to job fairs, but there were few jobs and many people looking. It was a terrible time to be unemployed.

Early the next morning, Ramon loaded up his car with his things. He thanked Jasmine for her hospitality.

Celeste walked Ramon out to his car and they embraced.

"Have a safe trip," Celeste said.

"I'll call you when I get back to L.A. I'll miss you," he said. And then he got into his beat-up old blue Honda and drove away.

Chance and Blondie sat at the living room window watching the drama unfold. As Celeste came back into the house, Chance grabbed his big rope toy and tried to get her to take hold of it and play tug-of-war, but Celeste was preoccupied and pushed him away. "Come on Chance, I'll play with you," Jasmine said as she grabbed the toy and started pulling it. Chance growled in a playful way and tugged and pulled until Jasmine let him "win." He looked at her, seemingly in surprise, and tried to get her to play the game again, but Jasmine wasn't willing. She opened the back door and both Chance and Blondie went outside to chase birds, bugs, lizards and anything else that might catch their eye. Chance had gotten into the bad habit of trying to catch bees that hovered over the flowering rosemary by the back gate to the alley, until he was stung. But he wouldn't learn; he would try again, as much as Jasmine told him not to.

Jasmine walked over to the sofa and sat down. She looked at Celeste as she was coming into the room and motioned her to sit down. "Are you sad?" she asked.

"Yeah, a little. I'm so confused about Ramon. I love him in a way, but don't in another. Does that make sense?"

"Being away from him might make things clearer for you," Jasmine said as she put her arms around her daughter and hugged her.

"Yeah, you're right. I guess you've always been right about everything, but I was too stubborn to accept that."

They sat on the sofa holding onto one another, Jasmine thinking that she didn't want to always be right. She just wanted to love her daughter.

"You know, Mom, I didn't plan on this happening. I don't want to be a burden on you. I want to be independent. And I especially don't want you telling me what to do, like I'm a child again," Celeste said as she pulled away from her mother.

"I don't want that either. And the sooner you're on your feet again, the better for both of us. So, what do you want to do?"

"I could model. I've done that before. Maybe get some TV commercials. They pay good money."

"That's a thought. But is it steady work?" Jasmine waited for Celeste to answer and then said, "No. And it would take money; you'd have to get a portfolio, a DVD together. And all those auditions. There must be thousands of people wanting to do that. You'd be competing with hordes of people chasing the same dream."

"It's not a dream. It's a profession just as much as being an accountant."

"It's not practical, Celey. It's not steady. Unless you find a husband to help support you."

"That's not an option right now." Celeste gazed out the front window, watching a woman across the street walking her slightly overweight Pug. "Why haven't you remarried?" she asked.

"I haven't had time; first I had a demanding job, and now I'm unemployed. And I haven't met the right person. I don't know if I ever will. But I'm content. I don't need a man to be complete. I love my painting, and if I can make some money at that, I'll be happy."

"I guess Dad is co-dependent. He needs a woman to do those domestic things for him."

"I was his handmaiden when we were married. He earned a lot of money, but I took care of everything at home, including you, my dear. And it was a lot of work."

"You just had one kid. What do women do who have two, three, maybe more? I can't imagine." Celeste shook her head as she thought about that. "I don't think I'll marry, either."

"Don't say that. You're young and it's better to have a partner in life. One of the things that I miss is having someone to depend on for making those big decisions. I'm not good at money decisions and I have no one I can totally trust. The financial advisors have their own best interests at heart, not mine."

"Don't you get lonely? Don't you miss the romance? The loving, holding? The kissing? The sex?"

"Sometimes. But, you know, my dogs fill up my heart. They're always there to hug me. And they never judge me. If I scold them for doing something bad, they're soon wagging their tails and happy to be with me. Husbands can carry a grudge for weeks."

Celeste laughed. "Yeah, I know what you mean."

"But back to the problem here. How about going back to school? You could get a grant. Our government is helping people like you."

"Why? What do I need to learn?"

"You might talk to a career counselor to find out what your strengths are and what you might be good at."

"No. I know who I am, Mom," Celeste said emphatically. "I don't need someone else to tell me. I know that I would never be a good nurse; I don't like to be around sick people. In fact I don't really like people all that much."

"I'm glad you know who you are. I don't quite yet, and I am a whole lot older than you are."

Celeste pondered this for a few minutes.

"We have a very good community college here in Phoenix, and I want you to go to the career center and talk to them and see if you could sign up for some courses. In the meantime, Celeste, you'll need to find some kind of a job to help me with expenses around here. It may be waitressing, or flipping burgers, even working at a call center, but you need to be doing some kind of work."

"Work a minimum-wage job? Mom, how can I? I don't even have a car."

"Well, there are some small businesses in the area, a major hotel just blocks away. We have good bus service and Phoenix just got light rail in the downtown area, finally. And there are lots of people with degrees working minimum-wage jobs these days, so don't think it's beneath you." And then she added, "I'll help all that I can."

Celeste knew that, as much as she hated it, she would soon be doing some drudge job for very little money. She'd always been fortunate to have work that was meaningful to her, fun and exciting. But that was about to change. The reality set in.

Chance and Blondie walked over to the water bowl and drank deeply. They were feeling the heat. They asked to come inside and when Jasmine let them in, Chance drooled all over the tile floor in the kitchen. Jasmine kept a towel by the back door just for the purpose of wiping dribbles from his mouth. Otherwise, he would shake his head and splatter saliva be all over the walls.

Chapter 15
Ramon Goes Home

Driving away from that little house in Phoenix, from Celeste, was the hardest thing Ramon had ever done. And now here he was zooming along on I-10, heading west, further away from her every minute. And where was he headed? Back to nowhere. Well, not exactly nowhere. Back to his friends and family, he guessed.

The road to L.A. stretched out in front of him, filled with trucks as far as he could see. The sun had only just shone itself over the buttes in the east and the landscape changed little between Tonopah and Blithe, muted tones of tans and browns with the soft greens of scrub cactus, a Palo Verde tree here and there and an occasional Saguaro cactus rising up like a soldier in the desert. He noticed a hawk, wings spread, lighting on a mesquite tree along side the road, likely coming back from its nightly hunt for rodents in the desert.

It was a road to lose your thoughts on, wandering in and out of life's pleasures and treasures.

These last two years with Celeste had been a conundrum. A series of highs and lows. . He had experienced pure joy and happiness along with incredible frustration. He knew the moment he saw her in that bar at the marina that this was the woman he wanted to marry, have children with, and live out his life. But he was not able to convince Celeste. He thought of her soft dark brown eyes looking at him, holding mysteries that he could not quite unlock. When she laughed they sparkled like gemstones, and when she was angry they clouded over like thunder in a rainstorm. There were times when he didn't know what to expect from her. Would she be soft and loving, eager for his kisses or would she shun him, lash out at him for some unknown reason? He attributed her behavior to the passage she was going through, trying to find her way in this complicated world.

Even though she had a degree in biology, she had come to L.A. to pursue an acting career.

"Why don't you work in your field of biology?" he'd asked her one night when they were having pizza after seeing a movie. Celeste hadn't had any work in over two months and she was complaining about her money running out.

"Because it's boring. It's just not me. Dad was the one who steered me in that direction, but I want some excitement."

"You need something to pay the bills. Excitement doesn't always do that."

"I know what you're saying. I hear it all the time from Dad. I don't need a lecture from you, Ramon," Celeste lashed out at him.

"Just trying to help. I'd be happy to support you as long as I have a job, but that's not a given these days." Ramon had been working for Mattel for two years in their accounting department and had been laid off recently, but he had found a six-month contract with a small accounting firm in Redondo Beach.

"Celeste, one of the things that attracted me to you is your intelligence. And if you have special training, a special skill, you should use it."

"I do have a special skill; I am attractive and I can act and I want to be able to show that to the world." Celeste played with her pizza, took a sip of her beer. "If I got a job as a biologist, I would most likely be doing research in a lab, long, tedious experiments for other people, until I'd get my PhD. It's grunt work and pays very little. I know somebody has to do it, and they make a huge contribution to the world. That's what attracted me to biology in the first place."

"Life is tedious, Celeste. Days full of repetitive tasks, some of them getting us nowhere."

"You're so pragmatic, Ramon. Just like my dad."

Later that night, Celeste rebuffed his efforts to make love. What was it? The argument they'd had earlier about her career? Or did it go deeper than that? He couldn't quite figure it out. And he certainly couldn't figure out Celeste. She was as much a mystery to him now as she had been the night he had first met her. Maybe that was what had attracted him to her. He would keep trying.

He had reached the Colorado River and was crossing over into California. He loved the desert landscape coming into Palm Springs. The sweeping sandstone sloping down into arroyos and little canyons of poly-colored rock, the starkness of it all. And then, to the traveler looking across the valley, the San Jacinto Mountains rose abruptly as if some Athenian god had designed this beautiful but harsh place.

He would be in L.A. in another hour or so. He would call his father and ask if he could bunk in with him for awhile. He knew Dad would be happy to take him in. It was Ramon who was hesitant to impose on his father's generosity. He felt he would lose his autonomy if he had to go back home. His dad could then feel that he had the right to tell him what to do, make decisions for him. And Ramon wanted more than anything to be independent.

A mirage loomed ahead, looking every bit like a pool of water in the middle of the road, but Ramon knew it was only the heat morphing itself, tricking the viewer into thinking otherwise. Life is like that, he thought. You see something ahead of you; a job, a potential mate, and you get excited about it only to find out that it isn't real after all.

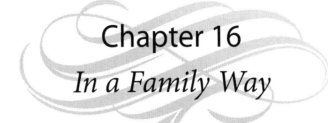

Chapter 16

In a Family Way

Puppies grow into their "teens" in six to nine months and go through a kind of puberty: the female ovulates and has a menstrual blood flow and the male dog's testes drop, preparing for mating. When these events happen, a male dog will travel miles to find a female in estrus, relentless in his hunt for a female to mate with. Not too different from young pubescent teens. This happens, of course only if the dog is not neutered or spayed. The urge to procreate is so strong in nature, among canines and humans alike.

Jasmine knew if she was going to keep Blondie, and she thought she would, it was time to take her to the vet and have her spayed. She thought the dog was seven or eight months old and if she wanted to get this done before Blondie went into heat, she had to act now. She loaded her into the car and drove to the veterinary's office. Chance hung around the front door as they were leaving and appeared to be wondering what was happening and why wasn't he going along on this trek.

Once she reached the office, just blocks away, she took Blondie inside. The waiting room was filled with owners with their pets waiting to see the doctor. Jasmine sat on a bench along a wall and filled out the necessary paper-work, while Blondie tried to make contact with the other dogs. Next to her, a young woman held a Chihuahua, shivering in a blanket. On the other side of her, another woman had an animal carrying case containing a cat meowing loudly, protesting the confinement and being in strange surroundings, no doubt. She turned in the paper-work and waited another half hour before she was given a room where they settled in. She found dog treats in a jar on the counter and gave one to Blondie, who seemed to be taking this in her stride.

The vet technician came in and took Blondie's vitals, temperature and pulse rate; all was normal. Then a young female veterinary doctor named Jackie came in and asked Jasmine to lift Blondie onto the table. "Well, what do we have here?" she scratched Blondie's ears, then took out her stethoscope and listened to her heart and thoroughly checked the rest of her body. "She's a healthy dog. Where did you get her?" Doctor Jackie asked. When Jasmine told her, she smiled and said, "You are kind to take her in. This is happening all too often these days. I suppose if you're going to dump a dog, the dog park is not a bad place. The animal has water and probably snacks from people and it won't get killed in traffic. But even so, it's sad." She examined her further. "So, what can we do for you today?"

"I want to have her spayed."

"Too late, I'm afraid. She's already pregnant," said Doctor Jackie.

"Oh no. That can't be!"

"How long have you had her?"

"A week. So she was likely pregnant when I got her, because she hasn't been in contact with any breeding male since I brought her home. My other dog, Chance, is male, but he's neutered."

"She's not very far along. Could have happened at the dog park, you know. Or maybe that's why her former owners wanted to get rid of her."

"Well, what do I do now? I can't take on any more in my household. My adult daughter just came back to live with me. She's unemployed, as am I. This is terrible news."

"We could do an abortion, but the procedure is costly."

"No, I don't think I want to do that anyway. I'll let her have the puppies and then have her spayed. I'll have to find homes for them, which is going to be difficult with this economy," said Jasmine as she petted Blondie, thinking that she didn't need this problem.

"She's really too young to be having puppies. You'll have to monitor her closely, especially when her time is near. I'll give you information on how to care for her. And then when the puppies are six weeks or so and eating on their own, bring her in and we'll spay her so this won't happen again."

"You've got that one right." Jasmine gathered up Blondie, paid the vet bill with her Visa card, and went home. She was in shock. This is all I need, she thought. Bad news often comes in multiples. She wondered what was going to happen next.

She brought Blondie into the house. Chance was there to greet them — wagging his tail, sniffing Blondie to see where they'd been. Celeste, dressed in jeans shorts and a white tank top, walked out into the living room.

"Blondie's in a family way," murmured Jasmine

"No way!. That's cool," said Celeste.

"Way! Not cool. She's too young, and we'll have to find homes for the pups. No, it's definitely not good. But we'll manage."

"She could get an abortion."

"Not a good option. Mainly because it's expensive."

"You could take her back to the dog park and then maybe someone else'll pick her up."

"I can't do that. She's ours, for better or worse."

"How long?" Celeste asked.

"A couple of months. They say about sixty-three days, and she's probably two weeks into her pregnancy, the vet said."

"I think this'll be fun," said Celeste, as she stroked Blondie.

"I'll let you clean up after the puppies when they're pooping all over. We'll have to get some kind of enclosure to keep them confined. I didn't ask for this."

"But you brought her home," Celeste reminded her.

Jasmine gave Celeste an icy look and took Blondie out the back door, with Chance following behind. She went out into the yard to clean up after the dogs and noticed that the drip system lines had been pulled out all along the back fence. "Blondie, did you do this? And Chance, what do you know?" Chance raised his ears and cocked his head to one side, and Jasmine thought she saw him point a paw towards Blondie, but she knew no one would believe that.

She was astounded. Now she would have to repair the drip system as well. She thought she could probably do that herself; she'd repaired the system before. In threes, she thought. Then she walked back to the covered patio to a wicker settee and two chairs with cushions and a coffee table. She noticed that one of the chairs had been chewed. "Oh, my god, I just bought this set last year," she screamed. She'd have to put the furniture in a safe place so the dog or dogs couldn't get to it. And she could never let them out in the yard unattended. Blondie was the most likely perpetrator because she was the youngest, but Chance could have participated as well. Then looking closer at the patio area, she saw that the supporting posts, heavy four-by-five inch wooden beams, had been gnawed, the brick wall had gaping holes, and the dog house had teeth marks around the door. "You've been busy, Blondie. You can't be trusted. Now I know why your owner dumped you. You are dangerous."

The rest of the week was mostly uneventful. Jasmine doled out household duties to Celeste, having her clean the kitchen, take out the garbage and pick up dog poop. Celeste seemed to be willing to co-operate, and Jasmine was beginning to enjoy having her daughter with her. She liked the company and the help around the house, too. I guess she's finally growing up, Jasmine thought. It sure took awhile.

But sometimes it takes a calamity for young people to understand responsibility to others and where they fit in the world. Jasmine could see that her earlier training, along with Richard's, was paying off. And Celeste appeared to have a good heart.

Chapter 17
Dogs Will Be Dogs

Dogs communicate with their bodies, wagging tails, ears perking and wiggling torsos. Reading the mood of a dog is incredibly easy if one is observant, and the tail is just one barometer of the dog's disposition. If, when one is approaching a dog, its tail is whipping back and forth and the body is twisting and turning, tongue hanging from its mouth, it is likely to be friendly. A wagging tail – however - can have different meanings: happiness – "I've found a bird and I am going to catch it!" or simply that food is on its way. On the other hand, if a dog approaches with bared teeth and tail down, the animal could be preparing to bite you. If this is happening, do not run away; the animal will chase you, and it will win. Dogs love the chase. Stand tall and firm, stamp your feet, and confront the angry dog. If you can pick up a rock or some other object to throw at it, that can help to be a deterrent. Most often the animal will back away.

If you are observant, you will notice that when you talk to your dog, its ears go up, saying that it is noticing and trying to decipher what you have said. if the words are familiar to your dog he will understand and act accordingly. People sometimes try to explain dog behavior in human terms. However, what we think is going on in a dog's mind is oftentimes far from what is really happening. Dogs may not be able to talk with words; they "think" with their noses, mouths and ears. Their hearing is far superior to ours, as is their sense of smell. That is why they are often used to find cadavers, drugs and even to detect cancer in humans. And that's what makes them wonderful watch dogs.

Dogs in the wild never bark. Wolves, coyotes, foxes, dingoes and other wild dogs howl and yip. But only domesticated canines bark. It is thought that this is because domestic dogs are communicating with humans, though this has not as yet been proven. The dingo, with populations mainly in Australia, was once a domesticated dog and then went back to the wild.

Chance was a very sweet-tempered dog most of the time. When Jasmine reprimanded him, he would hang his head and his tail would be between his legs. When he was happy, his tail and body were in motion, ears up, tongue hanging out, as if to say, "Yes, I want to go for a walk," or "Yes, I want to eat now." But when anyone strange came around the house or when he saw dogs and people across the street, he barked the loudest bark that he had in his repertoire. This, of course, made Jasmine, a single woman living alone as she had for years now, feel secure.. Having a big dog was like having a loaded gun at the ready in the house. And since Jasmine hated guns, having the dog served the two purposes of providing companionship and security. She didn't know if Chance would bite an intruder if someone came into the house uninvited. That had never been tested, thank goodness. But she hoped that he would. He was not attack-trained, but he was devoted to her and protective of the property.

One habit that she hated about Chance and couldn't break him of was jumping up on visitors when they came to her house. Because he was a big dog, some were frightened of him but most were just annoyed. He would jump and jump, trying to lick the new person's face. It was a friendly gesture but not pleasant, especially for those who were not used to dogs. She'd tried to give him the "off" command, told people to use their knee to push him away, turn away from him, but nothing seemed to work. He even did this in the morning when she was collecting his dish for feeding. Then she read an article about dog behavior and it said that this is instinctive behavior; that in the wild, puppies reach up to the mother to get regurgitated food from her. That explained it but didn't make it any less annoying.

Chance slept on her bed and Blondie in her crate. He was usually quiet all night long. But occasionally he would hear something outside, raise his head, perk up his ears, and then get off the bed and walk around the house barking his huge bark. It was not likely that anyone would want to enter her house to confront such an animal. During the night and in the daytime too, if he heard someone across the street in front of the house, he would go to the front window and stand up, pounding the glass with his front paws as he barked and barked. Some day he's going to go through that window, Jasmine thought. And one night it happened. When Jasmine woke the next morning, early as usual, she saw a small bloody spot on the comforter. What is this, she wondered? Then she walked into the living room, finding shattered glass on the living room floor below the large front window. Ah, that is where the blood came from. "Chance, come here," she said. When he came over to her she examined him and checked his paws. Sure enough, there was a small cut on his right front paw. "Chance, I hope you learned your lesson. I'm glad you weren't badly hurt, though," she said as she scratched his ears.

Jasmine measured the window pane and wrote down the dimensions. She called around for a handyman to repair the window and found one who would come out in the late afternoon. The sooner the better. Flies were coming into the house and the cold air from the air conditioner was escaping. She didn't want to be air-conditioning the outdoors.

"Celeste, how are doing with your job hunting? I haven't seen you go out looking for a job lately," said Jasmine. She had not seen Celeste making any effort to find employment, and it was critical for her to find something to do. Jasmine didn't want Celeste hanging around the house doing nothing; she needed to be busy.

"I'm going over to the Hilton this afternoon. They advertised in the newspaper for a bartender. I could make some decent money doing that kind of work. It would be fun, too, and I can walk to work." The hotel was a quarter of a mile from the house.

"Have you heard anything about the grant that you applied for?"

"No, I think it'll take awhile." Celeste had sent an application for an educational grant two weeks before.

"Tending bar? That's not a good job for you. I don't want you out late at night; it's too dangerous. The bar scene is not a good place, being out there exposed to men of all sorts, hitting on you. Aren't there any waitress jobs, or maid's jobs?"

"Mother, you're so old-fashioned! I'm not a baby anymore. I can take care of myself." Celeste always called her "Mother" when she wanted to make a point.

"That's what I'm afraid of. You're a beautiful young woman, and men will be attracted to you."

"I told you, I can handle myself. Don't worry so much."

"That's what mothers do, you know. Worry and want their children to be safe."

Celeste came home later that afternoon and said she had the job. "I think they liked the way I looked. I don't even know how to mix drinks, but I can learn. Mom, this is good. I can make good money and contribute to the household. Be happy."

"No doubt they liked the way you looked; you're beautiful. I'm skeptical. But whenever you are working late, I don't want you walking home alone. I'll come after you or you can use the car if I'm not using it." Jasmine was relieved, though, that she would be having some help with the bills. Groceries were expensive these days. Her income was just over the poverty level, and she couldn't qualify for food stamps. Maybe Celeste would see that being a bartender was not a career choice; she needed to get more education and learn a salable skill so that she could get a more meaningful job with a career path.

Now, on to her own job search and career. But for her it looked hopeless. No one wanted to hire a fifty-something woman unless it was for entry-level wages. She had submitted over two hundred resumes and had three inquiries, but no interviews. She thought about how this economy was a benefit for the big companies. They had the pick of many people, could hire the very best, and pay them lower wages. The worker gets short-changed again, she thought.

But she was still pursuing her own business and worked at that every day. She had written several articles for the Internet, one on labor relations in the U.S., and another on dog behavior. They had been accepted and were out on the World Wide Web for everyone to see. She wasn't paid for them, but that would come later. She was doing some miniature water color paintings as well that she hoped to sell in the fall to the shops in Scottsdale. She'd found some frames for the small desert landscapes and thought they were quite lovely and would sell well. Jasmine realized, though, that she was dabbling and knew she would have to make a choice if she was going to make any amount of money starting her own business.

Then she had an email from a man named Robert Sandesky. He had seen her Web articles and was looking for someone to write a feature article for *Progressive Engineer* about the new light rail system in Phoenix. Would she be interested? It paid $300.00.

Jasmine couldn't believe her eyes. This was her chance. Once she had one article, there would be others. This could be the beginning of her freelance writing career.

When Celeste came home at the end of the day, she told her about it.

"That's great, Mom. I think you'll be good at this. And if you can also make some money . . . ."

Chapter 18
Stormy Weather

Monsoon arrived with a vengeance. After many days of storms circling around the Valley of the Sun, with temperatures in the 100's and humidity rising, the thunderstorm hit late one evening with high winds, sideways rain, thunder and lightning. Hearing the rain pelting the roof and the sound of the thunder, Jasmine woke with a start and looked around the room. Chance yawned and laid his head on Jasmine's leg, but Blondie was whimpering in her crate. Jasmine took her out and pulled her up on the bed where she could be comforted and surrounded by her pack.

The rain was coming harder now, and Jasmine got out of bed and looked out the bedroom window. The street in front of her house was a rushing river, a torrent of water. She could see the level rising in the driveway and rippling towards the back of the carport. She pulled on some shorts and a t-shirt, put on her Teva sandals, and went to the front door. Just as she was passing the bathroom, Celeste came out, looking like she was not feeling well. "You okay, Celeste?" she asked. "I'll be fine," Celeste murmured as she went back into her room and shut the door.

Opening the front door, Jasmine saw that the water had risen to within an inch of the threshold. She opened the back door and saw that the water was covering the patio as well. She had to do something. The rising water would soon be high enough to come into the house if she didn't act. Slogging through the small lake, she walked to the tin shed in the corner of the yard to retrieve the push broom. The dogs were following her now and they looked at her quizzically, likely wondering what she was doing on this wild, rainy night. Lightning flashed and lit up the backyard, and minutes later thunder clapped, sending Blondie into the dog house near the back door. "Oh, Blondie, it's okay. You won't be harmed," she said as she leaned down to scratch the dog's ears. But Blondie shivered as another lightning bolt hit with the boom of thunder following.

Jasmine grabbed the car keys and ran to the carport to drive the car out into the driveway and park it. Might as well get a free car wash while I'm at it, she said to herself. Just as long as it doesn't hail. Then she took the broom and waded to the covered patio and began pushing the water back out onto the driveway and the street. It was a battle as she pushed and pulled the water out, then went back to push more. The water was everywhere, coming from the sky, streaming off the roof, and coming in from the street. Lightning, more thunder, and the acacia trees in the front yard were bending in the wind with sideways rain. Jasmine kept working, long hair dripping with water, her clothes clinging to her wet body, looking like she was near drowning. But she kept at it.

Celeste looked out the door and yelled at her mother over the storm, "What are you doing?"

"I'm trying to keep the water out of the house!" Jasmine yelled back.

"Can I help," asked Celeste.

"Yes! Go out back and clear the drain on the patio."

Thirty minutes later the drama ended, the storm passed. The rain slowed to a drizzle, and the water began to recede from the front patio. Jasmine breathlessly held the broom in her hands as she saw lightning in the distance. She thought how lucky she was that she'd averted the flood again. This was not the first time she had experienced this.

Water was flowing in the street like a river, and she thought back to when she was a child in Minnesota when a summer storm much like this would roar through the town and the streets became ponds. All the kids in the neighborhood would put their swimsuits on and run into the street, splashing and playing in the water. There was little traffic on the street, making it safe for the children. The homes didn't have swimming pools in those days; the closest place to swim was the lake, five miles away. She thought about how children in those days made their own fun with so very little.

She shook herself off, wiped her feet on the door mat, and went inside, after taking the broom out back to the shed where it had been. The water on the back patio had been close to coming into the kitchen as well, but it was fast receding.

"Wow, that was some storm!" exclaimed Celeste. "We don't get storms like that in California. How often does that happen here?"

"Every couple of years. That was a bad one, though," said Jasmine. "I think we'd better get some rest. No doubt there'll be cleaning up to do tomorrow."

Jasmine dried herself off, put her nightgown back on, gathered up the dogs, and climbed back into bed. Blondie was beginning to look pregnant, her belly rounding like a small football, with pink nipples hanging from her underside. Jasmine snuggled down into her bed, surrounded by the dogs. "Blondie, this is just for tonight. You go back into the crate tomorrow night." Jasmine still didn't trust her; Blondie had not fully grown out of puppy-hood.

The next morning the sun came streaming through the window at five a.m., announcing that the day was beginning and the storm was gone. Jasmine dressed in clean shorts and tank top and went out onto the back patio to survey the damage. Moisture hung in the air like a terrarium with a strong, musty smell of creosote. Jasmine loved the smell, but some hated it. In the desert when it is hot and dry there normally are few odors, even in the evening.

The leaves on the plants were washed clean of the ever-present Arizona dust but the patio was full of mud and debris. When she walked around the corner of the house to the north side she saw that her big, beautiful Palo Verde tree was down, covering the side yard. Time to get out the chain saw. And when she walked out to the front, again there were mud and debris and tree limbs in the street.

Celeste wandered out of her room, still looking peaked. Jasmine eyed her with concern. "Do you have to work tonight?" Celeste had started her new job two days ago. She said she was learning how to make all kinds of specialty drinks and she loved the customers, who were so nice to her.

"Mom, sit down. I have to talk to you," said Celeste.

Jasmine sat on the sofa in the living room looking at Celeste, almost knowing what she was about to hear. Chance and Blondie came into the room and climbed up and sat on either side of them.

"I'm pregnant. I took a pregnancy test yesterday, and it was positive."

"Oh, honey, I don't know what to say. But I almost knew. You've been throwing up every morning and, well, I didn't think you had the flu."

"What am I going to do?" Celeste started to cry.

"What do you *want* to do?"

"I don't know. I'm so confused."

Jasmine put her arms around Celeste, holding her while they cried together. After a few minutes she said, "I understand. I understand." She paused and then she said, "It's not the right time, but we'll figure it out. I love you, Celeste."

"I guess I should get an abortion."

"Is that what you want?"

"How can I start a new career, and have a baby, too? I don't think I can handle it."

"Well, you're not a kid anymore. Maybe you can. Obviously, Ramon is the father."

"Yes." She hung her head. "I don't know if he'll want the responsibility." Her head still down, she said, "Oh, Mom, I feel so bad. How could I have been so stupid? You told me when I was younger not get into this predicament. So here I am."

"Celeste, sweetheart, there is nothing to be ashamed of. You're not the first woman to have this happen. And I'm not going to lecture you. I love you, and I want to help you." Jasmine wondered if she should tell Celeste that she had been pregnant when she married her father. But that could wait. She remembered well, waiting for her period to come; they didn't have instant pregnancy tests in those days. The morning sickness and trying to keep the secret from everyone, especially her mom. In those days it was a disgrace to become pregnant before marriage. And her mother would not have understood. In fact, later, when her mother discovered that she "had to get married," she had belittled her for it.

Jasmine would never do that to Celeste. And for the first time since Celeste had been a teenager, she felt a bond with her daughter that she had never had before. They would work through this.

"Oh, Mom, I was so afraid to tell you. I thought you would be so angry. God, I thought you'd throw me out of the house."

"And what would that accomplish?"

"I love you, Mom."

"I know, I know," murmured Jasmine as she held her in her arms. She had her daughter back. "I love you too. I've never stopped loving you, you have to know that."

They cried and held each other. And they cried some more. The dogs moved closer, wanting to be hugged, too.

Finally, Celeste sat up straight, looked squarely at her mother, and said, "But what am I going to do?"

"Does Ramon know?"

"No, not yet."

"Have you heard from him?"

"Yes, he's called a couple of times."

"Are you going to tell him? It's his baby as much as yours."

"Not yet. Not until I know what I'm going to do. I know he would want me to keep the baby. He wants to marry me. And I'm not ready yet."

Jasmine was silent, absorbing what Celeste had just told her. It didn't make sense to her, but maybe Celeste had her reasons. She finally said, "I can't tell you what to do, but I think you should tell him."

"Do you think I should get an abortion?"

"You have to decide for yourself. If I told you to get an abortion and you regretted it later, you would forever hate me."

"But I thought you were for abortions."

"Sweetheart, I am for choice. There's a difference. I'm not "for" abortions. I truly believe that every child in this world should be wanted and loved and that we need to take responsibility for our bodies and prevent unwanted pregnancy if we can. Sweetie, I'm not admonishing or judging you. We're human and we make mistakes. And that's why women should have the right to choose."

"Mom, you're the greatest!" Celeste said as she looked at her mother adoringly.

"I'm just your mom and I love you, that's all."

"These dogs are way spoiled," said Celeste as she petted Chance.

"They are," Jasmine said. "But they know. They can feel our pain and our joy. These are two special dogs."

That night when Jasmine went to bed, she couldn't stop thinking of all the things that had happened to her in the past few months: losing her job, Celeste coming to live with her, Celeste getting pregnant. And then picking up a little lost dog in the dog park and finding out that she was pregnant, too. "What else can go wrong?" she asked herself. We've had so much happening; maybe we've had our quota and we'll all be on the upward swing from now on. Jasmine didn't believe in fate or angels creating destiny. She felt that we create our own futures, albeit with the help of many others. But people can have control over their lives, right? Yes, they can.

And two days later, she was tested again. She awoke early, about 4:30, for some reason, but the dogs weren't even stirring, so she went back to sleep. But then around seven, Blondie jumped off the bed; she had been sleeping there since the storm. That was Jasmine's cue to get up and put the dog outside before she had an accident in the house. Jasmine walked into the kitchen with bare feet and found herself sloshing in an inch of water. "What's going on?" she exclaimed out loud. She opened the back door and saw that the patio was flooded, too. "Did it rain last night? I didn't hear it."

Then she looked at the back wall and saw water streaming out of two holes in the brick. "Oh, my god, a broken pipe!" She ran to the front door and out onto the front patio to turn off the water from the street.

Just as she was walking into the house Celeste emerged out of her room. "What's going on? I heard you running out the front door." And then Celeste walked into the bathroom. "Where's all this water coming from?"

"Honey, I don't know. But I'm calling a plumber. The kitchen and the patio are flooded, too. I think a pipe broke last night. This house is pretty old, and that kind of stuff happens to older houses."

"How are we going to pay for this?" asked Celeste.

Jasmine liked the "we" in Celeste's statement. "I don't know. But we'll find a way. We have to fix it. Otherwise we are without water, and that means that we have no toilet."

"We're without a toilet now. How can I use the bathroom when there's no water?" Celeste shouted.

"Calm down. I'll turn on the water for a couple of minutes so that you can use the toilet and wash your hands. And I have some water in a plastic bottle for drinking."

"It could take all day. What're we going to do if it isn't fixed in a couple of hours? I need to pee often."

"Go across the street to Steve's house and ask if we can use his bathroom if we need to. I'm sure he won't mind."

Jasmine called Bird Dog Plumbing. The owner, Don, was a friend she had met at the dog park. She told him that she had a plumbing emergency. Then she got a pail and some rags and, after removing the sodden scatter rugs, started to sop up the water in the kitchen. Chance and Blondie ran in and out of the back door, making paw prints on the tile every time just as Jasmine tried to clean the floor. She didn't mind.

Don came right out within an hour and brought his dog, Avi. Chance and Avi were friends, and they immediately went into the backyard and started romping and playing.

"Tell me this isn't going to cost a fortune," said Jasmine. "Because I don't have very much money."

"Go and turn on the water in front," Don instructed her. Don looked at the brick wall with the water streaming out. "Have you had these pipes replaced recently?"

"No. But I did move the washer and the water heater off the patio and into the little room off the carport. I just didn't like the sight of a washing machine on my patio."

"The problem is right here," he said as he started to pound an opening in the block wall near a capped-off pipe. And sure enough, the pipe broke off completely. He took out all of the material around the broken pipe, cleaned it and soldered on a new cap. He completed the job in thirty minutes and then handed her the bill.

"Is this all you're charging me?" said Jasmine as she looked at the invoice for $100. "Thank you. You are good at what you do. You found the problem quickly and fixed it in no time." And she got her checkbook and wrote out the check to him.

"No problem. This happens to these old homes all the time. Let's hope you won't have any more pipes breaking for awhile. But if you do, call me." And Don called Avi and got into his truck and left.

"Well, we got off easy on this one, Celey. I was sure that we were looking at a $1000 bill here."

"I was thinking that we'd have to go out on the street with a sign "Work for Food," laughed Celeste as she hugged her mother.

"Take nothing for granted. You never know what will happen next."

And truer words had never been spoken. The very next week, on Tuesday, Jasmine put a load of clothes into the washer. The back door was open so the dogs could go in and out as they pleased. She was busily cleaning up the kitchen when she heard a bubbling, gurgling sound. "What's that?" she said out loud. "Couldn't be the pipe breaking again."

She walked out to the patio and saw water and debris bubbling up from a drain that she'd had put in years ago to drain storm water from the back yard. As she looked closer she saw what looked like wet toilet paper and sewage. "Oh, my god, my sewer is clogged!"

She went inside and called Don. "Hi Don, it's me again. You won't believe this but I have another huge problem. Can you come out right away?"

"What's wrong, sweetie?" Usually your plumber doesn't call you "sweetie" but Don was a good friend and he really liked Chance and Blondie and Jasmine, too. Jasmine hysterically told Don what was happening. "Don, there are *turds* on my patio. I can't believe it. *Turds!*"

"Take it easy. It's probably just some roots in your sewer line. We'll clean it out and you'll be just fine. I can't come over today, but I'll be there first thing in the morning. Can you live with that?"

"I guess so." Jasmine hung up the phone and sat down and cried. "One thing after another. I can't take this."

The next morning Don's truck, painted like a German Short-hair Pointer with spots all over, parked in front of her house. Jasmine let Don and his helper Rob in through the side gate. They connected a machine that they'd brought to an electrical outlet on the patio. Rob looked at the drain and opened the clean-out valve and proceeded to run a plumber's snake into the drain. Two hours later, after pulling up roots and what appeared to be fibers from rugs, the drain was clear.

"I bet you've been washing dirty rugs in your washer," Don said.

"Well, yes, I wash the dog's rugs. I have to keep them clean," Jasmine said defensively.

Don told her about a filter that she should put on the washer hose to prevent these fibers from getting into the sewer system and clogging it. He handed her another bill, this one for $120.00, and she paid him.

Jasmine went into the kitchen, made a cup of tea, and sat down at the table. There goes this week's unemployment money. What next? Let's see, she thought, all of her appliances were at least twenty years old—the washer and dryer, the dishwasher and the refrigerator. And the roof; that cost would be huge, $10,000 at least.

Celeste slipped into the kitchen and sat down with her mother. "Mom, it's going to be all right. We'll survive this." Jasmine just looked at her daughter and nodded with a blank stare. "There are people in the world who are dealing with a lot worse than we are. Look at the people in Syria, who are living in tents. They don't even have toilets in those places."

"You're right, Celeste. I need to keep this in perspective," Jasmine said finally, after some thought. "I'm glad that you're here to remind me."

"I love you too, Mom."

Chapter 19
Chance

There was something strange about Blondie from the start. She had an odor about her that I couldn't figure out and I didn't like. And now she's getting lazy and sleeping most of the day and doesn't want to play. I offer her my tug toy and she just walks away. She doesn't know what she's missing. I thought I was getting a playmate when she first came to live here, and I am disappointed.

They, the humans. are giving her way to much attention and I feel left out. I sit by my human and look up at her with pleading eyes to please pet me, scratch my ears, love me, but she doesn't even see me anymore so I just go to my bed beside the couch and chew on my bone. I'll have to admit that I've been ripping up toys and chewing on those black plastic pipes in the back yard. Blondie was blamed for it, and I don't care. And with the new person—one of them left awhile back—I don't get much attention at all anymore. Oh, there was that week when my person found Blondie that we went to the dog park every day, twice a day in fact. But we haven't been back since, and I miss all my buddies at the park.

I guess I'll just hang out with myself.

And now, the new person in the house, the young girl, Celeste they call her, has that same smell that Blondie has. What is going on here? I am confused. I guess I shouldn't complain, though, because I get good food twice a day along with fresh water and treats. And I get to sleep in my person's bed and it is so soft and comfy. But then one night last week we had this wonderful storm; I love storms. And do you know what happened? My person brought that Blondie into our bed. I guess she was afraid of the storm or something. She's a wuss.

And it's so hot outside I can't stand it. I refuse to go out unless I'm paid with a dog biscuit, and then I'm out there for an hour or two and I start panting and I drink as much water as I can, but all I can do is lie around. The patio is so hot when I walk on it that my feet hurt; I don't feel like doing anything. I have to wait until the sun is gone to play, but it's hot then, too. I try to come in where it's cool as much as I can. When the door opens I race to come inside. I am getting depressed. Tonight after the sun goes down I think I'll dig some holes in the yard. That always makes me feel better.

Chapter 20
Dog Hospital

L ife is complex, thought Jasmine as she was working in her office, paying bills and cleaning up her paperwork. Three months ago she had been living alone, unemployed, trying to find work and keep herself together. And today she had her pregnant daughter and two dogs, one of them pregnant, living with her. Where was this all going, she wondered?

To be sure, soon she would have another five or six puppies to take care of, maybe more. And, depending on how Celeste decided, maybe a grandchild, which didn't make her totally unhappy. And yet she was torn. Being a single mom in today's world was like juggling a hundred balls in the air. Finding suitable day care, working all day, and then coming home at night to a cranky baby, having to feed, bathe and prepare the baby for bed. Add mountains of diapers and baby bottles. If a working mom chooses breast feeding, it is an undertaking in itself; having to breast pump during the day to have the breast milk available for the baby, relieve the tension and keep the milk coming. Not all employers understand a new mother's needs, and they usually don't provide facilities; consequently the mother ends up in the women's rest room in a stall for privacy. Not a good option. And would Celeste be able to succeed in her new chosen profession? Jasmine remembered being a stay-at-home mom and how tired she was those first few months. She couldn't imagine how it would be with a full-time job too.

Celeste was working a six-hour day shift, five days a week for now. And since she was basically working part time, she had no benefits, no health insurance. She went to work at eleven in the morning and came home in the late afternoon, exhausted, going straight to her bed to rest. The morning sickness had stopped, but she was still so tired every day. She couldn't decide what to do, and time was running out. After trying every day to reach Ramon and failing, Celeste knew this would be her decision and hers alone. On the one hand, she had always wanted a baby, but she had pictured a very different scenario for her baby, with a loving father and time to love and care for the baby. All of the things she'd had when she was a child. And it wouldn't be like that if she had this baby now and kept it for her own.

She and her mother talked again late one night. Celeste trusted her mother more now, than she ever had before.

"I have a great idea. I could have the baby and give it out for adoption. I could even choose the mother," said Celeste one morning as they were having breakfast together on the patio.

"Adoption sounds good in theory, but isn't the perfect solution. I know there are loving adoptive parents, but there is no guarantee."

"I got on-line and there are all kinds of adoption agencies out there," Celeste said.

The dogs sat under the table waiting for tidbits to fall their way, which seldom happened.

"After you were born and we couldn't have more children, we were trying to adopt."

"Mom, I didn't know that. What happened? Why didn't you? I would have loved a brother or sister. Sometimes I feel so alone in this world."

"Your father and I were not getting along, and we decided not to go through with it. We were very close to getting a sister for you, though; we'd gone through the home study and had been accepted and were getting ready to select a child. And then, your grandmother said she wouldn't accept an adopted child as part of the family. And that was kind of the deciding moment. I thought about how having this child would always be cause for contention between your grandmother and me, and at a time when I was trying to get closer to her... well, it wouldn't have worked."

"I'm sorry." Celeste petted Chance, who moved closer to her, looking up at her with begging eyes. "I don't think I could give up a baby that I've carried for nine months anyway."

"Well, I know. I'm not saying adoption is bad or shouldn't be done; it's usually a fix for a bad situation. But I know in my heart that if I ever had to give up a baby that I had carried for nine months, I would wonder all of the rest of my life how that child was doing. If he or she was being loved, happy, healthy, getting along in life. It was just like when you stayed with your dad. I was devastated. I no longer could see you; I didn't know day to day how you were doing."

"I missed you too, Mom." Celeste thought for a moment. If she were to have this baby and adopt it out, she would have to detach herself in every way from the baby, and she didn't know if she could.

"Have you decided?" asked Jasmine.

"Not yet. This is life-changing for me in every way. I understand the impact on my life no matter which way I go. And then there is the baby."

"Soon the decision will be made for you."

And they left it at that for the time being.

The next day, a Saturday, Jasmine noticed that Chance was somewhat subdued. He hadn't eaten his breakfast and he was lying around, not playing or interacting with Blondie. "What's wrong, Chance? Are you feeling left out these days?" Jasmine thought it would pass. But as the day progressed, he seemed to be getting worse. Then, in the evening he ate but he threw up his dinner. Blondie ran in and tried to eat the kibble in the vomit until Jasmine shooed her away as she cleaned it up.

Jasmine knew now that something was very wrong. "Hey, Chance what is going on with you? I think we'll call the vet." But it was Saturday night. She tried calling the veterinary office. She got an answering service telling her the office was closed until Monday morning and that, if this was an emergency, she should call the Pet Emergency Clinic. Jasmine knew that if she had to take Chance into the emergency clinic it would be very expensive. She would watch him and see if he improved during the night.

Eight o'clock and Chance threw up again, only this time it was the head of a toy he'd been chewing on earlier that day. "Chance, this is good. That's what was making you sick. I think you'll be okay now."

But he wasn't. Jasmine went to bed, but she didn't sleep. She checked on Chance every ten minutes, pacing the floor, worrying. By midnight, he lay on the bed, visibly in distress. His eyes looked up at her, seeming to say, "Help me, I am hurting so bad." Blondie jumped on the bed and licked Chance's ears. Chance lifted his head to look at her with his amber eyes and then put it down again.

Jasmine called the emergency clinic and they told her to bring him in. She woke Celeste to tell her where she was going and then loaded Chance into the back of the car. He lay there in a daze. "Chance, I can't believe you ate that toy. Why did you do that?" She said as she was driving west on Glendale Avenue towards the freeway. She came to the emergency clinic and walked him inside. Even before they took him into an examining room, Jasmine was asked to sign papers to guarantee payment of the bill. Her Visa card was her savior again, but how would she pay this off, she wondered? Thank goodness for unemployment insurance at times like these.

They were shown into a room. The doctor, named Sarah Foster, entered the room. She was young, attractive, with large dark brown eyes and short brunette hair, dressed in multi-colored scrubs with dog and cat cartoon images on her top. "What have we here?" She scratched Chance's ears. Jasmine explained what had been happening to Chance for the last ten hours. She examined his eyes, took his blood pressure, and listened to his heart. "His vitals seem pretty good." She felt his abdominal area with both of her hands. "Something going on in there. I suggest we do an x-ray so we'll know more."

Jasmine agreed, and Chance was taken into another room. Jasmine waited and paced some more.

The technician brought him back, and Sarah came into the room with the results that told the story. "You see this mass here in the small intestine?" she said as she pulled up the digital images on the computer. Jasmine nodded her head, yes. "It looks like there's a mass of something, probably the toy that Chance ate, and he's not able to pass it because it's too large."

"What do we do now?" asked Jasmine, knowing what the answer was but not wanting to hear it.

"I'm afraid surgery is the solution. And we need to do it soon."

"Not a lot of options here, are there."

"No, I'm afraid not. You know, dogs have a strong digestive system and can usually pass most objects that they might ingest, but this is just too large and if it doesn't come out, Chance will not survive."

Since Jasmine's veterinary office would not be open on Sunday, either the surgery had to be done at the emergency clinic or they would have to find a veterinary clinic that was open on Sunday. Jasmine opted for the latter. She left Chance at the clinic. They would hydrate him and prepare him for surgery and then call around for her later in the morning to find a clinic that was open and would take Chance for the surgery.

Jasmine went home to wait. At least she knew what was wrong and how to fix it. But now she had to worry about how she would pay for what, no doubt, was going to be a very expensive surgery. What if it cost five thousand dollars? Would she be willing to pay that, or would she have to put him down? And what was her threshold? Three thousand, two thousand? What was Chance's life worth to her? She didn't know. What she did know was that she had grown very close to Chance. He was like another child. How do you put a price on a family member's life? It was four in the morning and she was so tired. Better get some sleep, and then she could make that decision in the morning.

Chapter 21
Chance's Big Day

The phone was ringing. Jasmine looked at the clock beside her bed. It was past seven. She never slept this late. She answered, and Dr. Foster was on the other end. "We've found several clinics open today. There's one on Seventh Avenue and Missouri, the Mountain View Clinic. They'll take Chance for the surgery. I talked with Dr. Paulsen and he said to bring him in. Do you want to pick him up, or do you want us to transport him?"

"I'll pick him up. How's he doing?" asked Jasmine, fully awake now.

"As well as can be expected, given the circumstances. He's hydrated and ready for the surgery. We'll send the x-rays along to Dr. Paulsen."

"I'll be there in half an hour."

Jasmine got out of bed and put on a pair of jeans and a t-shirt. She knocked on Celeste's door. "I'm going to the Emergency Clinic to take Chance to another veterinary hospital for the surgery. I'll be back soon."

She heard Celeste stir and then open the door. "Surgery? Chance is having surgery?"

"Yes, he has an obstructed intestine, and surgery is the only way to clear it out. Seems he ate the whole toy. He vomited the head yesterday, but the rest of it is still in him," said Jasmine. "I won't be gone very long. I'm going to take him there and come home and wait. You go back to bed. Get some rest."

As she drove to the Emergency Clinic, she thought again about the cost and decided, whatever it takes, she would save Chance. She would somehow find a way to pay. Hold a patio sale, sell some things on eBay.

Celeste didn't go back to bed. She went into the kitchen to make breakfast and wait for her mother to come home. She had something important to tell her.

The last few months had been the most difficult in all of her twenty-five years: losing her job, her apartment, and now getting pregnant. Deciding what to do next was the most difficult for her. She went back and forth every hour, it seemed, except when she was at work, where she had to concentrate on doing her job. If she had the baby and kept it, it could become a burden on her that might make her hate her child. If she aborted, she knew she would feel bad afterward, but she thought that would pass in time. If she gave it up for adoption, she would wonder all of the rest of her life about the child's well-being. If she was having this baby, she wanted to be the one to raise it. There was no easy answer, no easy out. No matter what she decided, it was going to hurt and be difficult.

And she kept beating herself up for not being more careful. She had been taught; she knew how to prevent this calamity. But this one night, they had been out drinking, came home late and fell into bed. And Ramon was extremely anxious for sex—he couldn't wait. She hadn't even thought about it until afterward, and then it occurred to her—they hadn't used protection. Just this one time, she'd thought. Surely after all of the times we've had sex, and all of the times she'd had sex with others in her short life, she wouldn't get pregnant this one time. But she did. And now it was on her to fix this. What a crock, she thought. Guys have all the fun and get off scot-free.

And now she hated her job. What was at first fun and exciting had become mundane and boring. She had learned all of the fifty-some combinations of alcohol that were served at the poolside bar of the Hilton at the Mountain Hotel—and that was that. There was nothing more to learn, except how to get bigger tips, keep the men from hitting on her, and fend off sexist remarks from her male co-workers. She was required to wear a bikini with a Hawaiian print sarong tied on her hips. This wouldn't faze her if she were at the beach or sitting around the pool as a guest. But, behind the bar, she was on display. She didn't know how to tell her mother that she wanted to quit. Now there would be extra bills with Chance, and she didn't have any health insurance. With a baby on the way, what was that going to cost? She shuddered just thinking about it.

Jasmine walked into the Emergency Clinic. The woman at the front desk greeted her. "I'm here to pick up Chance," said Jasmine. The woman, Chinese American with dark black hair and dark brown eyes, looked tired after working all night. She pulled up a document from the computer and handed it to Jasmine. Three hundred and fifty-two dollars. And this was just beginning. Jasmine again took out her Visa card and paid the bill. When the technician brought Chance to the waiting area, Chance looked at her with pleading eyes as if to say, what is happening to me? Jasmine gave him a hug and said, "Chance, it's going to be okay. We're going to get you fixed up. And I'm throwing away any toy that I think you might eat. This will never happen again, I promise." Jasmine remembered the exact toy he had eaten. It was one that she had ordered through a dog catalogue. It was long and furry and looked very much like a small fox. It had no stuffing, which was what attracted Jasmine to buying it, because the dogs would tear the stuffed toys apart and spread the white, fluffy material all over the house and yard. This toy would solve that problem. Well, it did, but now she had a bigger problem.

She took Chance to the car, and they drove the two miles to the Mountain View Veterinary Hospital. Upon entering, Jasmine gave the receptionist the x-rays of Chance's abdominal area. When they were given a room, they waited again for what seemed like hours but was really only fifteen or twenty minutes. Chance lay on the floor, exhausted and probably drugged. Then Dr. Paulsen, young, in his thirties, yet with thinning, sandy hair, entered the room. "Hi, I'm Dr. Paulsen. I'll be doing his surgery today." He pulled up the x-ray photos and reiterated what Dr. Foster had said earlier that morning. "We'll open him up and go in there and remove this foreign object, whatever it is, and he'll be good as new in a couple of weeks."

"How much is this going to cost?" asked Jasmine.

"I don't deal with the numbers. I'll have the assistant work up an estimate and you can take a look at it and decide. I hate to say this, but if you decide not to do the surgery the kind thing to do would be to put him down. It's your decision."

And he left the room. In another few minutes, the technician came in with the estimate: $1759.00. The list of charges was long: the blood work, the anesthetic, the antibiotics. Jasmine knew she couldn't short-change Chance and cut any of them; they were all necessary. She gulped, but it wasn't as bad as she'd thought it might be. She could do this. And she would find a way to pay for it later. She signed the estimate. The doctor returned and told her he would do the surgery that morning and would phone her as soon as he was done. "Have you done these surgeries before?" asked Jasmine.

"I've taken so many objects out of dogs, cats, horses—you wouldn't believe what these animals can eat. Yes, I've done this many times. Not to worry. We'll take good care of your buddy."

Jasmine went home, hopeful that Chance would now be okay. She pulled into the driveway, went into the house, and put on a fresh pot of coffee.

"How's Chance?" Celeste asked as she came into the kitchen. She had been putting on her make-up, preparing for work.

"He'll be fine. They're doing surgery this morning and they said they would call as soon as he's out."

"How much, Mom?"

"You don't want to know."

"Yes, I do. You can't afford this, I know that."

"I'll find a way. It's not that bad, a little over fifteen hundred, that's all," Jasmine said, minimizing the amount. "I'd thought it was going to be close to five grand and then I would've had to think twice about whether I could afford it. Chance is a part of our family."

"But you don't have the money."

"No, I don't, but I would have to put him to sleep if we didn't do the surgery. Would you want that to happen?"

"No, Mother. But I have to tell you that I want to quit my job. I can't do this job anymore."

"Why not?"

"You were right, the guys are hitting on me and my co-workers are abusive… and well…

"I hate to say this, Celey, but I was right. I told you this would happen in that kind of an environment. Have you gone to your boss about your co-workers?"

"Wouldn't do any good. Two of them are his best friends." Celeste gave her mother that look of "you're doing it again, treating me like a child." She combed her long brown hair, preparing to put it into a pony tail. "There's something else that I didn't tell you."

Jasmine looked at her expectantly. Now what, she thought.

"I have to wear a bikini at work. I wear a sarong, but the top is tiny and I worry all the time about falling out if it."

"That's it. You're done. No daughter of mine is going to be a sex object in a bar. You can call in now and tell them you're no longer working there."

"I can't. I'll go to work and give my notice. I might need a job reference."

"Let me know when you're done today. I'll pick you up."

"And, Mom, I've decided to have the baby and keep it."

Another bombshell. But Jasmine was prepared. Otherwise, Celeste would have gone to the doctor and had the abortion by now.

"I know, honey. I thought you would. I'll support you all that I can, but this is your baby and you are going to have to take full responsibility for the child. I can't raise another one this late in my life. You know that, don't you? And I'm not saying this in anger."

"Don't worry, Mom, it is my baby and I'll take care of it."

"How are you paying for the baby? Do you have the money?"

"No. You know I don't have any money. I don't know. I'll just have it at home."

"You can't do that. You have to get a baby doctor and you'll have to go to the hospital to have the baby and that's expensive. Probably several thousand dollars."

"I'll figure it out, Mom."

"If Ramon isn't stepping up, then I'd better call your father."

"No. I don't want Dad to know. Not yet, anyway. He'll have to know sometime, but not now. Please don't call him."

"Yes, he *will* have to know sometime, and now is as good a time as any. Maybe he'll want to help."

Celeste had never forgotten that conversation years ago when she was a teen out of control and what her dad had said to her —that if she were out on the street he wouldn't help her. If he felt that way then, how would he feel any different today? Would he view her behavior now as out of control? She didn't hold much hope for him to come forward and help her out of this predicament. But then she thought, I'm an adult now and it is time for me to help myself. I got into this and I'll find a way to resolve it. One way or another.

Chapter 22

Dogdom

Dog beds everywhere, beside the couch, by Jasmine's bed, and under her desk where she worked every day. Jasmine's house was devoted to dogs. Dog toys littered every room: knotted rope, nylon bones, and tennis balls. There was a water dish in the kitchen as well as one on the back patio, both freshened twice daily with clean water. A cookie jar filled with dog biscuits and a bowl full of dog treats had permanent places on the kitchen counter. A new white colonial-style dog house with a real shingle roof sat on the patio next to the back door. Unfortunately, Blondie had modified the front door, chewing around the frame, and Jasmine used duct tape to try to prevent her from further ruining the dog house.

One thing that Jasmine did not have for her dogs, though, was a doggie door for the dogs to go in and out of the house at will. The opening would have had to be large, and she didn't want to risk having intruders or, perhaps other critters coming into her house. Her dogs had to depend on someone letting them in or out. Since Jasmine was now at home most of the time, this was not a problem.

Blondie was looking very pregnant as the days went by, and Jasmine knew that her time was near. She confiscated a large cardboard TV box that had been abandoned in the alley. When she cut off the top and secured the sides, it was roomy and very sturdy, just right for Blondie and the puppies that were on the way. She put a soft blanket on the bottom and terry towels on top of the blanket, preparing for the big event. Jasmine then placed this whelping box beside her bed where she could keep watch on Blondie.

But when Jasmine showed the box to Blondie, the dog would have nothing to do with it. Blondie preferred sleeping either with Jasmine in her bed or in her dog crate. Being a patient person, Jasmine realized it would take some time for Blondie to get used to the new box and hoped she would eventually go there to have her puppies.

Jasmine had read everything she could about the birthing of puppies and felt that she was well prepared for this wonderful event that was about to happen. She would soon find out that one is never prepared.

Dr. Paulsen from Mountain View Veterinary Hospital called late in the morning to tell her that the Chance's surgery had gone well and he was in the recovery area. He recommended that she leave him in the hospital for at least three days so they could monitor him and get him back to eating and getting his bowels working again. She agreed; this was major surgery. The doctor told her that she could come as often as she wanted to visit.

What a relief, thought Jasmine. She would have her Chance back home in a couple of days. He was a young dog; he would heal fast and be back to his former, happy self in a matter of weeks. After hanging up from talking with the doctor, Jasmine sorted through the dog toys in the toy tub that she kept on top of her bookcase and evaluated each toy. She found at least five toys that were potentially dangerous: toys that had parts that could be chewed into pieces, swallowed, get into the digestive system and cause problems. She threw every one of them into the garbage and vowed to write an article, posting it on her Facebook page and other places, telling of her experience hoping to help others so they wouldn't have to go through what she had just experienced.

It came in the mail the next day, and none too soon; the grant money Celeste had applied for weeks before. She'd quit her job and was worried that she wouldn't find another, and she didn't want to be a burden on her mother. The week before, she had gone to the career center at Phoenix College for career counseling. After taking several tests and talking with a counselor, she decided on a career that she could be excited about. Celeste, like her mother, had always had an artistic leaning, and she loved the film industry. The counselor helped her put her skills and passions together, and they concluded that Celeste would be well suited to work in the computer animation industry, a growing field these days. And there was a school in Phoenix where this was being taught. Celeste was ecstatic. She thought she had found a career she would be happy working in. It did require some advanced computer skills however, that she didn't have, but she was smart and felt she could learn that part of it. Just using a cell phone these days required programming skills.

And now she had the money to carry out this plan. When Celeste told her mother, Jasmine was pleased as well. "Yes, that seems like a good fit for you. I think you could make a good living at it, and the film industry has, so far, been recession-proof. Go for it."

"The possibilities are unlimited. I could even start my own company," said Celeste. She was full of hope once again, along with being full with child.

"And now how will you pay for the baby? Have you found a way yet?"

"No. I'm still working on that."

"Unfortunately, Medicaid support has been cut in this state, leaving a lot of poor people without health care just when they need it the most. Why don't you call your father? And if you don't, I will."

"I'd rather you call him. I don't want to hear his rant when he finds out about how stupid I've been."

Jasmine visited Chance twice a day every day while he was in the hospital. The first time she saw him, he looked sad and forlorn. He had a tube attached to his body with a bag of saline solution to keep him hydrated, and he was undoubtedly still feeling the effects of the anesthetic; he had been out of surgery for only three hours. "Chance, I'm here to see you. How are you doing?" He looked at her and his ears perked up for a minute and then he laid his head down again. She opened the cage door and scratched his ears and rubbed his belly. He responded by licking her hand.

Chance was in one of the large metal wire cages stacked one on top of another, lining the perimeter of the large room. Many of the cages were filled with animals; cats, a rabbit, and dogs large and small. Two dogs, a Sheltie and a Dachshund mix, were crying and another dog was barking, wanting to be out of his cage. Chance was in a bottom cage in the corner.

"You have a lot of animals in here," Jasmine said to one of the technicians.

"Yes, we take in animals from the shelters if they need medical care," the young woman said.

Jasmine thought that was very commendable. "Has Chance eaten anything?" she asked.

"No, not yet. They're usually not hungry for the first twelve hours."

"I'll be back this afternoon," she said as she was leaving. When she came back a little later, Chance was sitting, his ears forward when he saw her. "Oh, Chance. I am so sorry you have to be here. But we'll take you home soon."

Jasmine called the next day and asked if Chance had eaten yet and they said no, that they tried to feed him and he refused. They told her that she could bring in some food and maybe if she fed him he would be more likely to eat. She cooked some ground turkey and rice, mixed it together in a plastic container and took that to the clinic. When she offered the food to Chance, he turned his head away and refused to eat it. "What's wrong, Chance? You've got to eat if you want to get out of here. I'll be back this afternoon and we'll try this again," She said. But in the afternoon it was the same story. He sniffed the food and licked it, but he wouldn't eat. When he still would not eat the next day, Jasmine became very worried.

"What happens if he won't eat?" she asked the technician.

"We'll force-feed him until he starts eating on his own."

Jasmine couldn't understand why he wasn't eating. He was such a chow hound at home, ate anything that was put before him and then some. She asked if she could take him outside for a walk, and the technician said that would be okay. After the technician unhooked his IV, Jasmine put a leash on him and took him out the back door. He seemed happy to be out of the cage, and when she returned with him and put him back in, he gave her that sad, why-are-you-leaving-me-here? look.

When Jasmine returned came back in the afternoon with fresh food she put it in a dish, opened the cage, and offered Chance the food. He sniffed, first took a lick and then a bite, and started gulping the food as if he hadn't eaten in days, which was true. "He's eating!" she shouted. "He can come home now, can't he?"

"Not until his bowels start moving and we know everything's working properly," replied the technician. Jasmine was dejected. She wanted to get Chance out of there as soon as she could. He was unhappy in the cage. She felt that she could take care of him now at home, and it was costing money to have him there.

Jasmine came back later in the evening and asked again if she could walk him. She took him out of the cage and out the back door. He immediately lifted his leg on a nearby bush. They walked down the block. He found a grassy area, sniffed around for a couple of minutes, and then did what they had all been waiting for.

"Hurrah, he did it!" she exclaimed as she came back in the door. One of the other doctors in the room laughed about what was happening as she said, "The only place in town where poop is celebrated."

"Can I take him home now?" Jasmine asked.

"Yes, I think you can," said the young woman doctor. "We had to take his IV out this morning because he was starting to chew it. That's usually a sign they're getting better."

Jasmine gathered up Chance, went out to the front desk, and paid the bill. Before she left, the doctor came out to the waiting room and handed Jasmine a package of medications and told her how she should give them to Chance. He then handed her an Elizabethan collar to put on Chance, saying, "You need to keep this on him at all times until his stitches come out."

"How soon will that happen?" asked Jasmine.

"In ten days to two weeks," said the doctor.

Jasmine put the collar on Chance and he gave her a look like what is this thing? She put Chance in the back of the car. He shook his head trying to get rid of the abominable thing around his neck, but he was wagging his tail glad to be out of the cage and finally going home. "It's a happy day, Chance. You're going home at last."

Chapter 23
Chance

I knew that eating that toy was a bad idea soon after I did it. The furry thing looked like a baby fox, and I hid it from Blondie right away. I took it outside and buried it in the dirt behind the bushes so she wouldn't get it. Then I went back when no one was looking and dug it up. What a sweet thing it was! I mouthed it and tossed it into the air when Blondie wasn't looking and then I started chewing and before I realized it, I had swallowed the furry thing, head and all. It slid down my throat and went to my stomach and sat there. I tried to tell my person, Mom, but she was busy with other things. I'll call her Mom from now on because that's what the new person who's still in our house, Celeste, calls her.

After a couple of days, my stomach really started to hurt. I tried, but I couldn't get rid of what was in there, that little furry fox toy. When I ate, I threw up my food and then I couldn't eat at all. I tried some more to get rid of it, and I did throw up part of it but there was more left in my stomach.

I'm not one to whine, so I just kept quiet. But I was just lying around and I guess looking pretty down and Mom noticed, especially when I was throwing up. She put me in the car and took me to this place where they took us to a small room that smelled like many dogs and cats had been there. I didn't like it right away, but Mom petted me and told me she loved me. Then another person came into the room and she reeked of dog and cat smell and some other terrible odors. After she poked this thing in my rear, she poked my stomach and that really hurt. But I didn't say anything; I am strong. They took me away to another room. There were lots of people there and they laid me on this cold, metal table and held me down and then this big machine came over me, I don't know what for. I was really scared.

Well, that wasn't the end of it. Then they took me back to the room where Mom was and talked to her for awhile, showing her some pictures on a screen. And then, I couldn't believe it, Mom kissed me on the head and said goodbye and she was gone and the people, I don't know who these people are and I don't trust them, took me back to another room and laid me on the table again and put one needle in me and then another and put me in this cage. I'd been in a cage before when my other owner took me to the doctor and they took my manhood away. I felt trapped then and I felt trapped now, but I was still hurting so much that I couldn't do much about it, so I just lay down and waited. I guess I was waiting for Mom to come back, but I didn't know if she ever would. Maybe she was going to leave me there like my other people left me in the back yard.

I slept for awhile, but the pain was getting worse. Then she came back; I was so happy. She took me out of that place and we went for a ride, but then she hauled me out of the car and into another place that smelled just like the place I was in before with the same kind of people. They put us in another room, and another person came in and poked me and then talked to Mom, and then took me away. What was happening to me?

They hooked me up to this water bag and put me in another cage. This is it. I'm a goner, I thought. She's getting rid of me for sure. What did I do wrong? And then my stomach hurt again and I just lay down and waited. I didn't cry, though.

It wasn't long before they came and took me out of the cage. I thought, she's never coming back for me, I might as well co-operate with these people. They took me to another room and put more needles into me and then everything went black. I don't remember anything after that until I woke up in my cage again and one of those people, a nice lady, was opening the cage and stroking me, asking how I was doing. And I thought, these are not bad people.

Well, I slept for I don't know how long, but I still had this pain in my stomach, a different kind of pain than I'd had before. But then the young girl gave me some medicine and the pain almost went away. I slept some more, still wondering if Mom was going to come back for me, but losing hope.

Some time later, I don't know how long, Mom showed up at my cage and she opened it and started scratching my ears. She's here. She's not going to leave me after all. Oh, boy. Maybe we can go home now and forget about this terrible experience I'm having. But, no, she left again. I am so confused. I guess I'll just go back to sleep. I don't know what else to do. If those noisy dogs would just shut up.

Chapter 24
And Puppies Make Ten

The gestation period for dogs is about sixty-three days, give or take a day or two. As the whelping time, birthing of the puppies, grows near, the belly of the mother dog, or bitch as she is officially called, will visibly grow in size as her breasts start to develop. When she is ready to give birth, she will look for a suitable place to have her puppies, even though you may have provided a soft, warm and comfortable whelping box for her. It is wise to let her be until you can move her without disturbing her.

As each newborn arrives into the world, the mother will lick the puppy, removing the membranous sack, and chew the umbilical cord. She may then eat the placenta. This is a holdover from wild days to keep predators from finding them. After all the puppies are born, she will nurse them, and she will bathe them often, cleaning their bottoms with her tongue, eating the small amount of excrement which stimulates bowel movements. This also is behavior from wild days. The mother dog will continue to care for and feed her puppies for a month or more or until they are eating and drinking on their own. During this time she is very protective of them and may become aggressive when people come near the whelping area, but after several weeks, when the puppies have become more independent, she will easily relinquish the care of the puppies and as they grow older, she is glad to see them leave. Her job is done.

Celeste was still so tired. She slept twelve hours every day and still wanted to sleep more. Fortunately, she was able to quit her job, but now she had other worries. She had doctor bills to pay and no money. Her mother told her about AHCCCS, the Arizona Health Care Cost Containment System. But when Celeste checked it out, she found that the program had become a casualty of the recession, and funding for people like herself had been cut way back. If you were already on the program you might be okay, but they were not accepting new people. So, Celeste did not know how she would pay for this baby. Maybe she should tell Ramon and he could help. But then she thought that he would want to marry her, and she still didn't know if she was ready for that.

Ramon had started calling her, and he called often. Celeste didn't return his calls. She guessed that she was afraid that she might let it slip that she was pregnant. And then he stopped calling. She hadn't heard from him in over a week. Now she was worried that she had lost him. He was not pursuing her anymore. Maybe he'd met someone else. Myriad thoughts flooded her mind. She tried calling him but couldn't reach him. His cell number had been canceled, and he wasn't listed in the land-line phone book.

Celeste decided to call his friend Roger in L.A. one Sunday afternoon. Roger Morrison was an old college buddy, and he and his girlfriend Debby had double-dated with her and Ramon several times in the two years that she had known Ramon   "Roger, this is Celeste. How are you?"

"I'm fine. How are you?" Pregnant pause. "I guess you're calling to find out about Ramon."

"Yes. I haven't heard from him in a couple of weeks. Have you talked with him?"

"I have. He's gone, Celeste."

Celeste's heart jumped into her stomach. "Gone? What do you mean gone?"

"He went to UK. He wasn't finding any jobs in L.A., in fact in California, so he decided to go to London and see if he could find something there."

Celeste's heart rate came back to normal. "When did he go? Have you heard from him since he left? And why didn't he tell me?"

"I think he tried to. He said he'd called you many times and you didn't answer or call him back, so I guess he thought you didn't want to talk to him. And no, I haven't heard from him since he left. If I do, do you want me to tell him to call you?"

"Yes, Roger, I do. I'm sorting through some difficult stuff right now and I... well, I haven't handled things as well as I could have. Have him call me. I do want to talk with him."

She closed her cell phone. That explains it, she thought. But now she wondered if he was fleeing because he had found out somehow about the baby and didn't want the responsibility. No, that couldn't be. And she had to ask herself, if Ramon did step forward, would she marry him? Forever is a long time. Then she thought that maybe Ramon had a right to know about the baby; he was the father. And what about the baby? Didn't the baby have a right to know its father? There were no easy answers, and Celeste was sure that millions of women had wrestled with these same questions for eons. Fortunately, in today's world, there was much less stigma attached to being an unmarried mother than there had been in the past. Celeste was thankful for that. And she was thankful that she had her mother's support. She could see now that her mother truly cared for her.

Maybe Ramon would come back, and maybe he wouldn't. The baby was on its way and she had to move ahead, regardless. Celeste signed up for computer animation classes at the Art Institute in Phoenix. The classes would start in two weeks. She wondered, though, how was she going to handle all of this? And the baby wasn't even here yet.

Jasmine knew something was wrong the minute she walked into the house with Chance, bringing him back from his three-day hospital stay after his surgery. Blondie wasn't there to greet her. Maybe she's outdoors, Jasmine thought. But, no, she looked out the back door and Blondie was nowhere in sight. Celeste's door was closed. She must be sleeping, although it was four o'clock in the afternoon. But Celeste was in the first stages of pregnancy, which were very demanding on a woman's body; she was still very tired and slept most of the time, day and night. Jasmine remembered what that was like.

Could Blondie be in with Celeste? Jasmine walked back to her bedroom with Chance following her, shaking his head still trying to get the large plastic Elizabethan collar off his head. She looked at the bed and there was Blondie, nestled in the middle of the white comforter, and she wasn't alone. Two little newly-born puppies, still shiny and slick from the birthing, lay near her as Blondie was straining to push out another. "Oh, my god, Blondie...well, what can I say?" Jasmine shook her head in dismay. She saw another puppy lying on the other side of Blondie. "Three and counting. We can't move you now. I'll wait until your family is all here and then move you to your box later," Jasmine mumbled, thinking, "There goes a perfectly good comforter."

Chance jumped on the bed to have a closer look and Blondie snarled at him, baring her teeth. "No, Chance, we'll give Blondie some privacy. This is her time," she murmured as she gently pulled Chance off the bed.

"Celeste, are you in there?" Jasmine knocked on her door. "I need you to take care of Chance. Blondie is having her babies."

Celeste opened her door, eyes wide with surprise. "Oh, I want to see," she said as she walked into Jasmine's bedroom. "So much for preparing the puppy box for her," Celeste giggled. "Maybe she wanted to have her puppies where she could be close to you. You're the super-mom around here."

"That's about to change," laughed Jasmine as she put Chance in Celeste's room and went back to check on Blondie. She'd had another one, and the count was now five. As each puppy arrived, Blondie reached around and started to lick the newborn, removing the placenta and chewing the umbilical cord. "Mom, it's amazing! As young as Blondie is, she knows what to do. I don't think I could have my baby without help," said Celeste in amazement.

"You could if you had to. Her knowledge is instinctive in all mothers," Jasmine said as she put her arm around Celeste.

"It's such a wondrous thing, that these little beings can be created from one," said Celeste.

"The problem is that too many are being created and there are not enough homes for them all," Jasmine said. "I just hope we can find homes for these little babies, and I want to make sure they're all spayed and neutered so we don't perpetuate even more overpopulation."

"Oh, Mother, you're so practical. What about humans? Do you want the same for humans?"

"Yes, there are too many humans in this world. Not enough food and resources for all of them. And, as you and I are seeing, not even enough jobs in our own country."

They watched until the last puppy was born, eight in all. Two black puppies; one female and one male, three black-and-white-and-brown-spotted puppies: one male and two females, two white females with black patches around their eyes, and one buff-colored female that looked just like Blondie. They all appeared to be about the same size and healthy and had all of their legs and toes. Jasmine placed the puppies next to Blondie for warmth, and they immediately began to search for their mother's nipples to start nursing. You could see that Blondie, although exhausted, was happy and proud of her new family. She looked up at Jasmine and Celeste and seemed to be smiling.

"If you asked me, I'd guess that the daddy of these puppies was black and white," said Celeste.

"I think you are right about that." Jasmine continued to watch as Blondie nestled her babies, still licking them. "We'll leave her alone for now." She paused and then said, "I guess I'll be sleeping on the sofa in the living room tonight."

Chance kept trying to get into Jasmine's bedroom to see the babies. The door was always closed, but he could hear little murmurs and squeals coming from behind the door and he was intensely curious. Jasmine had to admonish him and shoo him away repeatedly, but he persisted. That first night, Jasmine spent a sleepless night on the sofa. She had placed a bed for Chance beside the sofa, hoping he would sleep there. But that was too much to be expected of Chance. He was used to being in the big queen-sized bed with her, and he wanted to sleep with her now. He kept climbing onto the sofa, trying to find room for his large body, turning and pawing, and Jasmine kept putting him back in the dog bed. It was useless. No doubt, Chance was feeling insecure right now with just being home from his own traumatic experience, and having the new puppies in the house only added to the turmoil. Jasmine thought to herself that she certainly was putting up with a lot in her life, as she tried to give in to sleep at four in the morning. But these dogs were nearly as much her children as Celeste was. Well, not quite, but close. She loved them all and would do her best to take care of them. And she would help Celeste, too.

The next morning, a very sleepy Jasmine went in to her bedroom to check on Blondie and her new family. The puppies were all happily feeding, and if Blondie had been a cat, she would have been purring. Jasmine picked up the blond puppy and held it close to her. Puppies had a special smell that she just loved. She waited for them to finish feeding and then took Blondie outside so that she could relieve herself and then brought her back inside to feed her. She would need a lot of good food now that she was nursing eight puppies. Then Jasmine went into the bedroom, closing the door so that Chance couldn't follow. She took each puppy from the bed and put it in the whelping box by the bed. They squirmed and squealed, but then, as she placed each additional puppy in the soft bed, they crawled together and formed one big heap in the middle of the box and promptly fell asleep. Jasmine watched in amazement. They were the cutest things she had ever seen. She hoped she would be able to part with them, but the thought of feeding and cleaning up after ten dogs gave her courage.

When Jasmine brought Blondie back inside and showed her where the puppies were, she was afraid that Blondie would object and try to take them back to her bed. But she didn't. She sniffed the box, and then crawled in with her babies. Carefully examining each one to make sure they were safe, she then turned around once and lay down beside them. Jasmine gave a sigh of relief. She would have her bed back tonight.

Chance followed her everywhere now, but when he wasn't, she knew where to find him: sitting in front of her bedroom door. He would look up at her as if to say, "I want to see them, too." She couldn't have Chance in her room at night with Blondie and the puppies there, so he was put in Celeste's room. At first he protested, but then decided that he could climb up on Celeste's bed and sleep with her and be happy.

After a couple of days, Jasmine thought it would be all right to introduce Chance to the new puppies. She put Chance on his leash, just in case, and carefully led him into her bedroom. She watched Blondie's reaction. If Blondie had shown any objection she would have immediately taken Chance out of the room. But Blondie was cool. She just looked up at them and seemed calm and happy. Chance looked in the box, sniffed, wagged his tail and looked up at Jasmine, then sniffed some more. Then he started to get into the box with Blondie. Jasmine had to draw the line and pull him back.

"No, Chance. Not yet, maybe when they get older. You can be the daddy and play with them." And Chance seemed to understand. He sat down and just looked on with the same amazement that Jasmine and Celeste had several days earlier. Chance was a good and gentle dog, and she had no qualms about Chance being around Blondie and the puppies. He would not harm them. She knew that.

Now that the puppies had arrived, Jasmine's focus came back to Celeste and her dilemma of how she could afford to pay for her baby. She had insisted that Celeste find a doctor and make an appointment. Celeste told her that the several obstetricians she had called in the area had all turned her down because she had no health insurance and no money.

It was time to call Richard. "We must be practical," Jasmine told Celeste. And, while Celeste sat nearby and cringed, she picked up the phone.

After several rings, Richard answered. Jasmine was relieved that Deborah hadn't answered. "Hello, Richard, how are you doing?" Jasmine said. She needed to approach this carefully.

"I'm doing just fine. What is it that you want this time?" he asked, knowing that Jasmine always had something in mind when she called.

"Well, we need some help here." Jasmine paused, trying to think how she could sell this in a positive way. Maybe she should lie and tell him that Celeste needed money for school. No, lying was never a good thing. "Celeste is sitting right here and I'll let you talk with her in a minute." Celeste waved her arms and mouthed a big "No!"

"Hurry up. I have to get to work," said Richard.

"You knew that Celeste had a boyfriend, didn't you?"

"You mean that Mexican guy?"

"Celeste told me his family is from the Dominican Republic. Anyway, it seems that Celeste and Ramon were very involved. And after he left here in July, she found out that she's having his baby." Jasmine waited for the shouting.

There was silence on the other end. Then, "Why am I not surprised?"

"Well, Celeste is in need of some financial help right now, and we thought you might be able to do that."

"Where is the father?"

"She says he's in England right now looking for work."

"So he ran out on her?" Richard asked tersely.

"Not exactly. He doesn't know about the baby. Celeste has been trying to find him and hasn't been able to."

"Jasmine, I don't see why I should be paying for yet another of her mistakes."

"Because she's your daughter and you love her. You do, don't you?"

Jasmine motioned for Celeste to come to the phone and talk to her dad. She thought that he might soften up if Celeste talked to him directly. But she refused.

"Richard, this is your grandchild. Your first *grandchild*. If you don't do this you'll feel sorry the rest of your life," Jasmine pleaded, hoping to appeal to his self-reproach. "And you can certainly afford it," Jasmine added.

"Well, I'll think about it."

"Don't think too long. She needs to go to the doctor and get on some vitamins and get her hospital lined up. I'll help her all that I can, but if you could please send some money… It isn't as if you didn't have the money, Richard."

"I'll think about it. What a mess this is for Celeste!"

"That's why we have to help her now," implored Jasmine.

They hung up. "Why wouldn't you talk to him?"

"I can't, Mom. I'm so ashamed."

"Well, stop being ashamed and let's get on with having this baby. He said he would think about it, and I think he's going to help."

Chapter 25
Chance

I was finally able to come home. I was in that awful cage for what seemed like days, hooked up to a tube attached to my body. It was noisy. The other captives or occupants, I don't think they were there of their own free will, were constantly crying and barking, and when I wanted to sleep, they would wake me up. Every couple of hours strange people came and gave me pills and stuck more needles in me that hurt so bad. And then they would stick this glass thing in my rear and put a cold round thing on my chest.

Then Mom came to see me and I thought I would be going home. But, no, she left again. Am I going to be here forever? She came again with some food and I wasn't hungry, so I didn't eat any. My stomach was still upset. So I started to chew the plastic tubing. I didn't have anything else to do, and I had that urge to chew. All dogs know what that's like. Thank goodness they removed the plastic line.

Then a few hours later, or was it the next day, she came again. I could hear her footsteps in the hallway as she walked. Oh boy; I'm really going home now. They took me out of the cage and back to the room where two other dogs and one cat were sitting with their owners. Then they handed this big plastic thing to Mom and I thought, oh what a great toy. I can really chew on this. But Mom put it around my neck and snapped it closed and I was a prisoner in this thing. How humiliating! I shook my head until I was dizzy, but I couldn't get it off.

Mom took me out to the car and put me in the back. Whoopee, we're really going home! I gave a little squeal, and Mom reached back and stroked my muzzle and I heard the word "home."

After a time the car pulled into the driveway of our house and Mom took me out of the back and into the house. I had expected Blondie to greet us; she's always there at the front door, but no, she wasn't there—and I smelled something strange. Then we went back to the place where I sleep with Mom and there was Blondie on our bed and she had these little, tiny, wet things by her side and they were moving and squealing. And then I saw another one come out of her rear end, and I was dismayed. I wanted to get a closer look and smell and lick them, but Mom would not allow it. She took me into the other room where I was so worried.

Then that night, we didn't sleep in our bed. Mom was on the couch in the big room in front and I wanted to be with her, but she kept putting me in a bed beside the couch. I kept jumping up and trying to be close to her. I was stressed. I had just come home from a horrible experience, and now this.

Then, the next day, all day long, I heard these strange sounds coming from our room where we were supposed to sleep. But the door was closed. Blondie came out and I smelled her and she had that strange smell all over her and she wasn't very friendly. So I sat by the door and waited and waited. For two days I waited. I'm a patient dog. I can wait forever.

Finally, Mom put my leash on and took me into the room where Blondie's box was, and there they were—a bunch of little dogs, I guess that's what they were. One looked just like Blondie. I tried to get in the box to get a closer look, but Mom wouldn't let me. So I just sat there, and I was shocked that Blondie could do this; make these little dogs—"puppies" Mom called them. If I wait long enough, I know I can play with them, and that is going to be the most fun. I love Blondie; she's the greatest.

Chapter 26
Ramon Abroad

Ramon arrived in London on a Friday morning, taking the train from Heathrow airport to Paddington Station, just blocks away from his friend's flat near Hyde Park. He felt an excitement he hadn't felt in a long time, never having been out of the United States before, with the exception of a trip or two to Tijuana for a night on the town when he was in college. But in his mind that didn't count.

Here he was in a foreign country, where they spoke his language, no less. He had come looking for work after exhausting all possibilities in the States. There were so many people looking for work back in California that each time he applied for something, the job would be scooped up before he had a chance at it. So why not try something different, he thought. And coming to the UK was perfect, being an English-speaking country. His old college friend Dave Landers had a flat in London and was elated when he had contacted him with the idea of coming over.

"Hey, man you're gonna love it over here. The night life is out of this world and the women are extraordinary," Dave told him when he had called in late July. "I can get laid every night if I want to."

Ramon wasn't so sure that was what he was looking for. Another reason, and maybe the main reason he wanted to leave the States was that he needed to get his mind straight about Celeste. He couldn't stop thinking about her. No mater what he was doing, no matter where he was, he always had the picture in his mind of this beautiful woman with long flowing chestnut hair, sparkling dark brown eyes and olive-colored skin, so soft, so sweet, he wanted to eat her up. But she evidently didn't feel the same way about him. Soon after he had left Arizona he tried calling her. Day after day, his calls went to voice mail and she never called him back. He tried emailing, texting, and tweeting, and still no response.

So he would try something new. He had saved some money while he had been working for his dad, and British Airways was having a sale on plane tickets to London. Perfect. Even if he didn't find an office job, he could always work in a restaurant.

After going through customs, Ramon got on the train at Heathrow. He was amazed at the tight security. As the passengers got off the train and before new passengers embarked, Special Forces officers, looking like SWAT team officers in the U.S., dressed in black flak jackets and carrying assault rifles, went onto the train and swept through, making sure that it was safe. Ramon was dismayed. This wasn't done in the U.S. Although the U.S. had the 9-11 attack they had not had a terrorist bombing of trains like the London underground bombing several years ago. Ramon now recalled when that happened, was it 2004, 2005? He remembered that many people had died. Now he understood and was glad for the safety measures. He wondered, as the train sped toward London, where those Bobbies were and, as he recalled they didn't carry guns.

As Ramon was able to catch the Heathrow Express, the train whistled by the intermediate stops until it came into Paddington Station. It was ten in the morning and, since he had been on the flight all night, he was a little blurry-eyed as he got off the train. He was glad that Dave was there to meet him as he had promised. Ramon wouldn't have known where to go if he hadn't.

"Hey, Ramon, how was your flight?"

"Uneventful," Ramon muttered as he pulled his carry-on luggage behind him. "I tried to sleep during the flight, but you know how that is. I'm beyond tired."

"You'll have some jet lag for a day or two, but that'll go away. Any cute flight attendants?" Dave asked.

"You sound like you're horny as hell. Aren't you getting any? I thought the Brits were an agreeable lot," Ramon replied as they came out of the station and onto the street. They walked along for two blocks and then crossed the street, heading towards Hyde Park nearly getting run over in the process. "Wow, don't pedestrians have the right of way here?

"Negative. It's everyone for him- or herself on the streets of London."

Ramon breathed in deeply, glad to be finally at his destination and then coughed and wheezed, taking in the exhaust fumes from the many cars, trucks and buses whizzing by at break-neck speed.

"And no emissions standards, either? This air is bad," he said as he coughed again.

"You get used to it."

"Maybe you do, but my lungs are not liking this dirty air."

They walked another three blocks and came to a street with rows of walk-up apartments. Each of the old white buildings had a main entrance accessed by concrete or brick steps leading up to the oversized locked doors in different styles, some with large glass windows and ornate molding and others a simple design with small windows at the top. They turned to walk up the steps of one of the flats. Dave took out an electronic key, slid it into the appropriate slot, and then opened the door. They stood for a moment on the ground floor looking up at stairs to nowhere.

"Are you up for a climb?" asked Dave.

"Do I have a choice?" Ramon quipped.

"No. I could carry you, but I might drop you and you wouldn't like that in the least," Dave retorted.

And they started up the first flight of stairs with a none-too-stable wooden railing that wobbled when Ramon grabbed onto it. He decided to go it alone.

After the third flight, Ramon stopped on the landing to catch his breath. "Hey, Dave, you don't have to work out with stairs like these."

"You're right. Between that and having sex, I never have to go to the gym."

Ramon decided to let that one go. He was tired, and climbing these stairs was making him more tired. They finally reached the fourth floor and walked down a short, dingy hallway that smelled like stale cigarette smoke.

"Here we are. Home Sweet Home." Dave took out a key and opened the door with white paint peeling off and the number 402 at the top.

Ramon dragged his luggage into the front room and collapsed on a big, old slouchy couch covered in gray velour. He sat there for a few minutes, catching his breath, and then looked around the large room with a high ceiling, wooden floors and a well- worn red Persian area rug. The walls were painted a sea green and there was a large abstract painting in the style of Kandinsky on one wall. The far wall was all windows, and his curiosity got the better of him. He got up from the couch, groaning, and walked over to the windows to see what he could see.

"Wow! This is great. What a view. How'd you get this place?" Ramon exclaimed as he looked out over the expanse of green that was Hyde Park.

"From the same person that got your work permit for you. I have a cousin in high places." Dave came over and stood beside Ramon. "Look over that way," he pointed to the southwest corner of the park. "There, do you see the fountain?"

"No, I don't see a fountain. It looks like a small man-made stream. What is it?

"That's Princess Diana's Memorial Fountain. Really neat, isn't it? We'll walk down there tonight before dinner," said Dave. "In the meantime, here's your room," he said as he showed Ramon down the narrow hallway, past the tiny kitchen. "Maybe you want to catch some zzz's. There's sandwich fixings in the fridge. Don't drink all the beer. I'm going back to work for a few hours so they can pay my salary. I'll be home about five and we'll take that walk, get some fish and chips, and hit the pubs tonight."

Ramon took off his khaki pants and polo shirt, pulled back the forest green chenille bed spread, and fell into the single bed in the small, windowless room. Within minutes he was sleeping a deep sleep, no dreams. The flight was behind him, he had no thoughts of home, of his family, of Celeste. He just slept.

Chapter 27
Houseful

The end of September was near, and the never-ending heat continued, 107 degrees one day, 110 the next. But that was the norm for this desert city of Phoenix. Jasmine was used to it. Celeste complained every day. Celeste was attending school four days a week and working on projects the other three and loving every minute of it. The kitchen table had become the planning area, with drawings and storyboards laid out end-to-end. They now ate their meals on TV trays in the living room or on the back patio, where the dogs hung around under the tables begging for handouts. Jasmine partitioned the sole computer in her office so that Celeste could have a place for her digital assignments. At times there were conflicts when both of them needed to use the computer, but they soon solved that problem by working out a time schedule. Jasmine was so pleased that Celeste had found her niche in life that she seldom complained about something as minor as a computer conflict, except that her hard drive was fast filling up with digital images and she was soon looking at either getting a new computer or buying Celeste her own computer.

Celeste's pregnancy, now four months along, was beginning to show. This was, no doubt, one of the reasons she had such an aversion to the heat. Her doctor told her to expect the baby the last week in January. Celeste was not in any hurry to have this baby, but she hoped she would change her mind once he had arrived. She'd had an ultrasound and was told she would be having a boy. She wasn't particular about the sex of the baby; a girl would have been fine, too.

The puppies were growing as well. They were now old enough to start eating on their own, and when puppies eat, they also poop. So Jasmine had to move them out of the box in the bedroom and put them in a pen on the back patio. It was warm for them, but they didn't seem to mind. Jasmine turned on the mister that she had installed on the patio several years ago just for her dogs, and the puppies stayed pretty cool. Of course, Blondie had to sleep with her puppies, and Jasmine was worried that Blondie would be unhappy being on the patio at night. But she seemed to settle right in with the puppies.

The first night they were outside she kept checking to see if they were all right. All seemed to be fine so she went back to bed, with Chance sleeping on the floor beside her bed to keep cool. About three in the morning, she heard loud barking coming from the patio. Chance woke up, ears forward, jumped off the bed and rushed to the back door, with Jasmine following. Chance frantically pawed at the door as Jasmine looked out the back window and saw Blondie fending off a coyote that was trying to get to the puppies. She grabbed a broom from the broom closet and flew out the door with Chance right behind her. The coyote had grabbed one of the puppies and was preparing to run off with it just as Chance grabbed the coyote's leg and Jasmine hit it with her broom. The coyote dropped the puppy and ran for the fence, easily vaulting it, and disappeared into the night. It wanted no part of this gang.

"Oh, Blondie! Are the puppies okay?" Jasmine exclaimed as she looked at the puppies that were by now running around in their penned area. The puppy, one of the black ones that the coyote had had in his mouth was on the other side of the patio. She picked it up and carefully examined it and then put it back with the other puppies. It was crying, but other than that it seemed to be all right. Blondie went to it and nuzzled it to reassure it that it was safe. Jasmine examined

Blondie for any bites and didn't see any. "Good job, Blondie. I had no idea that a coyote would come into our yard like that. And Chance, you are a hero. You saved the puppy," she said as she stroked his ears. Chance stood tall, with ears forward, ready for any other catastrophe that might happen.

Celeste was awake by this time and standing by the door. "That was a close call. Guess they won't be sleeping on the patio anymore," she said.

"I've seen coyotes on the street before, very early in the morning. And I saw one a couple of months ago when I was driving up 12th Street. I thought it was a dog and I was going to rescue it, but as I got closer I saw that it was a coyote and it had a cat in its mouth."

"Poor thing," said Celeste. "Mom, don't you have a gun? You could've shot the coyote."

"No, Celey, I've never had a gun in the house. I don't like guns. Too many people are killed by guns these days. And I don't think I could shoot a coyote. I like coyotes, and they're just trying to survive like everyone else."

"But you could use it to protect yourself."

"I have the alarm system and a big dog. Why do I need a gun?" Then she started to pick up the puppies from the pen. "We'll put them in the house in the crate at night from now on. There are hawks and owls around here, too, and they could carry a puppy off just as easily. Oh, Blondie, I'm sorry. But fortunately we learned soon enough."

With the puppies growing bigger by the day, Chance could get a better look at them during the day when they were on the patio, and the playtime began. The first time Jasmine let Chance play with the puppies, she had to watch carefully to make sure he would be gentle with them. When she opened the pen, Chance went in and nosed and licked each puppy, all the time wagging his tail with joy. The circus had begun. They tried crawling up on him, chewing, clawing, nipping, and going down on their haunches, playfully barking at him. They moved out of the pen, first Chance, probably trying to get away from the sharp little teeth, then three puppies, then two more, and the chase was on. Chance went down on his front haunches, in play mode, and one of the black puppies climbed on top of him, pulling at his ears, chewing his nose. But Chance was cool. He didn't seem to mind. Jasmine and Celeste watched, laughing until their sides hurt. "You see, this is why I love dogs. The fun just goes on and on. Where else can you get entertainment like this? And it's free," said Jasmine with a chuckle.

"Well, not exactly free. Somebody has to do the cleaning up, and it's a lot of work," Celeste retorted as she stopped laughing as she thought about the two or more times a day she had to clean the pen and hose it down. Her mother asked her to do this, and she reluctantly agreed. Jasmine said to her in jest that she was preparing her for the days ahead when she would have diapers to change. Celeste didn't think that was funny.

Blondie had become a distant observer of all the antics, sitting by the dog house, watching, seeming not to care. If one or more of the puppies found her and tried to nurse, she walked away and sometimes nipped at them. Her job was done and it was time for her "children" to go out in the world and make their mark, so to speak. Jasmine had introduced the puppies to dog food, puppy kibble, and they were starting to eat on their own.

As much as Jasmine was enjoying the puppies, it was time to find new homes for them. She'd taken them to the veterinary for a wellness check, their first shots, and the removal of the dew claws that all puppies are born with. Now she had to figure out how to advertise them in such a way that people would be breaking down her door to have one of these exceptional puppies. In the laws of supply and demand, there was still an oversupply of rescue and shelter dogs in the valley, with people continuing to lose their homes or having to move in order to find a job.

She would be competing with these dogs and many others. How could she make her dogs sound like they were superior to all others?

Jasmine also had to find a way to make sure that the new owners would spay and neuter them. She visited a spay and neuter clinic to see if they would give her discount coupons for the procedure. To her surprise, they agreed. She then decided that she would offer the puppies for the price of the operation, then refund the money when the owners brought back a confirmation that the dogs had been altered. She hadn't wanted to make money on these puppies; she only wanted to make sure they were taken care of. Jasmine also typed up a list of questions, a contract for prospective owners. The title at the top read "Contract for Purchasing a Special Dog."

And the list read:

1. Is this your first dog?
2. Will this dog be part of the family?
3. Will the dog be a house dog and kept inside with the family, especially when the outside temperature is extreme?
4. If you move, will the dog go with you?
5. Do you have the money to provide for it: quality food, shots, veterinary care?
6. If you have young children, will you monitor them at all times with the dog? This applies even more so with infants.
7. Will you make sure the dog has appropriate training?
8. If you find yourself in a position where you cannot possibly care for the dog, will you find someone who can or take it to a shelter?
9. And will you love this dog with all of your heart for the rest of its life?

Jasmine then had a signature statement at the bottom for them to sign. She was determined that until they signed this paper, she would not sell a dog to them. It might not prevent them from abusing the dog, but at least she would have some assurance this would not happen, and that put her mind at ease.

"Mother, you're never going to sell the dogs with all these restrictions. And people will do whatever they want once they have the animal," murmured Celeste as she read the list of questions.

"You could be right. But at least I've tried and maybe created awareness. I think sometimes people get dogs, and other pets, too, for the wrong reasons. And then they find out that they don't want them, or can't take care of them, or a baby comes along and of course the baby becomes the priority over the pet. If they take these questions seriously, maybe that won't happen. I know I have no control once these sweet puppies leave my house."

With that said, Jasmine asked Celeste to make up flyers with photos of the puppies playing, to be posted around the neighborhood, on supermarket bulletin boards, and in veterinarian's offices. On the flyers Jasmine called them Celebrity Dogs, saying they were the most intelligent, most beautiful puppies she had ever seen and they would make their new owners wealthy. She also said they would become their best friends and make wonderful watch dogs to protect their property. Celeste objected again, saying that she was lying when she said that buying the dogs would make people wealthy. "Not so," said Jasmine. "If you think in terms of having a new best friend, you will have a richer life. And if the dog prevents burglaries, you have protected your wealth." Celeste just laughed at her mother's sanguine outlook on life. She hoped she could emulate that.

The ad was placed on Craigslist, in the *Arizona Republic*, the *North Central News*, and in other neighborhood newspapers. But then she did something else. She bought satin ribbon from the craft store, blue for the boys and pink for the girls, and tied bows around the puppies' necks. With Celeste's help she lined them up on a piece of royal blue velvet fabric she had been saving to make pillows for the living room couch and took still photos and a video of them. It took more than two hours; one or more puppies always out of place or running away.

Coincidently there was a local daytime television program featuring pets in the Valley. She sent the best digital photo and the video to the TV station, along with the copy from their ad. Within two days, the video was on air. A couple of days later she had a call from Channel 12. "Ms. Bailey, we saw your video with eight puppies on Channel 3," Alison Jackson, the program director, said when Jasmine picked up the call. "That's great. They're all here playing and growing," said Jasmine.

"We would like you to bring them in on Friday and we'll showcase them on our daily morning show. Could you do that?" asked Alison.

"Could I? Absolutely! We'll be there, all nine of us." Jasmine said with glee.

"Be here with the puppies by ten AM and we'll give you further instructions once you get here. And bring a helper, if you can," said Alison.

Jasmine told Celeste that afternoon when she came home from her classes.

"Yea!" yelled Celeste. "I think we'll find homes for these puppies after all."

"Good homes, honey. Not just "homes." And you doubted?" said Jasmine as she grinned at Celeste's delight.

"I'm afraid so. But I'm a believer now. There's something else we can do with this video. If we can put it on YouTube, maybe it will go viral."

"Great idea. I'll put you in charge of the YouTube project," said Jasmine.

Now, Jasmine thought, if I could market my skills as well as I'm doing with the puppies, I might find a job.

Chapter 28

Ramon in London

Ramon began his search for work in London, putting on his Calvin Klein gray flannel suit with a crisp white shirt and a silk navy-and-maroon tie. He could see his reflection in his highly polished black oxfords. Looking professional, if he could convince an employer that he also had the right qualifications, he might find a job.

Armed with his resume, letters of recommendation from his prior employers, and his work permit, Ramon set out on the streets of London in search of a job. He decided that he would take almost anything; it didn't have to be an accounting job. He knew that he could work as a business analyst or a data analyst, and he would even work in sales, just to have some money coming in to pay his half of the rent and food and drink.

Every morning, Ramon walked four blocks from his flat to the nearest newsstand to get a copy of the *London Times* and brought it back to peruse the want ads for employment while he drank his morning coffee. If there were any jobs listed he would make note of them on a log that he kept on his computer. He then went to on-line job sites to see if there were any postings for his type of work. If there were, he would submit an application with his resume and a cover letter. But then he decided that he would go in person to some of the large, well-known companies in the city.

First on his list was British Airways, and then he would go to Lloyds of London and Harrods. He went on-line to find the addresses of the headquarters for these companies. If he could he walked, or took the Metro or a bus or, as a last resort, a cab. After he found the office building, he went to the Human Resource Department, introduced himself, telling the human resource person that he was an experienced accountant and was looking for work in that field. He would then hand them one of his resumes with his business card and telephone number where he could be reached. He did this every day for two weeks.

And, by night, he and his roommate Dave were becoming pub crawlers, visiting a different establishment every night. Dave, shorter than the six-foot tall Ramon, was blond, blue-eyed with a ruddy complexion, and always on the make, looking for women. He could literally charm the pants off them—and often did, leaving Ramon to go home alone. Ramon couldn't see why these women were attracted to Dave. Was it possibly because he was American? Ramon thought that Dave was acting like a freshman in college, and he didn't want to participate. Even though women, attracted to his Latin looks, would flock around him as well, he wasn't interested. He had one woman on his mind: Celeste.

"Hey man, what's with you? You're turning down these beauties. Why?"

"Dave, I have other things on my mind. I'm just not into bar-hopping I guess."

"You're in London. There are gifts to enjoy here. Take advantage of it."

Ramon finally told Dave he should go without him. That he needed to get his rest and be ready for the next day's job search. He didn't mention Celeste.

"But you are the best chick magnate I've ever had. They all adore the Latin lover."

Ramon held firm but said he would go occasionally. He hated being in these places; they were dark and full of smoke. There were no smoke-free places in London. With the automobile, bus and truck exhaust on the streets and the smoke-filled bars, he felt like his lungs were being ravaged.

So he continued walking, riding the streets of London by day and spending his evenings in the apartment, reading or watching BBC. At times he would gaze across Hyde Park, watching joggers, cyclists and couples walking together, thinking of Celeste and wanting to be back home again. If he were to get a decent job, he could work for a few months and then go home with money. Then maybe Celeste would marry him. He certainly understood how she would not want to marry a loser, and he felt like one since he had lost his job.

He thought that if he delivered enough resumes, eventually one of these companies would call him in for an interview. It wasn't happening. So he put Plan B to work, looking for a waiter's job or something in the kitchen, prep cook, or even as a chef, thanks to his experience in his father's restaurant. And it wasn't long before he had a call back from the Mango Room, a Caribbean restaurant near Regent's Park, for a job as prep cook. He went in for the interview, telling them that his father owned The Islands in Los Angeles. Tony, the owner and head chef, was so impressed that he gave Ramon a job as chef, a step above prep cook, with more money. He was to start in a week. Ramon was pleased. Now he would be working nights and had a valid excuse not to go out trolling with Dave. And if he got a better offer for an accounting job, he could always quit the chef's job. He needed to be working. He needed the money.

After several weeks of working in the restaurant, Ramon was exhausted. He was working twelve-hour shifts, six days a week and the work was intense, especially during the dinner hour. But he wouldn't quit. Sometimes coming home at two in the morning, he would take off his clothes and roll into bed and fall asleep in minutes. Then he had the mornings to himself. Dave was at work, and the apartment was all his until noon, when he went back to the Mango Room and started all over again. It was these mornings that he would try to call Celeste. After he'd been trying for weeks, she finally answered the phone. He was overjoyed.

"Celeste, is that really you? I've been trying to call you for weeks now, and you never answered the phone."

"Ramon," Celeste paused. "How are you?"

"I'm fine. How are you?"

"I'm doing okay. Where are you? I heard you went to Europe. You sound like you're next door."

"I'm in London. I've been here a few weeks. It's pretty exciting. We've been seeing all the sights—Buckingham Palace, the Tower of London." There was another pause. "So you're just okay?"

"No. I'm fine. I got a grant and I'm going to school, learning computer animation. It's really fun." Celeste was wondered who the "we" was that he was seeing the sights with.

"I've missed you. I think about you all the time."

"I miss you, too," Celeste said. She wasn't sure she meant it, but she had been thinking about Ramon a lot lately. Especially since she was carrying his baby. Should she tell him? She was in a quandary. "When are you coming back?"

"I don't know right now. I've been trying to find an accounting job over here, but the job market isn't much better here than it was in the States. So I took a chef's job at a Caribbean restaurant near Regent's Park, which isn't too far from where I'm living."

Celeste was thinking that Ramon was sure hard-working. He had that going for him.

"I'm bunking in with Dave Landers. I don't think you ever met him. He was one of my roommates in college. He has connections here in the UK and got me my work permit. You should see our apartment. It looks out on Hyde Park, and I can see Kensington Palace from my window."

"I bet the weather is cooler there." Celeste was relieved that Ramon was living with a male friend at least. "Although it's finally cooling down here in Phoenix."

"I didn't call to talk about the weather, Celeste. I felt your ambivalence the last few weeks we were together. I guess I have to know if we have a future. I love you and I want to be with you." There, he'd said it. But that was the truth. He always tried to tell the truth.

"I think I love you, too."

"You think. You don't know?"

"I'm in such turmoil right now."

"We all are. And I know how that feels. Can I call you again?"

"Yes, call me anytime. I do want to talk with you." He doesn't have an inkling of how I feel, she thought. No man does. They don't have to carry and birth all the children of the world. And Celeste couldn't tell him right now. She didn't want him to feel obligated to marry her. But if he loved her?

Ramon said he would call next week, and Celeste said that would be fine with her. After they hung up, she thought about how much he must care for her if he was calling all the way from London. Surely he was meeting single women every day. But yet he still thought of her. That was worth a lot.

Chapter 29
Puppies Go Home

Jasmine had to admit that having Celeste come back to live with her had been a positive thing. When she'd first heard from Celeste some five months ago, just the thought of having to worry about another person was daunting. She had her own concerns, being jobless and paying bills on a limited budget. As the weeks and months had gone by, she was happy to have Celeste sharing her life, albeit a little in disarray right now for the both of them.

They spent endless hours talking: about dogs, people, politics, relationships. Jasmine hoped she had picked up where she left off when Celeste, as a young teen, had gone to live with her dad. She soon found their relationship to be more of one adult relating to another instead of the parent-child relationship they had when Celeste was younger. But she could still give her advice and guidance when asked. They had become closer than she'd ever thought possible.

Celeste certainly had her own ideas, and they didn't always agree on everything. She was in some ways more realistic than her mother in that she recognized that not everyone in the world could be fed, not every animal could be rescued. She chided her mother for taking in Blondie when they could barely buy food for themselves some days. And then she had been dismayed when it was discovered that Blondie was pregnant, putting more of a financial burden on them.

"But you can try," Jasmine implored. "If everyone who could would take on one homeless person, one homeless dog, the world would be a better place."

"But, Mom, we don't have the money to help anyone right now. Last week we didn't have enough to buy hamburger. And we never go out to eat," said Celeste. They were sitting on the sofa late one evening, Chance lying at their feet snoring.

"Nonsense. We have a roof over our head, and we have money coming in, even though it's from the government. And I'm hopeful that I'll find work or I will be able to bring more money into our household. And look at you. You're on your way to a great new career. In another year you'll find a good-paying job, and the baby will be almost walking by then."

"The baby." Celeste looked down, picking at her frayed jeans. "I'm so afraid. I don't know how I can do this. Work and take care of a baby the way he should be taken care of. You stayed home with me and devoted all of your time to taking care of me. I just can't imagine working in a demanding job and coming home to a crying infant every night."

"It's going to be hard, but you'll get through it."

"I'll be grumpy. I'll just want to relax in front of the TV. But I'll have to feed him and bathe him and love him in the small amount of time between dinner and his bedtime. What is that, three hours? How do other mothers do it?"

"I'll help for awhile, until you're making enough money. You'll see. It'll work out. Everything always does."

"Mother, you're such Pollyanna. I wish I could be like you, but I can't," said Celeste. "I guess everything does always work out one way or another, but not always for the better."

"What do you have to lose by thinking positive thoughts about this? Nothing. When I first thought about you coming to live with me, I was worried. But, you know what, honey; it was the best thing that could have happened to both of us. I'm glad you're here at this time."

Celeste also kept telling her mother that she should have a man in her life and Jasmine was adamant that she wasn't ready. "Why would I want a man? I make my own money. I do almost everything around this house, keep up the yard, and trim the trees. I've even done plumbing jobs, if the pipes aren't stuck. I go to bed every night with the dogs, and I'm thankful that I'm safe and have a warm bed. We have enough to eat, good books to read, and wonderful dogs. And I have you here with me. I don't need anything more or anyone else right now."

"I love you too, Mom. But some day you'll want someone else. It's not just about taking care of the house." Celeste posed.

"When the time is right. And I'll know when that is."

Calls were coming in for the puppies from all over the Phoenix area and beyond. One woman called from Prescott, Arizona, 100 miles north of Phoenix. Jasmine tried to screen people over the phone, to ensure they were serious dog people. Only then would she make appointments for them to come and see the puppies. She was somewhat apprehensive about strange people coming to their home. This would be the time to have a man around, she thought. But they would manage. If, when she met people at the door, she didn't like the way they acted or looked, she wouldn't let them inside. That was how she would handle it. And she would try to make the appointments when Celeste was going to be there: thinking that the two of them together would be better than her alone. Thinking back through the years, these things had never occurred to her. She would sell cars, furniture without a thought to any danger. Either she was getting older or the world was more dangerous. A little of both, she guessed.

The first couple came in the middle of the afternoon. They had two little children with them, ages two and five. Jasmine took them to the back patio to see the brood, and they picked out the black one with white feet and took it out to play with. The two-year-old picked up the puppy by the wrong end. It was dangling from the toddler's arms and finally fell to the ground, which fortunately wasn't very far. But still Jasmine cringed.

Jasmine watched and waited for the couple to intervene, but they didn't. "Why do you want a puppy?" she asked.

"For our kids," the husband said. "How much are these puppies?"

"$250," said Jasmine, jacking up the price by a hundred dollars.

"You can't be serious," said the woman, who was wearing very tight jeans and a light-blue low-cut tank top.

"I am serious," said Jasmine.

"Com'on, honey, let's go. She doesn't want to sell us a puppy," said the husband as he grabbed the two kids by their hands.

Jasmine felt that she had done the right thing. She had visions of these children, maybe not meaning to, but abusing the puppy with no parental intervention. And buying a puppy for little toddlers is a bad idea, she thought.

Later, a young woman called and asked to come and see the puppies. She arrived at five in the afternoon, just as Celeste was coming home from school.

Her name was Sandra and she was a registered nurse at Phoenix Baptist Hospital. She was in her thirties, had long, straight brown hair and was wearing scrubs. She picked up one of the black puppies, the male, and held it very carefully, stroking it until the puppy melted into her arms.

"Do you have a yard for a dog?" asked Jasmine.

"No, not right now, but I'm looking for a house. I would take it out and walk it though. I live right near the hospital."

"You must work long hours," said Jasmine.

"I do. Twelve-hour shifts. But I have a roommate, and she's unemployed right now like everyone else. She could take the dog out."

"Have you raised a puppy before?"

"Yes, we've had dogs in our family all of my life. I know what a pain they can be when they're little. But they're so much fun."

Sandra asked the price and Jasmine told her $100, a little lower than she had intended to ask, as she really liked this lady. She told her that the money would be refunded upon getting the dog neutered. Sandra put the puppy down and watched as it played with its siblings. Then Jasmine handed her the contract. Sandra read it thoroughly and then looked at Jasmine and smiled. "I wish everyone would do what you do," she said. "If you approve, I'll take the puppy. He's a sweet one and I promise to take good care of him. What kind of food are they eating?"

"I have a bag of kibble for you to take home with you. They are used to eating this food. But you can buy whatever brand you think is good."

Jasmine handed her the food as she thought, one down, seven to go.

Every day, calls came in and people came over to see the puppies. Jasmine rejected only two more people: one couple who she knew couldn't afford the expense and a man who said he wanted a watch dog and wouldn't let the puppy in the house. But, one by one the puppies were leaving, until only two remained.

As each puppy left, Jasmine worried. Would they be taken care of? Would they be loved? But she thought she had done everything she could to make sure that these puppies had good homes.

The last two were the black female and the blond puppy, a female that looked like Blondie. She wondered why no one chose the blond one, but she supposed that it was because of her gender. Jasmine went out to play with the puppies and picked up the blond puppy. It looked up at her and licked her face. Jasmine looked down into the puppy's eyes and said, "I think we should keep you. Do you want to stay here with us and your mommy?" The puppy licked Jasmine again, and Jasmine took that as a yes. She would keep the blond puppy. As the weeks had passed, she had become very attached to it, and she thought one more dog wouldn't be a problem.

And now she had to name her. Sugar. She would call her Sugar because she was so sweet.

"You're kidding," said Celeste when she told her. "I'm not going to pick up after her."

"Yes, you are. We'll share the responsibility. She's so sweet, and you'll come to love her in time just as I do."

"Oh, Mother, you're such a sucker for these dogs."

Jasmine thought about how Celeste was her father's child, pragmatic and sometimes a little cold-hearted. But Jasmine felt that she was doing the right thing.

Chapter 30
Life Changes

The problem with puppies is that they are puppies. Although cute as can be and playful and fun, they can cause a lot of trouble if they are not monitored when they are very young. You can start training immediately, teaching your new puppy to go outdoors to relieve himself. You do this by taking him outdoors often and he will soon get the idea. It is good to spend as much time with your new puppy as possible in the first few weeks to bond with him. Tether him to you when you are watching TV or working on your computer in the evenings. At night it is beneficial to put your puppy in a crate to help with housebreaking. Make sure the crate is small enough that he can't go to a corner and get away from where he might have urinated. Being kept in a crate isn't cruel. Dogs think of the crate like a cave, a safe haven, and as they get used to it welcome their time there. However, crating them all day is not a good idea.

At six months it is time for your puppy to go to school for some basic training. You can either do this on your own or take him to puppy training at the many dog training schools available or even at the local PetsMart. You can also have a trainer come into your home. By doing so you will learn many tips on how to teach your dog manners, leash training, leaving undesirable objects alone, and obeying commands, like Come, Stay and Down and Off when he jumps on people. This will be very useful later on in controlling him.

Most likely your puppy will chew, for example on furniture and shoes, but you can try to prevent that by giving him chew toys after telling the dog "no!" when you see him chewing something that he shouldn't. Digging is another habit that is difficult to break. Putting his feces in the hole sometimes cures that, but not always.

By the time your dog reaches the age of two or so, he will begin to become an adult and stop most of the bad habits that are so distressing. It is during this first puppy phase that many people give up on their dogs and take them to the shelter to give them up. But you don't give up on your children, and you can't give up on your puppy, either.

It looked like a giant snow globe at Christmas time, feathers floating all around the room. Jasmine couldn't believe her eyes. And in the middle of the bed sat Chance and Sugar, looking as sweet as Sugar's name implied, cocking their heads and wagging their tails as if to say, "What's the problem? We're just having some fun here."

"What are you two doing? My best feather down comforter. You've ruined it! What a mess," Jasmine yelled. She shooed them both off the bed and examined the softball-sized hole in the corner of the comforter with feathers spilling out everywhere and tried to determine if it could be repaired. As she walked into the living room, she watched in dismay as Sugar was making a puddle in the middle of her pristine white area rug that she had just shampooed a month ago. "Oh, no. No, no," she repeated as she carried Sugar outside to where she should be wetting.

I don't know if I can take this, Jasmine said to herself as she thought about another two years of dog messes to clean up. She went back into the house to clean the wet spot in the rug and treat it with a solution to neutralize the odor so the dogs would not wet there again. Fortunately, Celeste was at school or Jasmine would have heard from her about how silly she was to keep the puppy and how much work she was making for herself. And now Jasmine saw the value of such wisdom. She hated to admit that sometimes her daughter was practical and a good decision-maker.

Jasmine looked out the back window to check on the dogs. It was like having a two-year-old in the house again. She couldn't trust them even for one minute. She had to keep an eye on Sugar to make sure she went outside about every hour to relieve herself. If she didn't do that, it was guaranteed that there would be a puddle somewhere or a spot on the carpet. She'd even found dog feces behind the couch. At least Sugar knows this is wrong or she wouldn't have hid it. After she cleaned it up she put boxes at either end of the couch to keep her from going back there again. Sugar was in the crate now at night, so Jasmine didn't have to worry about her having an accident during the sleeping hours. But Sugar was still very young and she couldn't go eight hours without having to relieve herself. Invariably there would be whining coming from the crate at three AM and Jasmine would then have to take her outside and wait while she did what she needed to do.

And the chewing had started in a big way. Sugar was chewing the patio furniture, had shredded one of the patio pillows, and had managed to chew a hole in the living-room couch. The couch more or less belonged to the dogs now. They lounged there every afternoon and in the evening, leaving only the two easy chairs for Jasmine and Celeste. Jasmine didn't mind; however, when she had guests she had to clean the dog hair off the furniture before they arrived, knowing that not everyone was as tolerant of her dogs as she was.

With the bedroom incident and the amount of work involved with another dog, Jasmine was rethinking her idea of keeping Sugar. It had taken more than an hour to clean up the down feathers in the bedroom. It seemed like she was cleaning up messes all day long, and she had work to do. She had to get some money coming in to pay the bills. As much as she loved Sugar, maybe it would be better if she found a good home for her. She had been successful in finding good homes for the other puppies; surely she could do it again for Sugar.

The deciding factor came late one evening, as she was getting into bed. She pulled down the sheet and was settling in for a good night's sleep when she felt bites all over her leg. "What is going on?" she wondered out loud. She turned on the light on her bedside table, got out of bed, and pulled back the sheet. There in the middle of the bed was a rope toy. Now that in itself wasn't a problem, but the fact that it was covered with fire ants gave her a surprise that she was not ready for. She still felt the biting on her legs and looked down to see ants crawling over her feet, onto her ankles, digging in for a meal. Unbeknownst to her, one of the dogs (she didn't know which one) had brought the rope toy into the house and had "buried" it under the blankets on her bed in hopes of keeping it from the other dogs. And evidently the toy had been sitting in the grass on top of a fire ant nest.

"Oh, joy," Jasmine said under her breath. She didn't want to wake Celeste. "That does it, Chance. We're going to find a home for Sugar. Sorry, buddy," she said as she climbed back into bed. Her legs were on fire, and it was a couple of hours before she finally fell asleep.

The next day, with a heavy heart, Jasmine placed an ad on Craigslist; "Sweet as Sugar" "Golden, Lab mix, four-month-old puppy, female. We call her Sugar and you will love her, too." She clicked the save button and the ad was placed.

"I heard from Ramon!" exclaimed Celeste early one morning, several days later.

"And so did you tell him that he's soon to be a father?" asked Jasmine. She was in her office writing a magazine article on dogs and their behavior as puppies that she was going to submit to *Modern Dog* magazine.

"No, I didn't."

Jasmine invited Celeste to come into her office and sit in the other chair that she had for guests. Blondie was curled up on the dog bed in the well of her desk, napping. "Don't you think it's time that you tell him?"

"I guess so. He's in London working as a chef. Says he's making a lot of money."

"Well then, he can help pay for the baby. He's partially responsible for its existence."

"I didn't want to turn him off. But he said he would be back in a few months."

"Celeste, are you taking full responsibility for this child? You have to decide. And you need to let Ramon know about his child, and then he can make up his own mind about what to do. I think Ramon will want to do the right thing, and he needs to contribute. Babies don't live on air—they cost money. There's the formula, the …

"No formula, I'm nursing. Mom, you knew that."

"The diapers, the clothes and toys, and then school and college…"

"I know, Mom. I know."

"I don't think you really have a clue. Go Google it. You can see just how much money it takes to raise a kid these days. And you want to give this kid the best possible start in life, because it's a cruel world out there. If you give kids the tools to survive, hopefully excel, they'll have a chance at a happy life."

"Mother, you're preaching again. I don't like it when you preach to me."

"You may not like it, but you've got to face reality here. You can't just live in a cartoon world, like the drawings you do for school. Unless you're rich or have a trust fund. It's nasty out there. I mean, look at what's happening to all of these people, these workers looking for jobs.

They thought they had it made: good jobs, nice homes, and poof! it's gone, all of it. Jobs gone, can't pay the mortgage and so the house goes back to the bank; the stock market ate everyone's 401K, so the savings for retirement are gone. It's like the flood waters of Katrina, that swept away everything, and now people have to start all over again. And it used to be that people could retire at age sixty-five. Not anymore—not in America."

"What about you, Mom? Do you have to start all over?"

"I'll be okay. I have some savings and I am going to do a redo here. I worked for fifteen years at a job that I really didn't like, just for the money, and I'll not sell my soul again like that."

"That's what I've been trying to tell you. And that's what I'm doing...or not doing. I love my art animation classes. And I think I can make decent money."

"Celey, I'm happy for you. And I think you're practical *most* of the time. But.... getting back to the baby. You're going to have to tell Ramon and lay it on the line. If he wants to be a part of the baby's life, then he'll have to contribute."

"You're right, Mom. I will."

"What about marriage? Are you in love with him? Would you want to marry him? That's certainly an option. I just think going it alone is not the best for you."

"I should've known you'd go into a tirade like this. It's just like it used to be when I was in high school. You don't trust my judgment, ever, at all...."

"It's not that I don't trust your judgment. I just think that sometimes you live in a dream world. You've got to wake up and face reality. The baby is on his way, and he's real."

Celeste softened her tone. "I don't think I want to marry Ramon. I do love him in a way. But ....." and Celeste's voice trailed off.

"But what? If you love him, marry him. You seemed to enjoy each other. Do you have the same values, goals? He's smart and good-looking. If he's honest and caring and dependable...."

"Do you like Ramon?" Celeste asked in earnest.

"Yes, I like him. But I don't know him well enough to make a judgment."

Celeste felt the baby kick. She put her hand on her swollen belly. "I can't put my finger on it. I just can't see spending the rest of my life with him."

"You don't have to spend the rest of your life. Marry him, raise the child, and by then you'll know whether you love him or not. I'm sure other women have done that."

"You think I should marry Ramon even if I don't really love him? That's not right."

"Celey, you and Ramon decided consciously or unconsciously to conceive this child. You and Ramon owe it to the child to provide for him, and that's at least a twenty-year commitment. You can marry Ramon and do it together or not marry him and spend those years haggling over who is going to pay for what. Unfortunately, it all comes down to money. That's the reality here."

Celeste looked out the window, twisting her hair, while absorbing what her mother was telling her.

"You see how your father doesn't want to cooperate right now in helping you. He has a wife who, no doubt, would not want to spend any of their money on you."

"But I don't think Dad would be happy about my situation no matter if he was married to another woman or not. Just the fact that I got pregnant without being married. Very untraditional, in his way of thinking. "

"I suppose so." Jasmine reached down to pet Blondie, who was licking her hand. "And, oh, by the way, Celey, I'm taking your advice. We can't keep Sugar. It's just too much for us to handle right now. I put an ad on Craigslist on Tuesday, so if you get some calls, let me know."

Celeste looked at her mother and smiled. She guessed that her mother did trust her judgment, sometimes.

The puppy antics continued. Everything and anything in the house was fair game for chewing. The electrical cords, rugs, chair legs. Jasmine couldn't even leave her sun-glasses lying around; Sugar grabbed them one day, but fortunately Jasmine caught her in time. And when Sugar wasn't chewing, she was digging in the back yard. As fast as Jasmine filled in the holes, more "magically" appeared. She tried everything to keep Sugar from digging, reprimanding her, filling the hole with feces, but nothing seemed to work.

One thing was true about Sugar; she was always sweet. She never growled when Jasmine or Celeste tried to take away things that she wasn't supposed to have. She would never bite anyone.

Jasmine thought that if she made sure Sugar had plenty of plenty of toys and chew sticks, she wouldn't chew the furniture and dig. And she rotated the toys so they were always new to Sugar. But it didn't seem to matter. Then one day she walked out into the back yard and saw that the whole drip system had been dug up again around the perimeter of the yard, and there were pieces of black hose and the drip heads scattered everywhere. Jasmine had been working on an article for about two hours that she was hoping to sell to a magazine and she had forgotten that the dogs were outside, alone.

"Oh, Sugar! You really did it this time. And Chance, were you helping?" Jasmine didn't think Blondie had been involved in this caper. She'd recently had her spay operation and had calmed down considerably since. Jasmine picked up the pieces and thought about all of the hard work it would take to put it back together. She would have to do it herself, because hiring someone was out of the question with the way her finances were going.

And the phone wasn't ringing for Sugar. Until one morning, Jasmine picked up her mobile and a male voice on the other end asked "You have a Golden Lab mix puppy?"

"Yes, we do. Do you want to come over and see her?" Jasmine asked, hoping he would be there soon.

"I'll be over later this afternoon, if that's okay with you."

"Yes, that'll be fine," Said Jasmine, The sooner the better, she thought. This dog is ruining our house.

Celeste was at school, and Jasmine would be alone. She was concerned, but the man on the phone had a nice-sounding voice. She hoped he'd be as nice in person as his voice sounded.

At 3:30 there was a knock on the door, and there stood a man with a young boy at his side. He introduced himself, "Hi. My name is Bill Carlton, and this is my son, Chas. I called about the puppy. May we come in and have a look?"

Jasmine could hardly hear for the noise Chance was making while jumping up and down at the screen security door. "Yes, come right in. Let me put Chance away first and then we'll go out on the patio and see Sugar. Just a minute." She took hold of Chance's collar and pulled him into her bedroom and shut the door. She then went back to open the front door. "Yes, come on in. Glad to meet you, Bill and Chas," Jasmine said as she shook Bill's hand. It was a soft hand. He must work in an office. Maybe he's an accountant or a programmer, thought Jasmine. They walked out to the back patio and Sugar, along with Blondie, came to greet them. Sugar jumped on Chas despite Jasmine telling her "off."

"Oh, that's okay, said Bill. I didn't get your name."

"Jasmine. And my daughter, Celeste, should be here any minute. She's at school right now."

Bill and Chas sat on the settee, and Chas pulled Sugar up onto his lap. Sugar licked his face and then started licking his ears and neck in exuberant puppy fashion.

"Do you have a yard?" asked Jasmine.

"Yes, we have a house over off Missouri and Seventh."

"Do you have other children, Bill?"

"I do. I have two daughters by another marriage. But they're grown and gone. One, Sandra, is married and lives in Oakland, California, and the other one, Beth, works for Charles Schwab here in Phoenix."

"I used to live in Oakland," said Jasmine. "And my ex-husband is still there."

Chas put Sugar down on the patio floor and picked up a tennis ball and threw it. Sugar ran as fast as her legs could go to get the ball and brought it back to Chas.

"Smart little dog," said Chas.

"She's going to be a big dog, though, if you look at the size of her paws," said Jasmine. "Was that the father that you put away in the bedroom?" asked Bill.

"No, we don't know who the father was." And then Jasmine told them the story about finding Blondie at the dog park and how she soon realized that she was pregnant. "I found really good homes for all of the other puppies; there were eight altogether. I was thinking of keeping Sugar, but I'm finding that, with two other dogs and working at restarting my career, I just can't keep up with another puppy. I don't have the time to train her or take care of her the way I would like."

"I was wondering why you were giving up this precious dog. She's adorable," said Bill. "What do you think, Chas, do you like her?"

"Yeah, Dad, I really do. And she likes me, I can tell." And Sugar jumped up on Chas's lap again and starting licking him and gnawing on his hands, as puppies will do.

"Have you raised a puppy before, Bill?" Jasmine asked as she handed Bill the contract that she had given to all of the other people who had adopted puppies from her.

"Yes, I've had dogs all my life. I know about puppies and what a pain they can be. But once their grown and they bond with you, they make wonderful companions."

Chas took the puppy out into the yard to run with her. Bill looked at the contract and then looked up at Jasmine and said in a low voice, "This dog is for Chas. He lost his mother, my wife Helen, three months ago to breast cancer. He needs a special companion right now to be his friend, and I think Sugar will help to fill that empty space in Chas's heart."

As Jasmine looked at Bill, tears came to her eyes. What a sad thing for a boy to lose his mother. And how thoughtful of his father to buy him this puppy. Could a dog fill that void? Well, maybe. Then she looked at Bill again, sitting there on the patio, checkbook in hand. He was about her age, maybe a little younger. He was dressed in Levi jeans and a light gray PF Chang marathon shirt, and he had dark hair, a little gray at the temple, cut short, and gray-blue eyes. He had a marathoner's body, slim, not too tall, but tall enough. Her heart went out to him

"I'm so sorry" Jasmine said. "It's never easy. Especially for the kids."

"Are we approved?" Bill asked with a twinkle in his eyes.

"Yes, you're approved. You do understand that I want the best for these puppies."

"I commend you. You're doing it right. If more people would be as caring as you...." Bill gave Jasmine a wide smile. "How much for the puppy?" he asked as he started to write out the check. "And you do take checks, don't you?"

There was a loud screech out in the yard. Jasmine and Bill both looked in that direction and Bill started to get up to see what was happening. "No! Sit, stay," ordered Jasmine. Bill was taken aback, but then they both laughed. "I'm sorry, I've been with dogs too long." She went out to the yard and saw that Chas and Sugar were playing joyfully with a rope toy. They looked fine.

"Seventy-five dollars." Jasmine really wanted Bill and Chas to have Sugar. "Yes, I'll take a check," Jasmine said as she came back to where Bill was sitting. "They're fine. Sugar is pretty excitable." She paused for moment and then asked, "What do you do for a living?"

"I'm unemployed. Have been for six months. But when I'm working I'm an accountant, so I figure that when the economy picks up, I'll get something. I send out resumes every day."

She was right about his profession. And would she be right about his character? He seemed to be a caring, loving person. But she'd been wrong about people before. "Sugar's had her first shots, but she should have two more boosters. You can go to the Humane Society to save money. And here is a certificate for spaying."

Chas, carrying Sugar in his arms, walked back to the patio where his dad and Jasmine were chatting. "I think she's yours, son. And your responsibility too, to feed and train. And now you can have a sleeping partner at night." Chas grinned.

Jasmine gave Chas a bag of kibble and got the leash that she had for Sugar and walked Bill and Chas to the front door with Sugar still cradled in Chas's arms.

"You can come and visit any time. We don't live very far from you," said Bill as he noticed a tear on Jasmine's cheek.

"You know, I just might do that."

Chapter 31
Chance

They're gone. I miss them. When the little dogs, Mom called them puppies, were here we played until we dropped and then slept and played some more.

It took a long time for the puppies to get big enough to go out and play with me. I waited and waited, sat by the bedroom door day after day. Mom was always watching when I went near the box where Blondie had her puppies. And Blondie was snippy, too, and didn't want me to be there at first. But then after awhile, the puppies, there were lots of them, started climbing out of the box. And then Mom moved them into a pen on the back patio and that night a wild dog came into our yard. If I had been out there I would not have let him in, but it was just Blondie and the puppies. He was trying to carry off one of Blondie's puppies when we ran out the back door. I grabbed his leg and Mom hit him with a broom and he ran off into the night. I sure hope he doesn't come back again. I've smelled these wild dogs around here before but I didn't think they would come in our yard with me around. Mom called me a hero. I guess that's something good.

So the puppies were getting bigger every day, and we started playing. Blondie would lead them out of the pen and they romped and peed and pooped all over the patio. I don't think Mom and Celeste were happy about that.

But then they got big enough, like real little dogs, to really play and that's when they'd jump on me and play tag and tug-o-war. We'd all take a nap together and then get up and drink some water and eat and play some more.

We dug holes in the side yard, too. Then Mom came out and saw the holes and yelled at us, mostly at them, although I did it too, but I wouldn't 'fess up to it. Blondie just sat by and watched.

One day these new people started coming to the house to look at the puppies. And Blondie didn't even care anymore. It was like they weren't even her puppies. I was shocked. I thought she would defend them to the end.

But I guessed early on that they would be leaving. And they did; one puppy at a time. Until there was only one left. And I thought she was going to stay with us forever, but no, Mom got rid of her, too. I guess the day that Sugar, that's what they called her, chewed the feather blanket on the bed and then wet on the living room rug, Mom had enough of the puppies and wanted them gone. So this man came with a young boy and, poof! Sugar was gone, too.

I'm sad. I had a lot of fun. Blondie's still here. I hope they don't get rid of her. But she's no fun anymore. I guess motherhood took a lot out of her. And then she went somewhere, and I think it was the same place that I went to have that operation, because she came home with a red place on her tummy that looked like mine after my toy eating operation.

And then I got to thinking that they might send me off as well, so I've been on my best behavior these days. And I'll have to say that life has gotten back to normal. We never went to the dog park when they were here. And neither Mom nor Celeste played with me when the puppies were here. They were too busy cleaning up. And now we go to the dog park again and Celeste plays ball with me in the back yard.

It's still pretty hot here some days, but I don't care. I drink a lot of water and I don't have to work too hard. But I'll always remember those crazy days with a bunch of puppies crawling all over me. It was great fun.

Chapter 32
The Search Continues

Another job fair. Lines of people, men and women of all sizes, ages and races, lined up from out the door and around the corner of the America West arena in downtown Phoenix. Even in October it was still hot and those who wore business suits, which were most of the people, were copiously sweating. They tried to stay in the shade but when that wasn't possible, they fanned themselves with resumes and drank from clear plastic water bottles.

Two hundred jobs, that's what was advertised in the full-page ad in the *Arizona Republic* on Wednesday. And 2,000 people showed up. The outcome would not be good, Jasmine thought. She hoped she would get into the arena to talk to some employers. This was not her first job fair. She had not fared well in the two others she had attended earlier in the fall. It was going on a year now since she lost her job and, even though she was trying to find other means of making a living, she had to keep trying to get a regular job with a regular paycheck. She had skills and she should be able to do this.

The line moved forward; she moved closer to the door. Someone, a short dark-haired man, tried to get in front of her.

"Hey you, take your turn. Get in back and wait like everyone else," she said.

"I guess people are getting desperate."

"Yes, when you've got a mortgage and three kids, that's desperation," said the woman in front of her. She looked younger than

Jasmine, Dressed professionally in a charcoal pants suit with a tailored white cotton blouse, she looked younger me, thought Jasmine. But they all looked younger to her. Jasmine had never felt so old.

"How long have you been unemployed?" Jasmine asked.

"Only six months. I thought I would have a job by now, but not in this economy."

Jasmine asked her what kind of work she did. She said that she was a business analyst with a multinational firm and that they had brought in some people from India to do her job and laid her off.

"The worst of it was, I had to train my replacement. How bad is that?"

"That's pathetic. My name's Jasmine. What is yours?"

"Patty Johnson. Yeah, it is, and my husband got laid off a month before me and he's still looking as well."

Jasmine shook her head, commiserating with the woman. It's good she thought, that people were sharing their stories. Maybe she should start a blog for unemployed people to talk to one another. They could tell stories, vent their feelings. It might help some who were depressed to know that they were not alone. She would think about this.

Jasmine was finally able to get in the door. There were multitudes of people milling about inside, moving from one table to another. She could see some approach a potential employer, hand them a resume, and then walk away after being told that they had nothing for them.

She approached a table with several young male recruiters sitting and talking to people. They were dressed in the standard uniform of dark suits, white shirts, and neckties. They had shed their jackets and looked like penguins in the arctic. This was a large bank. Jasmine had heard that banks were doing well these days, sitting on buckets of cash. They'd had a bailout from the government to encourage them to start lending money, though they hadn't done so. It was nearly impossible to get a loan to buy a house these days, and banks were foreclosing on homes all over the Valley.

Jasmine gave one of the young men her resume; he looked at it and then looked her over thoroughly. "You have good database skills?" he asked.

"Yes, I've been working with databases for the past ten years."

"Well, we'll take a look at this and call you if we have an opening," he said.

Jasmine continued from table to table, handing out resumes and picking up brochures from the companies so that she could follow up when she got home. It was the same every time. They take your resume and say they will call and they never do. With so many people competing, Jasmine didn't think she had a chance. She had great work history and salable skills, but she had one strike against her from the start: she was middle-aged, and these companies, when they did hire, more often than not would hire the younger people and pay them less money. She thought about how a recession was really good for employers; they had the pick of the best people and could pay them less money. The worker these days had little room to negotiate.

After about an hour she walked out of the arena into the brutal sunlight. She put on her sunglasses to protect her eyes. Time to go home and regroup, she thought. What a waste of time. No more job fairs for me.

It was early Saturday morning. Celeste was sleeping late as usual. Jasmine took her coffee and the newspaper outside to the table under the Texas Ebony tree in the corner of the patio. She sat down, took a sip of the strong, black brew, and gazed at the cloudless sky. Three doves flew overhead and Chance looked up with ears forward. She glanced at the headlines on the front page of the *Arizona Republic*. "Immigration Laws Need Reform Says Governor Jane Warneke," then in the lower corner "Unemployment 9.5 Per Cent." Jasmine knew all too well about unemployment. But the immigration article interested her. Governor Warneke was asking the federal government to do their job and keep illegal aliens out of Arizona. She said they were costing the state too much money and that if the Feds didn't step up, she would take matters into her own hands.

Chance and Blondie were romping in the yard, racing back and forth along the patio walkway. Jasmine wondered what steps the governor would take. Were Hispanics going to be under siege in Arizona? Because, if that were the case, she and Celeste could be affected. Jasmine and Celeste looked more Hispanic than Caucasian, with olive Latino skin and hair the color of dark mahogany. The Sheriff had been doing sweeps for illegals in South Phoenix for months now. She and Celeste never went there, but if they were profiling people she would have to be careful not to have a traffic violation.

Both dogs came up to Jasmine and jumped on her to give her their morning kisses. "Oh, I love you, too," she said. "What would we do without you two to keep our sanity?"

Later that morning, Jasmine packed up the dogs in the back of her car and took them to the dog park. She thought she needed to go as much as the dogs did. When they drove into the parking lot, she could see there were more than the usual numbers of dogs this morning. Blondie and Chance pulled at their leashes until they were inside the chain-link fenced area. Jasmine waved to some of her friends and started to walk with the dogs around the perimeter of the park. Chance and Blondie ran freely, ears and tongues hanging, happy to have the space and the freedom. Chance saw a pigeon and stopped to stalk it and after a few minutes tried to run it down. He was never successful, but he always kept trying. Kind of like me, thought Jasmine. The jobs were out there and she kept pointing to them but when she pounced they were gone.

She and the dogs came full circle to the water faucet at the north end of the park where several people and dogs were gathered. Chance put his face in the water bucket and sucked the water in his mouth, as was his habit. A man came over with his yellow Lab and said hello and Jasmine returned the greeting.

"Your dog gets right into the water, doesn't he?" the man said.

"Maybe that because he's a water dog," said Jasmine.

"Do you come here often?" he asked.

"A couple times a week at least," Jasmine responded.

"I'm here on the weekends mostly. Working during the week."

"Oh, you have a job. You are fortunate. What do you do?"

"I'm an architect. Self-employed. But the work is slow for me, too."

"Work is more than slow for me. It's non-existent. But I'm hopeful."

He asked what type of work she did, and they talked about the terrible economy. The dogs circled around and played in the water. Blondie walked over to a huge mud puddle and lay down right in the middle of it. No matter. She would hose her off when she got home.

"I'm hopeful, though. I see this as just another adventure in my life, and I will come out of it better than before," said Jasmine.

Then the man looked at her in a strange way. "My name's Ted, by the way. And if you're looking for adventure….." and then he trailed off and looked at Jasmine again. Is this man hitting on me, she wondered?. She looked at his hands for rings. He kept his left hand in his pants pocket.

"I don't understand. What're you saying?" Jasmine looked at him, questioning him. "Are you saying that you want to see me? I guess we could have coffee some time."

"No, I couldn't do that," Ted said.

"Are you married?" asked Jasmine point blank. Might as well get right to the truth, she thought.

"I am. You see, my wife is taking care of her mother who is very ill and, well, she doesn't have much time for me anymore and I thought maybe…."

"I don't think so," said Jasmine as she started to distance herself from Ted. Incredible that he should approach me like that, she thought. But at least he's honest. And why was he attracted to me? I don't think I sent those signals to him. Then she thought about what she said to him about adventure. He must have taken that as an entrée to approach her for sex. To her, adventure meant exploring uncharted territory, like where was she going with her new career. But leave it to a male to misconstrue what she said into something sexual. He must be really starved for sex, she thought, but then that's just the way some men think. She vowed to avoid him if she saw him again.

Celeste was just getting up when Jasmine arrived home with the dogs. She sure was good at sleeping these days, Jasmine thought to herself. But then growing a baby takes a lot out of a woman.

"What would you like for lunch, Celey?"

"I'm so hungry that I don't care. Whatever you're having." Ever since the morning sickness vanished, Celeste had the appetite of an elephant. She wanted to eat anything in sight all day long. And she was gaining considerable weight.

"You had better watch your weight," Jasmine said with a knowing smile on her face. "You don't want to gain too much. It's not good for the baby or for you. Didn't your doctor tell you that?"

Fortunately, she had been able to help Jasmine get on a Medicaid program to help with the expenses of the baby. The governor had tried to cut the program, but when she found out that the state would lose federal funds if she did, she then reinstated it. Life was indeed precarious these days for those who were in need. And that seemed to be the majority of Americans. She hoped that this was only temporary and she and Celeste would be bringing in money to pay their own way soon. But in the meantime, they would take all the help they could get.

Jasmine's cell phone was ringing and she'd forgotten where she put it. She was in her office and she could hear it, but where was it? There were papers all over her desk. She shuffled them around and finally found the phone and answered it. "Hello, this is Jasmine," She said, trying to hide her frustration.

"Hello Jasmine, this is Bill calling. How are you?"

"Bill?" she said, wondering who Bill was.

"Yes, Sugar's dad. Remember?"

"Oh, *that* Bill. I'm sorry. You caught me at a bad time."

"You must know a lot of Bills."

"No. In fact, you're the only one that I know right now. How's Sugar doing? You aren't bringing her back, are you?"

"No. We love her. We wouldn't part with her for anything. She and Chas are inseparable. You should see them cuddled up at night in Chas's bed. And when Chas leaves the house, Sugar waits by the front door until he returns. I don't know what we're going to do when Chas is in school. Sugar will be spending a lot of time at the front door waiting."

They both laughed. "I'm glad Sugar is working out for you. She's a challenge sometimes."

"I was calling to ask if you might want to come over and see her."

"Sure. I'd like that. Things are kind of hectic right now, but we could do that. When is a good time for you?"

"How about tomorrow, about one in the afternoon?"

"That would work for me, seeing as how I am pretty free of appointments these days," she said sarcastically.

Bill gave Jasmine his home address and she promised that she would be there.

Well, she thought. This should be interesting. He's quite nice, and he's single, too. You never know.

Chapter 33
Opportunities

Jasmine opened her email. The subject of the third one down caught her eye: one word in the subject line, "Interview." Was she seeing right? She opened it and sure enough, she was being called in for an interview. The email said that if she were available she should go to Maricopa County DOJ, 620 W. Jackson, at 9:30 AM on Thursday of next week. She almost jumped out of her chair. This was wonderful. Her prayers had been answered—after all of the job searches, the resumes sent out, albeit a few rejections. It seemed that most often she sent resumes and heard nothing back, like a black hole. But here it was, right in front of her eyes. She started to get excited, and then she told herself to calm down. There were probably a dozen or more people competing for this job, and she *was* older. They wouldn't hire her. But she had experience. Wouldn't they see that?

Now, what to wear? Jasmine had gained five pounds in the past year. When she was first laid off she purchased two new interview pant suits from Macy's on sale: a subtle gray plaid Evan-Picone and a charcoal gray Tahari. She didn't know if they still fit. Going to her closet, she tried on the pants to both of the suits. As she turned in front of the mirror, there was no doubt, they were a little tight. But that was the style and when she tried on the jackets, her tummy bulge was less obvious. She could get by. And with a tailored white blouse she would look quite professional.

She went back to her computer and sent off a reply saying that she would be happy to be at the interview. Happy; was that the right word? Ecstatic was more like it, but she didn't want to seem overly anxious.

Now, she thought she had better get out her old computer books and brush up on her craft and she could go on-line as well. She knew that once she started refreshing her memory, it would come back to her. Like riding a bicycle; you never forget.

Jasmine was now an accepted member of the unofficial dog park gang. It was a small, diverse group of people who gathered daily around a well-used picnic table under a Chinese Elm in the southwest corner of the park. The size of the group varied from day to day, anywhere from three to five people. Most were unemployed like Jasmine or retired, but some worked part-time schedules and, of course, in the summer there were always a couple of teachers.

They were all very different. Jack, who was tall, maybe mid-sixties, always wore a straw hat and used a cane. His dog Jordan, a scruffy-haired terrier mix mutt, was his service dog. A thin angular man in his seventies named Reggie showed up daily with his coon hound Andy. Sheri, a pixy of woman with deep wrinkles and a pallid skin who spoke with a thick accent, had a medium-sized bull dog mix named Rascal. She always had a cigarette in her hand and said she would never quit smoking, even if it killed her. Jasmine thought it probably would, but she wasn't going to say it. Then there was Tex, a large older man in a motorized wheel chair whose dog's name was Max, a yellow lab mix. Another guy, Ken, probably younger than the others, was missing two of his front teeth. He lived across the street with his mother and was an admitted felon. But Jasmine liked him. He lied a lot and you could never believe what he told you, but he was thoughtful of others and had taken in three rescue dogs. That meant a lot to her. Sandy, a retired nurse, was the anchor of the group and if she was missing, everyone asked where she was. She always had a book in her lap, although she seldom read while at the park because she was interacting with all the others.

As different as these people were, they had one thing in common: they all loved dogs. They loved their own dogs and everyone else's dogs. And they would gather around in the early summer mornings with the dogs milling in the middle of the group. Dogs fetching a random tennis ball. Dogs wrestling with one another, sniffing rears, barking and sometimes humping one another. The funniest was when Tyco, a black male Chihuahua, jumped on a Weimaraner, trying to mate with it. But when the dogs misbehaved like this or started to become aggressive, someone was always watching and would reprimand them and keep order in the chaos.

Conversation in the group was sketchy. Most were watching their dogs, making sure they were having a good time and staying out of trouble. They talked about training and care of dogs and about the best vets in town, what kind of dog food was best and where to find bargains on pet supplies.

But then there were times when the talk would turn to world events. Sheri was born and had lived in Austria and would occasionally share her view of the world events. She was one of the most patriotic of the group, saying that she appreciated the United States for being the country of opportunity more than most places.

Some talked about jobs or the lack of and how to survive on a small income. Those who had jobs were thankful, and those who didn't and were not retired were always looking for some way of earning a living to buy the dog food and pay the vet bills. Politics and religion were, for the most part, not discussed and when they were, heated exchanges would sometimes erupt. But in the end most everyone agreed to disagree and the conversations continued on in a friendly manor.

Jasmine remembered her first encounter with this group, how unfriendly they had been to her and then how she misjudged them.

Some had not attended college, but she found that they had degrees in life and had much to offer in the ways of ideas. And of course everyone was dressed in Dog Park chic, herself included, sandals, jeans shorts, and vintage t-shirts with ventilating holes, looking like they had been riding the rails when in fact all were riding the journey of life.

As she got to know everyone, she gained respect for them and they for her. She even began to like some of these unlikely people gathered in this place by the very fact that they had dogs. And Sandy became one of her good friends, sharing books with her and an interest in dogs and humanity in general.

This day Jasmine was particularly ebullient, after receiving the request for an interview. Should she share with everyone? She had a hard time containing herself, she had to tell someone.

"I have an interview next week," Jasmine blurted out.

"Oh, that's wonderful. What kind of work?" asked Jack.

"I'm a computer programmer. Database analyst. It's with the Maricopa County Department of Justice."

Jasmine could see the raised eyebrows around the tight little circle. Should she have told them? But there were professionals here. Marge sitting next to her was an attorney who looked at Jasmine and said, "Oh, you have to contend with all those high-and-mighty attorneys."

"Not really. I'd be locked in a cubicle all day long writing code to capture the data so they can do their work," said Jasmine. Then she began to think, was this what she wanted? For a year now, she'd had freedom from schedules to do what she pleased. "But the money is good," she continued. Then she started thinking about the extra money to help Celeste with her baby, not having to worry about where the money was coming from for the vet bills, maybe even taking some trips. She had thought about going back to Minnesota to visit her parents. They were getting older and she wanted to spend some quality time with them before they were gone.

"That's wonderful," said Sheri. "I hope you get it."

"I'll keep you all posted," said Jasmine, still wondering if she had done the right thing by sharing this personal information with the group. If she didn't get the job, would they view her as a failure?

"Mom, I got a check form Dad. He sent me a thousand dollars. Isn't that wonderful?" Celeste rejoiced as Jasmine came in the door from the dog park with Blondie and Chance that Saturday morning. She put the dogs outside and then sat down at the kitchen table to go over the mail that she'd just brought in. She started sorting out the bills: pay this one, wait on this one, pay part of this one. Then she looked up at Celeste. "That's wonderful. It'll be a help, but a thousand dollars doesn't go very far these days in paying medical bills. You're probably going to need about $10,000 just for the delivery alone."

"I have Medicaid, remember?" Celeste said as she joined her mother at the table.

"Well, then you'll have to save it for buying baby clothes, a crib, diapers...."

"Mom, I've been doing some research and I've decided that I want to have my baby at home."

"At home? Here?" Exclaimed Jasmine. "What if you have complications?"

"The hospital is only five miles away. We could get there in minutes if stuff doesn't go right. I already talked to my doctor about it, and he said that I'm healthy and I should have a normal healthy birth. And I don't want to be drugged out when he comes into the world," Celeste said pointing to her bulging belly. "I want that moment to live in my memory forever."

"Celey, I don't know. There's so much that can go wrong. Tearing of the vagina, a breech baby, bleeding. It would be better to be in the hospital where doctors and nurses can take care of these emergencies."

"Oh, Mom, women have been having babies at home since the beginning of time and they've been able to do it. Why can't I? And look at Blondie. She didn't have to go to the dog hospital to have her babies, and she had a lot more babies than I'm having."

Jasmine laughed. "You've got a point there, sweetheart. We'll consider it," she said as she thought about birthing Celeste's baby at home, in her house. She was doubtful. But then other women have done this, why *couldn't* they? And it might be a wonderful family experience.

"No, I've decided," exclaimed Celeste.

"I'm still skeptical. I would like to talk with your doctor and the midwife myself."

"Sure Mom. You can come with me to my next appointment. I'll tell the midwife to call you."

"I'm going over to Bill's house to see Sugar. Want to come along?"

"I don't think so. I have homework to do. I have a project due tomorrow. You go ahead, Mom, and take some pictures."

Jasmine drove to Seventh Avenue and tried to find the street where Bill lived. It was a quarter to one and she wasn't having any luck with the streets intertwining like a maze in a cornfield. Finally she found Rose Lane and turned onto the street. Let's see, he said that his house was four houses from the corner on the west side of the street. There it is. It was a nice looking 'fifties ranch-style home. There were two large trees in the front yard, with a flagstone walk-way leading up to the front door. She parked in front under the shade of one of the trees and walked up to the front door, rang the bell, and waited. She heard footsteps inside and then the door opened and there was Bill, standing with a glass of iced tea in his hand.

"Please come in. The house is a mess; I hope you don't mind."

Jasmine looked around the large living room. A light brown leather couch with a chair to match filled most of the room. A half-filled coffee cup and the morning newspaper were still on the coffee table, and a pair of sneakers peered out from underneath the chair as if to say, I dare you to claim me. But other than that the room looked quite orderly. "Your house is clean compared to mine."

"Can I get you something to drink, some iced tea? Let's go outside and see Sugar. She's been pretty active this morning. She's probably taking a nap now."

And she was. Sprawled out on the patio, eyes closed until she saw Bill and Jasmine open the door and then she sprang to life, jumping up on Jasmine as if to say, where have you been?

"Oh, she's grown even in the two weeks since you got her." And she paused as she was literally being attacked. "Just some water would be fine," she said as Sugar pummeled her.

"Sugar, off. You know better than that." Sugar kept jumping and Bill shook his head in disbelief. "She has an excellent appetite, to be sure. Here, sit down and maybe Sugar will settle down a bit," Bill said as he pointed to a patio chair. He went into the house and returned with a glass of cold water and handed it to Jasmine.

"Thank you." She took a long drink. "How's your son doing?"

"He has good days and bad days. But having Sugar has helped. I see them curled up in front of the TV and they look so natural together. And then as I told you on the phone, Sugar sleeps with Chas at night. I think Sugar is a great comfort to him."

Sugar mouthed Jasmine and then tried to jump in her lap.

"You gave her the right name. She's as sweet as sugar," said Bill. He threw a tennis ball for her and she ran and retrieved it, bringing it back to Bill. "How's your job hunting going?"

"I have an interview next week with the Department of Justice at the County. I'm so excited and hope I get this job, but you know how it is, so many people looking for work these days. Employers have their pick."

"Yes, I know. It's really tough out there."

"Hopefully this recession will be over by next year and then we can all get back to work again."

"I wouldn't count on it. This one is more serious than any we've had since the 'thirties. It could get even worse," said Bill as he scratched Sugar's head.

"What are you going to do? Have you had interviews?"

"I may have to relocate. And this is a good time for us to do that. Start out fresh in another city. I'm thinking about moving to Seattle. There seem to be more jobs there, especially accounting jobs. Boeing is doing well with defense contracts these days, and then there's Microsoft."

"What about your son? How old is he? Sixteen?"

"He's fifteen. He's starting his junior year this fall. Yeah, it might be tough on him. But then he's having a tough time anyway with the family situation, with losing his mother. They were pretty close."

"You could be right. Maybe moving, making new friends, new surroundings. I hope you would take Sugar with you."

"Of course. Sugar's part of the family. We wouldn't leave her behind."

They talked more about family. Bill asked about Celeste and how she was doing and when her baby was due. He didn't seem to be judgmental about her being pregnant and not being married. He seemed to be kind and thoughtful.

"Well, I had better not take up your whole afternoon. I'm sure you have things to do," Jasmine said as she started to get up to leave.

Jasmine walked into the house with Bill following. "I've enjoyed talking with you this afternoon," she said as she took her car keys out of her handbag.

"Would you like to have coffee some time? Or dinner, maybe get a hamburger?" asked Bill.

Jasmine thought for a few moments. His wife hasn't been gone that long. Shouldn't he still be in mourning?

"I know what you must be thinking. I'm just looking for friendship right now, nothing more. This is a lonely time for me."

"Sure. Call me. I would love to meet you for coffee. After all, you're almost part of the family after adopting Sugar."

And she walked out the front door and got into her car to drive home. He's nice, she thought. I really like him. A man who has real feelings.

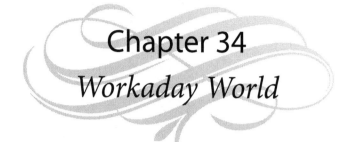

Chapter 34
Workaday World

The days of 100-degree heat were nearly over, and in Phoenix that was cause for celebration. The mornings were pleasantly cool and the evenings brought a fresh, cool breeze into Jasmine's bedroom window, making for ideal sleeping weather.

Jasmine spent the first hour of every morning taking care of small chores before she got to her writing. She washed the dishes and cleaned up the kitchen, dust-mopped the floors and made her bed. She tried to keep the house clean and clutter free, but with two people and two dogs living in such a small house, it was sometimes futile. She thought of people with housekeepers to clean up after them, and she had to admit that she was envious. It took a chunk of time out of her day to bring order to the chaos in her life. But then she also disliked having strangers come into her home, her refuge. And her motto was if she could do it herself, she most often did, and cleaning her small house was a relatively easy task.

Some mornings Jasmine would turn on the TV and work out with Lilias Yoga on Public Television. She would move the furniture to make room for her mat and follow Lilias, trying to get her body into the same contortions. Then Chance and Blondie would come into the room and lick her face and pull at her pony tail, and Jasmine laughed and giggled until her sides hurt. Eventually she would have to put the dogs outside so they wouldn't interfere with her work-out time. It was the same when she worked out with free weights. Blondie would invariably come up to her as she was lifting her eleven-pound weight and lick her face and want attention. And because Jasmine was worried about dropping one of the weights on the dogs she had to keep them out of the room when she was using them.

After the morning workout, she would sometimes put Blondie's and Chance's leashes on them and take them along with her on her morning run. Jasmine had a couple of routes in the neighborhood, or sometimes she would take them to the canal. They loved these outings. They checked out the new smells and tried to chase any birds or ducks that might be nearby. Chance, the garbage dog, would invariably find something to pick up and eat and Jasmine then had to pry it out of his mouth.

After her workout she would go outdoors and sweep the patio, water the potted plants, pick up the dog poop in the yard, and refill the dog's water dish. It was a ritual.

And this morning Jasmine could feel fall in the air. Even though she didn't mind the heat, she was glad it was almost over. She could now open the house at night and let the cool breeze filter through, instead of having to listen to the grinding of the air conditioner all night long. And this had been a summer of record heat, especially the nighttime heat, with a record number of nights where the temperature never went below ninety degrees. Jasmine often thought that this is what is must be like in Iraq or Afghanistan in the summer. Except that many of those people didn't have air conditioning.

As Jasmine looked around the yard, she took note of the plants that had survived the hot summer. Every year she would plant flowering shrubs and plants in the late fall after the weather cooled and they would bloom all winter, bringing joy to her heart. But then, come summertime, as much as she tried to save them, they would wilt and die as the temperature reached 105 and more. She watered everything, but she just couldn't keep up with the heat. And then the cycle would start all over again. Fall in the desert, unlike other places, was a time for renewal, a time to clean up and replant for the cooler winter months in the desert. And for Jasmine, that meant a lot of work, trimming and pruning, pulling out the dead plants, weeding and preparing the flower beds with mulch.

She did most of the work herself. She recalled the days when she was married and she and Richard had other people to do most of the work around the house. Their cleaning lady, named Nellie, who was recommended to them by a friend, was sixty years old. Jasmine always felt that Nellie was honest and trustworthy, and there were times when she could even leave baby Celeste with her when she wanted to make a short trip to the grocery store. And they had Jorge, the gardener who came on a weekly basis to cut the lawn, do the pruning and trimming and any planting they wanted done. Needless to say, their home always looked like it could be featured in *Better Homes and Gardens*, sans the daily clutter and toys that found their way into each and every room and the back yard when Celeste was a small child.

But Jasmine didn't have the money to spend on domestic help, and even when she was working and had more money, since her divorce, she wanted to take care of her own home. Scrubbing floors and cleaning toilets was a lowly kind of labor and she felt there was something demeaning to other people in having them do this work in her home. This could be due to her Hispanic heritage and the fact that many of the people who were maids and cleaning people were also Hispanic. She wasn't sure. But she liked the autonomy of "doing it herself."

Because of this, the house was not always magazine-picture-clean and the yard would not have won any awards in *Sunset Magazine*, either. But Jasmine was willing to accept that. She overlooked the weeds if she couldn't get to them. She dismissed the dust and dog hair in the corners and on the furniture, saying to herself, I'll get to it when I can, and in the meantime a little dog hair never killed anyone.

The one job, however that she could no longer do was trim the palm trees. There were three Mexican palms in her front yard, two on the south side and one on the north. Every year they needed to be trimmed. When she had first moved into the home they were small enough for her to reach and she could trim them herself. But they had grown and were now twenty feet tall, requiring a person to either climb the trees or reach the fronds from a hydraulic lift. When she called tree-trimming companies, the cost was prohibitive, up to $300. So she waited, hoping for another solution. In the days that followed, Mexicans came by periodically, asking if she wanted her trees trimmed. When she asked how much they charged, they told her twenty-five dollars per tree. That was much better than what she was quoted from the tree companies. So every year, they would come around and they would climb the trees and get the job done. She never knew if these people were in the country illegally. She never asked. They did a good job, and that was all that counted for her.

But there was always another problem when these trees were trimmed. Palm trees make wonderful homes for many types of birds, and invariably there were nests in the trees when they were being trimmed. She told the tree trimmers to tell her if there were any baby birds and if there were to bring them down, as they would surely fry to death if they were left without the shade of the palm fronds. The first few years, there were always one or two pigeons, a sparrow one year. She would put the baby birds in a box and take them to a bird rescue organization. Jasmine in fact hated pigeons; they were dirty, messy birds leaving excrement all over her driveway. But even so, she couldn't kill a baby pigeon. And then she gave the bird rescue people a donation and that made them happy.

One year, the tree trimmer climbed down from the tree leaving a mother dove sitting with her babies in the hot afternoon sun. He had told her that the babies were big and about to fly away. Jasmine hoped that was true. But after he left, she watched that mother bird sitting in the hot sun for a week or more, and there was not much she could do. She felt terrible. Then one night there was a drenching rain and the poor mother was sitting there exposed, pelted by rain and buffeted by the wind. Eventually the mother bird flew away and was gone. Jasmine hoped the babies survived. After that experience she never had the trees trimmed in the summer. She waited until fall when it was cooler and there were no nests in the trees.

After doing the morning chores, Jasmine would come into the house with the dogs following after and settle down at her desk to view her emails and then do some serious writing. Chance always settled into the dog bed she had placed in the well of the desk, and Blondie sprawled out beside her chair for a morning nap. When she went to the kitchen to get another cup of coffee or tea, they followed along, coming back and resettling into their places when she came back to her desk. She would reach down periodically and pet Chance or Blondie. It was a happy, tranquil scene.

Thursday came too fast. Jasmine had studied every day so that, if the interviewer asked technical questions, she would be able to answer them. She had gone to bed early the night before, but unfortunately Chance came to the side of the bed at about three in the morning asking to go out. And when Chance asked to go out she believed him. The one time she hadn't there was a wet spot on the rug in the TV room the next morning. She had told Chance to go back to sleep and she rolled over and did the same. Well, he had asked her. It was clearly her fault.

She was wide awake when she came back into the house after taking him outside to relieve himself. Trying to sleep, Jasmine couldn't help worrying about the job interview, the money, and how little she had of it. She was tired this morning, and her mind was not functioning as it should have. She made a fresh pot of coffee and had two cups while going over her notes on database administration.

Chance and Blondie sat around her, looking at her expectantly.

"No, we are not going to the D O G P A R K, today," she said spelling it out so they wouldn't get excited for nothing. "I have important business downtown today."

The interview was at 9:30, and she would make sure that she wasn't late. Being late for an interview was one of the worst things a person could do. Jasmine remembered several years ago, when she had an interview with Catholic Health Services West on Central and Thomas in Phoenix. She was dressed and ready and had gone out to start her car and the battery was dead. The engine would not turn over. What a horrible time for this to happen. Her mind raced; what to do? There was no way to get the battery jumped; nobody was around. And if she called her mechanic, it would be too late by the time he got there. She went inside and called a cab and then called the person who was to interview her and told her the circumstance. She told her she had called a cab and would be there as soon as she could. Well, she didn't get the job, but the interviewer praised her for her quick action in getting to the interview as soon as she did.

Celeste walked out of her bedroom just as Jasmine was getting into the shower. "Mom, I have to use the bathroom."

"You'll just have to come in and use it then. I have to take my shower now. I have my interview in two hours and I can't be late."

"It sucks having only one bathroom."

"You're spoiled, Celeste. When I was growing up that was all people had. I even knew some families where I grew up that didn't have a bathroom. They had an outhouse out back."

"Oh, Mother I don't want to hear that," said Celeste as she flushed the toilet.

Jasmine toweled herself off and, wrapping the towel around herself, went into her bedroom to dress. She pulled on the pants, just barely buttoning them, and then put on the tailored white shirt. Viewing herself in her full-length mirror on the door of her closet, she thought she looked professional. She put on small silver button earrings, her watch and a simple sliver ring and bracelet; nothing too gaudy. She then combed her long graying hair back into a ponytail, and she was ready to go. No fragrance—she never wore it for business feeling that doing so sent the wrong signal.

Putting on her suit jacket and grabbing her brief case, she went out to her car with her Map Quest map in her hands. Shouldn't take more than twenty minutes to get there, she thought. She had to stop by a convenience store to get change for the meters. The administrative assistant had warned her that she would have to park on the street.

Driving down Seventh Avenue, she came to the streets that were named after presidents and Jackson wasn't among them. Had she passed it? She drove over the bridge, into South Phoenix. "I've gone too far and it's getting late," she said to herself. "I had better turn around and go back, and then if I don't find this street I will ask someone."

She looked at the map again, and it showed Jackson coming off Seventh. She turned east on Jefferson and pulled into an auto repair shop. A man dressed in working blues walked over to her car as she rolled down the window. He told her to turn on the street before going over the bridge, then go east to Fifth Ave, south on Fifth and she should come to Jackson. She thanked him. Rolling up her window, she looked at her watch. She had fifteen minutes to spare. Sweat was rolling down her face. Doing as she had been instructed, she found the street, parked the car and got out to feed the parking meter. Putting in one quarter, ten minutes only. She fed the rest of her quarters, four dollars' worth. What a rip-off she thought. Looking at her watch, ten minutes to interview time and she had to go through security yet. She was sweating under her arms now. So much for getting there on time.

After going through security, she took the elevator to the second floor, as she had been told to do. When she got off the elevator, she walked down the long hallway and saw that all of the offices had security pads. Now what? She read a sign posted on the wall that told her to go back to the office closest to the elevator and knock on the door and someone would come and open it. She was now officially late for her interview.

As Jasmine knocked, a security guard opened the door, and she told her that she was here for an interview. Walking up to the receptionist desk, she signed in and told the woman behind the desk that she was here, a little bit late but she was here. The woman looked at her and smiled and said it would be okay. She was only ten minutes late.

She sat at a table in the reception area, now thoroughly distraught. Calm down, she thought. It will be okay. Minutes later a tall, lanky man with sandy hair in his middle thirties came out to get her and take her to a conference room. She introduced herself and shook his hand; his name was Terry.

Jasmine followed Terry down a long hallway. "This building is larger than it looks," she said.

"Yes, it is. It was built only four years ago," Terry said without looking back at her.

When they came to the conference room door, Terry opened it and there was another, younger man seated on the long side of the large conference room table. He rose as they entered. Terry introduced him, "This is Scott. He is our technical lead and I am the IT director. I will ask you some administrative questions, and then Scott will delve into the technical area." Jasmine shook his hand, said her name, and thought, this guy is young enough to be my son. She sat at the head of the table with the two men on either side of her and settled in. This is going to be a long interview, she thought

Terry went first with the interview questions. He asked about her former job, about what she liked most about programming, and what she liked least. He asked how she worked with other people. His face showed no emotion, but after several of her answers he said, "That's good." Jasmine was encouraged.

Then it was Scott's turn. Even though he was the technical person, he seemed friendlier, smiling and giving her positive nods after she answered his questions. And then, as quickly as it had started, it was over. She got up, shook each of their hands saying their names in succession, thanking them for the interview, and then they walked out of the room. The pressure was off and she exhaled deeply.

Scott walked her back to the exit door. He thanked her for coming in and said that they would let her know. As she was riding down the elevator, she thought, "That went okay. I'm still alive." Getting off the elevator, she noticed that there were many more people coming into the building, probably for hearings and trials.

Jasmine went to her car. It was hot inside with the sun shining on it. She took off her suit jacket and got into the car and started it, opening the driver's side window to get some air as she drove slowly home. She had no idea how well she had done, but she wanted this job. It would be a good job for her, and it would pay well. Not as much as she had been making, but enough. Wages were down with the recession. With so many competing for the jobs, employers could pay what they wanted. Sometimes she wondered if the system wasn't rigged to bring wages down. And she thought of all those CEO's making a thousand times what workers were making. They weren't taking a cuts in pay while workers were losing ground every year.

Chapter 35
Chance

We got through the dog days of summer. I heard my humans saying that and I don't know what it means, but I didn't think the hot weather would ever end. It did get exciting when the rains came and there were even little ice cubes falling from the sky one night. Our Mom was really harried, running around with a broom pushing the water here and there. I didn't get it. Blondie and I went out back and splashed and ran and played until we were exhausted. And for the first time in a long time we were cool and feeling good. There was a lot of noise, though, big booming coming from somewhere in the sky, and bright flashes of light. I wasn't scared, but Blondie was. Maybe she'd had a bad experience in another life. So every time I heard the loud noise I looked around for her and she was hiding under the settee on the patio. I would go over to her and pull her out to play again, and she seemed to be all right until the next loud noise.

All in all, we had a wonderful time that night. In the morning there was all this mud and leaves and branches. Our mom got out the broom again and swept and pushed the dirt and leaves until they were all gone. I sort of liked having all that stuff around; it smelled good, and there were more bugs and lizards to chase.

Life has gotten to be pretty boring lately, though. Our Mom and Celey don't pay much attention to us. They just come and go and come and go. Mom dresses up in funny clothes and takes this leather case with her. And then she comes back and I don't know where she's been or what she's been doing. I try to smell her to find out but I don't smell any animals on her, just other humans.

We do go to the dog park some days, and that's the best. We meet all of our pals there and chase tennis balls and sniff one another and hump one another. Sometimes there are fights, but I try to stay out of those. Some days there are big dogs that come with a bad attitude like they own the place and we should all play by their rules, and if we don't they start attacking and bullying. Sometimes a dog will get hurt, and then the humans all gather around and scream at one another and have a fight of their own. I don't know what good that does. But I watch now when these bad dogs come and I try to stay out of their way, because they are trouble.

After the rains, there was this big puddle of mud at the dog park where we all went to lie down, and I rolled over and got down in it. It felt so good. It cooled me, and it smelled the best. Our Mom was not happy, though; she tried to keep me from getting in the mud, but I showed her that I can do what I want at the dog park, and if I want to lie in the mud I will. But then when we got home, I got a bath and I hate that. I don't know why humans always want to give us dogs baths. They use this awful-smelling soapy stuff on us and scrub us and the water gets in my ears and up my nose. But I get back at them. As soon as I'm out of the tub I shake all over and get water all over everything. That'll show 'em.

Most days now, I just get up and eat and go outside and do my business in the yard where I was told to do it. And then I lie down on the patio and watch the bugs fly over, and sometimes I catch a fly and eat it. If I hear anyone in the alley, I race to the gate, get my fur up on my back, show my teeth, and bark as loud as I can. Nobody is coming into this back yard that doesn't belong here. But to be honest, I don't know what I'd do if some stranger did leap over the fence. Would I bite him? Would I corner him and just try to frighten him out of the yard? If he had a treat, I might just wag my tail and lie down and roll over. I don't know. Thank goodness it hasn't happened, yet.

Chapter 36
The Waiting Game

Jasmine was sure she'd blown the interview. Her answers were too short, incomplete, and didn't go into enough detail, and she couldn't answer one question, about distributed applications. Well, it wasn't her area of expertise. She decided over the weekend to write a thank-you note to the person who had interviewed her and explain that she knew she'd fallen short. A thank-you letter for an interview is always a good idea in any event she thought.

She wrote the letter on Sunday morning while Celeste was sleeping. They still needed another laptop computer, and this job would give Jasmine the money to buy one. Mailing the letter the next day, she could only hope that it would help her cause. Then on Tuesday, the phone rang. When Jasmine picked up it was a woman from the County. Oh, no, she thought; they're calling me to tell me that I didn't get the job.

"Is this Jasmine Bailey? "

"Yes, who's calling?"— Jasmine's standard question when she didn't know the caller. If it was a sales call she always nipped it early by saying that she didn't need any but thank you for calling. She didn't have caller ID, another one of her ways of saving money.

"This is Janice Trent from Maricopa County Department of Justice."

Here it comes, Jasmine thought.

"We would like you to come in for a follow-up interview on Thursday at 2:30 PM. Please bring three references from supervisors of past employers, and there will be a written test. Will you be able to make it?"

"Will I? Yes! Oh, I'm so happy. Thank you. I didn't think I'd done that well," exclaimed Jasmine. Not too transparent, she thought. I'm definitely going to have to get my emotions in check if I do any more interviewing.

"We'll see you on Thursday, then. You can park in the Jackson Street garage across the street from our building and tell them you are interviewing with CTS."

"Thank you, thank you," said Jasmine as she petted Blondie and Chance. She hung up the phone and danced around the room. "Finally, after sending out hundreds of resumes, I'm going to have a chance. Did you hear that, Chance?" Chance's ears perked forward and he wagged his tail as if he knew all about it.

Celeste came out of her bedroom, groggy with sleep, wearing pajama bottoms and an oversized t-shirt. "What's happening, Mom? I heard the phone ring. Was that Ramon?"

"No, it was the County calling to tell me that I have a second interview on Thursday. They liked me. I'm surprised. I thought I had messed up, but I guess not. Oh, Celey, this is so exciting. I'm going to study every day, and make sure that I have the answers this time. This will be a technical interview, and I need to brush up. I haven't worked in over a year."

"Mom, I hope you get it. Let me know if Ramon calls. I really want to talk with him," said Celeste as she went back into her room to dress for the day.

Jasmine started pulling all her files with documentation on .Net, database and windows application development. Chance and Blondie settled in under her feet, Chance in the well of her desk and Blondie to her side.

Celeste hadn't heard from Ramon in over a week and she was worried. They had been talking twice weekly. There were thousands of miles between them. Had he met another woman? She couldn't call him because it was so expensive calling overseas and Jasmine had told her that, until she started paying the phone bill, she couldn't make those calls to Ramon.

"No more calls to London, Celeste. We can't afford it. Let him call you. He has a job and money coming in," Jasmine told her one morning when she opened her telephone bill and saw a twenty-five-dollar charge for a call to UK.

Celeste had a cell phone, but it was prepaid and didn't allow for overseas calls. Jasmine made sure, even though they were paring back on everything to save money, some things were important and she knew that cell phones were indispensable, especially in an emergency.

But then Celeste discovered Skype. That solved everything and cost nothing. The problem was, again, that the computer wasn't always available to her, and when it was, she needed to be doing her school work, not talking to Ramon. She told Ramon that he would have to call her as she wasn't allowed to make calls out of the country. But he hadn't called.

Jasmine was sitting at her computer one evening studying for her next interview. She'd found to her amazement that everything she needed to know was on-line. The phone rang, she answered, and it was Richard calling.

"Richard," Jasmine exclaimed in surprise. "And why are you calling?"

"I wanted to know if Celeste received the money that I sent."

"Yes, but it's not enough. A thousand dollars doesn't buy anything anymore. She has doctor bills and she needs to buy things for the baby.

She needs at least ten grand." Jasmine thought she would go for the most. Richard could afford it. She didn't mention that Celeste had Medicaid. Even with help from the government, having a baby these days is expensive.

"Jasmine, you know I can't send that kind of money."

"Are you saying that Deborah is in charge of the money at your house?"

"No. I'm not saying that. But she knows what comes in and what goes out. And she wouldn't like it if she found out about the thousand dollars."

"How do you hide that from her?"

"I have a separate account. She has one of her own. Her family has money you know, and she has a trust account."

"Is that why you divorced me? To marry someone with a trust account?"

"Jasmine, you know that's not true."

"I don't. You were seeing her while we were married. But this is all not important. What's important are your daughter and your future grandchild. Aren't they worth more than a thousand dollars? I mean really, Richard."

There was silence on the other end. Jasmine knew how to bring out the guilt in Richard, and it was a good thing. In fact most of his actions toward her and Celeste were guilt-driven.

And Richard couldn't deny that he'd been seeing Deborah while he and Jasmine were still married. It was true. He'd met Deborah at work. She worked for the assistant administrator and they were working together every day, sometimes on projects. The affair blossomed when Richard took her to lunch one afternoon after they'd finished up a very important, grueling project to increase the profitability of Highland Hospital, where he was the head administrator. They'd had a couple of glasses of wine and Richard looked into Deborah's blue eyes. Yes, she was young and pretty and with a great figure, albeit she had breast implants. But Richard didn't know that and he most likely didn't care. It was the package he was interested in. They ended up going to the Waterfront Hotel for the rest of the afternoon, and Richard was hooked. And, yes, he later found out that she came from a prominent family and had money of her own.

"Jasmine, I was really calling to find out how Celeste was doing. Is she okay? Can I talk to her?"

"Yes, she's doing fine. I'll get her on the phone."

Jasmine called to Celeste who was doing homework in the kitchen.

"Your dad is on the phone. He wants to talk to you."

"I heard you arguing. I should have known it was Dad," Celeste said as she walked in and brusquely took the mobile away from her mother.

Celeste walked out to the back yard for privacy. Jasmine heard her giggling a couple of times, and then she came back into the house with the phone in her hands. Chance wagged his tail and gave her a lick on the hand. Blondie looked up from where she was napping and then laid her head down again.

Jasmine waited for Celeste to tell her what her dad had said to her, but Celeste went back to her work in the kitchen without a word.

Chapter 37
The Big Day

Jasmine had been studying day and night for the past two days, setting up test questions and going over the material again and again. She was amazed at how much there was to cover in such a short time, but felt that if she hit the high points she would be able to answer most of the questions. This was like being in college and cramming for a test the next day, she thought. And then she was also a bit put out, because as every programmer understands, it's not always what you know, but knowing where to find it.

After walking the dogs, Jasmine put on her nightgown and prepared to go to bed early. She called the dogs, "Blondie, Chance, it's time for the book club to meet." That's what she called this special time they had together when they would gather around her on the bed while she read her favorite novel or magazine for the thirty minutes or so before she turned out the light and went to sleep. But this night, sleep would not be her friend. She adjusted her pillow just so, and the sheet and blanket, and then turned on her side, hoping for slumber. Too many thoughts. She turned again to the other side. Would she pass the test tomorrow? How would they get through Celeste's pregnancy? Would Ramon come back and help her? She couldn't turn it off. The luminous dial of the clock beside her bed showed 12:15. She turned again to the other side, and the dogs got down off the bed. I guess I'm keeping them awake, too, she thought. The clock now said one o'clock.

Enough. She got out of bed and went to the kitchen to get a sleeping pill. Just one over-the-counter little blue pill and she would be asleep in thirty minutes. Fortunately, the interview wasn't until 2:30 in the afternoon. If she was tired she could sleep late tomorrow, she thought as at last she slipped into that never, never land of peaceful sleep.

He called Celeste's cell late that night. She was so relieved to hear from him.

"Ramon, where have you been? I haven't heard from you in over a week."

"Dave and I went to Paris. We took the Euro Star and went through the Chunnel. It was really groovy."

"That's wonderful, I think. But I was worried when I didn't hear from you."

"I'm sorry, Celeste. I should have called. But Paris was just so beautiful. It's the city of love, you know."

"That's what I was worried about." There was silence. "Have you met someone else?" Celeste asked, almost afraid to ask.

"Oh, no Celeste, I thought only of you. There were couples holding hands and kissing along the Seine, on the Champs-Élysées, everywhere, and all I could think was how I could bring you to Paris to see this extraordinary city."

Celeste was feeling better, but she thought that she should tell Ramon about their child now. Then he could make up his own mind about what to do.

"Ramon, that's so sweet. Do you mean that?"

"From my heart, I do. I see only you. I haven't been seeing anyone else."

"Ramon, I have to tell you something."

"This sounds serious."

"It is." Celeste took a deep breath. "I'm expecting a baby. Your baby. Next month. I was afraid to tell you because….. I don't know why, to tell the truth…."

"You're having a baby? Wow! That's huge. My baby! I'm going to be a father…." Ramon blathered on.

"Yes, you're going to be a father. And it's a boy. I didn't care what it was, just so long as it's healthy."

"Are you okay, Celeste? I mean, are you feeling okay?"

"Yes, I'm fine. I had morning sickness for awhile, but that's gone now. I'm getting big and none of my clothes fit, so I had to get some maternity clothes. I went to a thrift store, because it was cheaper."

"Why didn't you tell me sooner? I wouldn't have left the country. I would have come there to help you."

"I don't know. I don't want to force you to be with me. But if you love me…"

There was a long silence on Ramon's end of the line and Celeste thought he might have hung up.

"Are you still there, Ramon?"

"I'm here. Celeste, this changes everything. I'd better get back there and find a job in the States. And we need to get married."

"Whoa, hold on. Ramon, I don't want you to feel like you have to marry me. I can take care of myself and the baby too."

"Have to? I want to marry you. Celeste, will you marry me?"

She thought for a few moments. Is this what she wanted? Did she love Ramon enough to spend the rest of her life with him? She still wasn't sure.

"Wait until you come home. I love you, Ramon, but let's talk about it when you get back here."

"Celeste, do you have money to pay for things? You know, the doctor and the hospital?'

"I'm not going to the hospital. I'm having the baby at home. Yes, Dad sent some money and I suspect he'll send more. Mom laid a guilt trip on him."

"When's this baby due?"

"January, late January."

"Here's the plan. I'll give my two weeks' notice, catch a flight back to LA, and I'll be over there as soon as I get back. We can get an apartment. Do you want to live in Phoenix?"

"It's as good a place as any. And I want to finish my school and get a computer graphics job. I hate the politics here, though."

"I'm sending you some money." Ramon paused. "Are you having the baby at home because you don't have the money?"

"That was how it started, but the more I looked into it, the more I liked the idea. It just seems so much friendlier, and I don't want all those procedures that they foist on women. I'll have a mid-wife to help. They know what they're doing, and if there are complications, the hospital is not far away."

"I love you, Celeste. Never forget that. We can be a family."

Celeste believed it now. "I love you, too."

Chapter 38
Another Interview

The day had arrived, and Jasmine was as nervous as a first-day kindergartner. She wanted this job so badly. She'd slept until ten and now decided to get up and have a leisurely breakfast, go over her notes and work on some writing in the morning, and then start to get ready by 1:00 o'clock. She would not be late this time.

Chance and Blondie circled around her, asking to go to the dog park.

"No, not today. I have an important meeting today. We'll go tomorrow."

They didn't seem to understand. When she said "Go," their ears perked up; "go" to them meant *they* were going. Chance kept giving her head butts as she was working on the computer, and Blondie walked around her office whining. But before long they realized that she wasn't taking them today and they settled down in their favorite places, Chance in the well of the desk and Blondie beside her chair. Jasmine always had to be careful when she was working at her desk not to back her chair on an ear, a tail, or a paw lying behind her in the path of the chair rollers.

At 1:00 o'clock, Jasmine took her shower and carefully dressed. By 1:45 she was out the door and on her way to success or her Waterloo. She turned onto Jackson and pulled into the Jackson Street Garage. This is a dingy-looking garage, she thought, but it was better than parking in the hot summer sun on the street. And then she thought about how, when she had a job, she liked to walk at noontime for exercise. Looking around the area, she didn't think she would want to walk in this neighborhood day or night. Maybe she could find a nearby gym.

Jasmine went through security and took the elevator to the second floor. Fortunately, this time she knew exactly where to go. She rang the bell for the CTS area. When a guard answered and she told her that she had an interview, the guard let her in. Walking to the reception desk, she signed in and told the receptionist that she was here for her 2:30 interview. "I'm early. I apologize," said Jasmine.

"Perfectly all right. I'll tell Anthony that you're here."

Minutes later Anthony, a very tall, dark-haired man in his early thirties dressed in blue jeans and a green cotton polo shirt, came walking up to her. "I'm Anthony, the DBA here. You must be Jasmine. Let's go down to the conference room and talk for awhile," he said as he led the way down the narrow hallway.

This is the guy she would be working with, she thought. She liked him right away. He had an easy, friendly way about him, not at all pretentious. Jasmine had worked with some real jerks in her career, and that always made her job more difficult. She remembered when she was working at Intel and had been the token woman developer among twelve men. The dress code in the summer allowed everyone to wear shorts and flip-flops. She would sit with her team in a meeting, with the guys' hairy legs draped over the chairs, and they would be scratching their crotches. She realized that this was done purposely to intimidate her. And it did. She lasted only a year in that job but went on to something much better.

They reached the conference room and sat at the large table, Jasmine at the end and Anthony to her side. The conversation was about databases and how they are built, how they work, and all such talk concerning the technology.

SHE SLEEPS WITH DOGS

"This is an especially nice place to work," said Anthony. "I'm happy to come here every day, and I couldn't say that about other jobs I've had."

This is encouraging, thought Jasmine. She asked how many people worked in this area and how long they'd been there. She eyed the sheets of paper that Anthony was carefully guarding. And then he handed them to her with a lead pencil and an eraser. "Take your time. If you can't answer all of the questions, don't feel bad. No one does." And he left the room.

Jasmine perused the questions; there were two pages, with ten questions on each page. As she browsed through the questions, her hands became sweaty and she could feel her heart beating a little louder in her chest. She knew about half the answers. She was sure that wasn't good enough to get the job.

Jasmine worked on the questions for over an hour, reading each very carefully, making sure she understood each one. She answered the ten questions that she was sure of first and then went on to the others. None of these questions covered anything that she had been studying. She would have to make educated guesses and give it her best. That's all she could do. After completing the test, she looked it over and checked her answers one more time. She had left only one unanswered, but she was unsure of her answers to at least half the questions. She had done the best she could.

Ramon came home early on a Sunday morning after working all night. Working in a restaurant was one of the hardest jobs he'd ever had. Of course he knew there were harder jobs, like working in the fields picking strawberries. Fortunately, he had never had to do that. Now he was concerned. He had told Celeste that he would quit this job and be back in the States in a week or so, but now that had changed. When he told his boss, Tony that he was quitting, Tony said that he couldn't do that right now. The holidays were coming up and he needed Ramon more than ever. He would double his pay, and if Ramon wanted to stick around, he could be promoted.

Money was important to Ramon at this point. He decided to stay through the holidays, earning the extra money and putting it aside for when he did go back. After all, it might be awhile before he would find a job in Phoenix. And the baby wasn't due until late January anyway. Telling Celeste would not be pleasant, but he was sure she would understand.

He collapsed on his small bed and was soon at one with the gods. Hours later he heard his roommate crashing around in the kitchen and thought he might get up to see what was happening.

"Hey, pops, finally getting up, are you?" said Dave as he took a beer from the refrigerator. After Ramon told Dave that Celeste was pregnant, Dave started calling him by this name, and he wasn't fond of it. "Want a beer? It's the middle of the day."

"No thanks. And I want you to stop calling me "pops." Sounds like I'm your father," said Ramon. Since Ramon had been working and not going out with Dave, Ramon thought that he was unhappy having him there. Like all that Dave wanted was to have a buddy to make the rounds at the pubs.

"So when are you going back to the little lady?"

"I'm staying through the holidays. Tony, my boss just offered to double my salary if I would stay. And I'm going to need the money."

"You can say that again. You're going to have two more mouths to feed soon."

Ramon, dressed in his shorts and a t-shirt, sat down at the small, 'fifties-style stainless kitchen table. "You know, Dave, I used to like you. Back when we were roommates in college. But you've been getting on my nerves lately."

"Ramon, Ramon, Ramon. If only you hadn't hooked up with that woman of yours. You're just no fun anymore. We used to have fun in college. You fucked the women and got drunk and did some tokes.

Now you're all business, won't even look at another woman. What's happened to you, man?"

"I guess I've grown up, Dave. When's that gonna happen for you?"

They sat there sniping at each other, Dave standing by the kitchen sink drinking his beer and Ramona drinking a cup of black coffee, trying to wake up.

"Look, let's be friends. I've got only about three weeks left here. I'm going to be working some pretty long hours. But when I'm not working, I want to see the rest of this little country. It's a pretty neat place. And I'd like you to be my tour guide. Deal?"

Dave looked at the ceiling, took a drink from his beer. "Deal. I'll show you the best of England. The castles, Shakespeare's house, the White Cliffs of Dover, the Lake District. We'll have a blast."

"Great. I might not be back for awhile."

And they ended on that friendly note. Ramon still worried about what Celeste was going to say when he called her about his delay in returning. But he'd deal with it when it came.

Arriving home later that afternoon, Jasmine let the dogs inside and changed her clothes, putting on a pair of cotton shorts and an old t-shirt. Celeste was most likely at school. She took the bus every day. They had only the one car, and Jasmine seldom let Celeste use it.

Jasmine sprawled out on the living room couch and the dogs climbed up with her, both licking her face at the same time. "Wow, that's a lot of love. At least somebody wants me."

Now the wait begins to hear if she got the job. Not likely, she thought, but miracles do happen. In the meantime, she knew she had to get back to her writing and submitting magazine articles to see if she could bring in some money. And she wanted to do some more painting. She had done some miniature watercolors of the desert that she thought she could sell. She would, however, continue in her job search, submitting applications and resumes. She thought about how many people were having the same experience as she; many in much worse financial shape than she was. She wondered to herself if this was the American dream that everyone talked about. You work hard for years, try to save for retirement, along comes a recession, you lose your job, your retirement money and maybe your house and car. There must be a better way. And then all of those at the top run off with the money. Jasmine had read on the Internet how some CEO's make $16,000 an hour. Is anyone worth that much money? And then some get fired and get a golden parachute in the millions. All of this is taking away jobs and money from the middle class, she thought.

Jasmine stroked the dogs' heads. "I'm glad I have you guys. I can always count on you two, Blondie, Chance." They both looked up to her, with ears forward and tails wagging. There is nothing in the world better than having wonderful dogs, she thought.

And just as she was settling in with the dogs for a short nap, her cell phone rang. Oh no, who could be calling me now? It wouldn't be the County in so short a time. She reluctantly got up from the couch and went to her office to retrieve her phone.

"Hello, Jasmine. This is Bill. Did I catch you at a bad time?"

"No," Jasmine lied. "I was just sitting here with the dogs. What's happening with you?'

"Not much here. I was just calling to see if you would like to go for dinner tomorrow night."

Jasmine thought for a minute. She wasn't in the mood to see anyone now. But she liked Bill. "Sure, that would be nice."

"I'll pick you up at seven. There's this little bistro on Seventh Street that I think you'll like. I'll see you then."

It would be good to get out for a change. Jasmine couldn't remember the last time someone had invited her for dinner. Maybe it would take her mind off all of her problems.

When Bill arrived the next evening promptly at seven, Jasmine was not quite ready. "Come in," she said as she opened the door. "I'm not used to people being on time. I just need to brush my hair and put on some lipstick. Have a seat on the couch. I won't be long."

"You look lovely without the lipstick," Bill said as he settled in on the couch and picked up a book about San Francisco from the coffee table. Bill noticed the dogs looking at him through the window from the patio. "I think the dogs want to come in," he said loudly enough for her to hear.

"No they don't. Unless you want to be mauled. They're fine. I'll leave them out when we go to dinner," Jasmine called from her bedroom.

Jasmine went into the bathroom to finish getting ready. She brushed her long dark hair back into a pony tail and then twisted it into a bun and secured it with a hair pin. She looked for her coral lipstick and applied that to her lips, then added some lip gloss while thinking about what he had said about her looking lovely without lipstick. "Something tells me that he wants to court me, even though he says he doesn't," she thought. She went to her bedroom and looked in the mirror. Her jeans were too tight, but her cotton blouse covered the tummy bulge. She went to her jewelry box to fish out her aqua-marine earrings and necklace that she liked to wear with the ocean-blue blouse that she loved so much. She was ready for her date. Yes, this was a date. How long had it been since she'd had a date? Years, she thought, as she spayed some cologne behind her ears and on her wrists.

"Hi, I'm ready," Jasmine said as she came into the living room.

"You look great," said Bill.

He would say that no matter how I looked, thought Jasmine.

"I thought we could go to this little Italian restaurant down the street. We're fortunate to have so many nice restaurants in this area," Bill said as he opened the car door for her.

"Well, that's probably because this is a tourist town," Jasmine said as she got into Bill's light blue Honda Civic. And he's a gentleman too, she thought. When was the last time someone opened a car door for me?

There was little talk between them on the way to the restaurant. They arrived and parked in the lot behind. As they went inside, the crush of people was overwhelming. Bill went to the hostess stand and asked to be seated. He had called ahead for a reservation, but the hostess said it would be a few minutes and asked if they would like to sit in the bar and have a drink. The bar was full of people as well, so they sat on a bench in front of the restaurant.

"Have you eaten here before?" asked Bill trying to make small talk. It was very noisy and difficult to carry on a conversation.

"No. I haven't. I don't go out that often. When I was working I didn't have the time, and now I don't have the money."

The hostess came to seat them. She took them to a little table in the far corner of the room. When the waiter came by he asked if they would like something to drink. Jasmine ordered a glass of cabernet wine and Bill ordered a Miller beer.

"How's Sugar doing?" Jasmine asked.

"She's a delight. She's doing some digging in the back yard, though. I don't know how to stop a dog from digging."

"I don't either. I've tried everything. Putting poop in the hole, booby-trapping it with a balloon. The trick is knowing where they're going to dig next." They both chuckled.

"Chas is in love with Sugar. He has been really depressed since his mother died, but since we got Sugar, he seems to be coming out of it. I guess having something to care for helps to take his mind off his mother's death."

"How long have you lived in the Phoenix area?" asked Jasmine as she sipped her wine. She wanted to steer Bill away from talking about his deceased wife. She was sure it would stir up sad memories.

"My parents moved here in 1965. I was only three at the time. Dad had gotten a job with Motorola; he's an engineer. I barely remember it. Except that it was in the middle of the summer and it was so hot."

"You're almost a native, then."

"I guess you could say that. What about you?"

"I moved here about ten years ago. I was able to get a good job in computing. I said I wouldn't stay, but here I am." Jasmine didn't want to go into her past history about her divorce. At least not yet.

"I think I understand. Phoenix can be a difficult place to live, with the heat and all. I've threatened to leave many times, but then I look at other parts of the country and every place has something that's not easy. California has earthquakes and mud slides. The Midwest has tornadoes. There's no perfect place. And my wife, Helen was a native .She loved Arizona and wasn't ever agreeable to moving."

"So you're thinking about relocating now. Seattle sounds like a lovely place to live. Except for the rain. I guess you're right: every place has something that's not totally likeable,"

"I love the Northwest. I'm a hiker and a backpacker."

"Arizona has lots of opportunity for those activities. The beauty of this state is that when it's hot down here, you can go to the rim country and when it's cold up there you can stay in Phoenix and bask in sunshine. Are you a skier?" Jasmine inquired.

"Yes. I love skiing. How about you?"

"I am. Both downhill and cross country. Have you ever done snow shoeing? It's so much fun. A lot of work. You burn a bunch of calories."

"I cross country ski but I've never snow shoed. You'll have to show me how some time. You, my dear lady are multi talented."

Jasmine blushed.

The waiter brought their food, sea bass for Jasmine and steak with spaghetti on the side for Bill. They talked on into the evening about careers and raising children, enjoying the food and wine. Bill talked about his wife again, but Jasmine thought that was only natural. He must have loved her very much.

The waiter came back to ask if they wanted desert.

"Let's share one," Jasmine spoke up. And they ordered a decadent chocolate mousse. "I've been gaining weight since I lost my job."

"It doesn't show. You have a great figure, I've noticed," said Bill.

There were very few people in the restaurant when they left, but then it was nearing ten o'clock. Bill drove her home and when they arrived there he walked her to the door.

"I've had a wonderful time this evening. I hope you did as well," Bill said as he took her hand in his. "I would like to see you again."

"Sure. I'm going to be a little busy in the next couple of months. With the baby coming and all. But I'll make some time."

Bill then kissed her on the cheek and turned around and left her. Oh my, what am I getting into? she wondered. He's just lonely. He can't be near ready for a serious relationship so soon after his wife's death. She turned and went into the house. Celeste was sitting in the living room watching TV. The dogs were lounging on the floor by her feet, and they got up to greet Jasmine as she walked in the room.

"How was your date, Mom?"

"It was good. So what are doing up so late?"

"Just had to make sure that my mother came in before curfew," Celeste laughed.

"Don't be so silly. In a few years you'll be that parent worried about where her teen is at midnight. Payback time." Jasmine headed back to her bedroom, and the dogs followed. "Have these dogs been outside recently?"

"Yes, they just came in," Celeste said.

"Well, I'm going to bed. I am exhausted." Jasmine took off the tight jeans that seemed to have gotten tighter with the all the food she had eaten. She put on a large t-shirt and then went to brush her teeth and wash her face. As she was applying her face cream she wondered what Bill was up to. Did he want a relationship? She liked him. He had good qualities and he was an outdoor person; she liked that.

She went into her bedroom, where the dogs had already staked their claims on the bed. Chance, as always, was right up near her pillow. "Chance, you have to move, you know that." And he did move down toward the end of the bed. Jasmine pulled up the covers and turned out the light. I guess I have to decide on whether I sleep with dogs or a man, she thought. Dogs are easier to deal with. Men can be difficult sometimes. And she drifted off to sleep.

Chapter 39
Time Is Near

The holidays were fast approaching, although there wasn't a lot to celebrate this year. Jasmine received a letter in the mail from the County a week after her second interview, and she knew without opening it that it was a rejection letter. Oh well, she had given it her best. But because she had no job and Celeste was still in school every day, with a baby on the way, the money had to be stretched as far as it could go. She had four mouths to feed; in addition to herself and Celeste, two hungry dogs. And soon there would be another little person in the house.

Celeste's middle section was protruding far out in front of her now. She could barely reach down to put on her shoes, and the few maternity clothes she had barely fit her. She had trouble sleeping at night, partly because she couldn't get comfortable and partly because she was apprehensive about the birth. She had heard so many stories about how painful childbirth is, how sometimes women spent days in labor. She still wanted to have a natural birthing, but did she have the courage to go through with it?

"All of the mothers of the world have had to endure this, Celeste," Jasmine told her one evening after Celeste let on about her fears. "And most of them lived to tell about it."

"I know. But I've heard horrible stories about women lying around for days having excruciating labor pains. I don't think I could take that." Celeste then thought about what her mother just said. "You say *most* lived? Women do die giving birth, don't they?"

"Well, yes they do, but fewer die these days with modern medicine. You could go to the hospital and have an epidural. But they can't give you anything until the baby is starting to come out anyway. So you're going to have to endure some pain. Didn't the mid-wife tell you?"

The mid-wife had been preparing Celeste. And Celeste had been taking classes at the hospital teaching her how to relax and breathe. She had exercises to do every day to strengthen her abdominal and back muscles, and she had been walking every day as well, taking Chance and Blondie with her when she went.

"Why don't you have the baby in the hospital?" Jasmine repeated. "Then maybe you wouldn't be so worried."

"No, I'm going to do this my way; all natural, no drugs, no c-sections. I want to be fully awake and watch this baby come into the world. I just hope Ramon can be here."

"Celey, you can do that in the hospital. If you tell your doctor that you want a natural child-birth, they will abide by what you say and then you'll be right there in case something happens."

But Celeste was adamant about having the baby in a natural setting, in her own bed with family and friends surrounding her. She hated hospitals, in fact had feared them ever since she was a little girl. When she was seven she'd had her tonsils taken out. When the nurses were ready to take her to the operating room, they brought a large needle to give her a shot to calm her down and they literally had to chase her around the room to catch her to give her the shot. She had never forgotten.

Celeste had received a call from Ramon a week ago, and he told her that he wouldn't be coming back until after the holidays. That worried Celeste. She feared that he might not be there when the baby was born. Celeste had wanted him to be with her, coaching her, helping and witnessing the most wonderful event of their lives. And what if he called again after the holidays, to delay his homecoming again? Maybe he wasn't coming at all, she thought. She worried every day, but there was nothing she could do. He'd said that he was staying through the holidays to earn more money and would be back the second week in January. She had no choice. She had to trust him.

Jasmine put up the artificial Christmas tree, although there were few gifts under it. She had purchased the tree five years ago, and it had paid for itself over time. As much as she enjoyed the fresh pine scent of a real tree, having a tree in a box was more efficient in many ways: no watering, less fire hazard, no tree to dispose of.

As they were decorating the tree, Jasmine thought about how joyful it was this year to have Celeste help decorate the tree. While Christmas music played on the radio, they ate Christmas cookies that Jasmine had made and drank eggnog, Celeste's being non-alcoholic due to her pregnancy. Other years, when Jasmine was living alone, she had always put up the tree at Christmas and more often than not she did it solo. True she often had "help" from the dogs, trying to chew the light strings or play with the ribbons and ornaments, but that only made the task more enjoyable.

"Are you going to invite Bill for Christmas dinner?" Celeste asked.

In the weeks leading up to Christmas Jasmine had been spending a significant amount of time with Bill. They had gone hiking in the mountain preserve with the dogs. They had been to movies, and Jasmine had cooked dinner for Bill on a couple of Sunday evenings. Jasmine loved to cook, try new recipes. They were now fast friends. In fact, they were on the verge of becoming more than friends.

"Yes, I thought I would. Is that okay with you?"

"Mom, I like Bill. He's a really nice guy. You need to invite Chas, too."

"Yes, I agree. But Bill does have family in town. Maybe he won't want to come."

She called Bill that evening and asked if he and Chas would join them for dinner on Christmas Day. He said that he would be delighted. He told her that his extended family traditionally gathered on Christmas Eve to open gifts and have a meal. And he wasn't looking forward to Christmas Day, their first without his wife, Chas's mother.

"Oh, and bring Sugar with you. You don't want to leave her alone on Christmas Day," said Jasmine.

Jasmine was happy that he and his son would be coming. She wanted to buy them each a gift and didn't know what to get them, but she would think of something.

Jasmine bought two hen turkeys from the local Bashas store at forty-nine cents a pound, a weekly special, one to donate to another family and one for their Christmas dinner. Two weeks before Christmas, Jasmine had visited Toy-R-Us and purchased toys for the Toys for Tots program in the Valley. She couldn't give much this year, but she wanted to do something for needy families. Celeste complained to her mother for giving so much away when they had so very little. "Celeste, we have abundance," Jasmine told her. "We have a roof over our heads and food to eat. There are people going to bed hungry every day in America and around the world. We certainly can give this small amount." And Celeste must have realized that her mother was right. She gave some of her money that she had been saving to her mother to buy something for a needy family. She wondered, though, what these families did the rest of the year. They had all of this help from many people during the holidays, but the holiday season lasted only a couple of months. Would poor families go hungry again in January, February....?

Christmas day arrived, bright and sunny but cool. Jasmine took the dogs for a walk on the canal early in the morning while Celeste slept in late. She came back to the house and started to prepare the dressing for the turkey. She would be putting the turkey into the oven at around one in the afternoon so that it would be ready by five or six when she had invited Bill and Chas and Sugar to join them.

Jasmine saw Celeste come out of her bedroom, sleepy-eyed, hair disheveled. "Merry Christmas." She went to give her daughter a hug. "You know, Celey, this is the first Christmas we've been together in a long time. I'm glad you're here with me."

"Thanks Mom. Even though I'm unemployed and pregnant?"

"Yes. Even though you're unemployed and pregnant. You know, I'm looking forward to being a grandmom."

"That's not what you said a couple of months ago."

"It just took me awhile to get used to it. These things happen for a reason. I truly believe that."

"Yeah, right," said Celeste as she went to the bathroom to brush her teeth.

Bill and Chas arrived right on time: five o'clock on Christmas day, with Sugar in tow. "It sure smells good in here," Bill said as he took the leash off Sugar. Chance and Blondie were ecstatic to see Sugar again. They both surrounded her and sniffed her everywhere as if to say, where have you been these past few weeks? We've missed you.

"Celeste, put the dogs outside so they can roughhouse and play without getting in the way of the cooking," said Jasmine. "Bill, can you carve the turkey?" Jasmine asked as she was preparing the candied yams.

"Sure, I'd be happy to," Bill replied.

"Chas, would you like to mash the potatoes?"

Jasmine believed in involving everyone in the last-minute preparation of the Christmas meal. It made it easier for her, and she felt that it made Chas and Bill feel more at home.

They at last gathered around the beautiful Christmas table, set with Jasmine's best china, sterling silver and crystal goblets from her former marriage. There was a large white candle in the center of the table and two candles on either side with fresh pine boughs that Jasmine would get for free from the nursery every year to decorate the house. The candles were lit, giving a soft, peaceful glow to the room.

"Let's all hold hands," said Jasmine. She closed her eyes and then said, "Our thoughts tonight are with those who are less fortunate, those who don't have a home, or family to be with, or food to eat. We hope for peace around the world so that families and little children will no longer have to suffer. And we hope that all of the animals of the world, domestic and wild, will be able to have a place on this earth. And finally we hope that each one of us at this table will have a healthy and prosperous year."

"Amen," said Bill.

"Amen and let's eat," Chas said as he reached for the mashed potatoes.

"Hold on, Chas, pass the dishes and then take your portion. Where are your manners?" Bill asked looking at Chas in a disapproving way.

"That's okay, Bill," said Jasmine. She was glad that Chas was feeling so much at home.

"Do you believe all that stuff that you just said, Mom?" Celeste asked as the turkey platter was being passed.

"I want to believe it, but I know in my heart there will always be suffering in this world. And as much as I would like to do something about it, I don't think it's possible to feed and clothe and provide shelter for everyone. There are millions of people without fresh water in Africa. And those people, especially the children, often die from dysentery and disease. If someone could solve that problem alone we will have made a dent."

"I think the problem is that there are too many people on this planet and not enough resources," Bill chimed in. "and until that's solved we'll be seeing famine and wars into the foreseeable future."

"I agree with you, Bill, and no one wants to talk about it. Because to curtail births means cutting economic growth, and that involves money," said Jasmine with a mouthful of turkey. "People supply labor, and the more people the better to keep labor costs low. And then people are consumers, buying the products that the companies make."

Celeste squirmed in her chair. "So I guess I shouldn't be having this baby then."

"Not you, honey. If each of us only reproduced ourselves one time, meaning one child per person, that alone would bring down the rate of the population growth. It's those who have a half a dozen kids and then those kids have kids and so on and so on…."

"Jasmine, this is sure good turkey dressing," Bill piped up. "Not to change the subject or anything"

And everyone around the table laughed. "It's a recipe from my grandmother," Jasmine said laughing with everyone else. And what a joyful time this was, she thought as she ate more dressing.

"Chas, you're sure quiet," said Jasmine as she watched him stuff a roll into his mouth.

"As long as he's eating, he's happy," Bill said.

Chas gave his dad a dirty look. "All I can say is that everything seems to be about money and greed. Big companies care about the people only when they are buying products from them."

"That's about it," said Jasmine, surprised that Chas was paying attention to the conversation.

"The dogs are enjoying this," said Celeste as she pointed out how they were quietly lying under the table. "I think they're looking for a handout."

"Don't you feed them at the table," warned Jasmine. "That's one of the worst things you can do."

"I know, I know. You don't have to tell me," Celeste complained.

The light conversation continued. "Seconds, anyone?" asked Jasmine.

"Oh, no, I couldn't. I'm so full, I'll have to waddle out of here," said Bill. But Chas took more turkey and dressing when it was passed.

When everyone had finished eating, Jasmine and Celeste cleared the table and then Jasmine brought pumpkin and mincemeat pies to the table and cut slices for everyone.

"Let's go into the living room and open our presents," Jasmine said as she cleared the desert dishes. As they settled on the sofa, Jasmine handed Bill a brightly wrapped box and then found another gift for Chas under the tree.

"You shouldn't have done this. We didn't bring gifts for you and Celeste," said Bill as he looked at his package.

"You brought yourselves, that's your gift," said Jasmine. She then took three small misshapen packages off the tree and gave one to each of the dogs. They tore into the paper revealing rawhide bones for each dog. Blondie, Chance and Sugar quickly settled down to the job of chewing and were, for a change, very quiet.

Bill opened his package and held up a royal blue cotton knit polo shirt. "Thank you. I can certainly use this. I live in these at work."

And Chas opened his present from Jasmine and Celeste, a book on fly fishing. "How did you know? I love fly fishing. Thanks."

"Your dad told me, Chas," said Jasmine.

They all sat around, full from the dinner, until Celeste finally said to Chas, "Hey, let's take the dogs for a walk and work off some of this dinner"

"Good idea," said Chas.

And they gathered up the dogs, put leashes on them, and were out the door.

Now that the kids were gone, Bill moved closer to Jasmine on the couch. "It was a lovely Christmas. Thank you for inviting us."

"It was, wasn't it. Well, in fact it still is. The evening isn't over."

"What are you doing New Year's Eve?" Bill asked.

"Oh, the usual, an early supper, watch a little TV, and then to bed early."

"Want some company while you watch TV? I'll bring some food and a bottle of sparkling wine, and we could celebrate together."

"I would like that. What about Chas, though?"

"I think he's going to a party one of his friends is giving. He doesn't want to hang out with us. And Celeste?"

"She'll be here. I don't want to leave her alone."

"The three of us can celebrate together then."

"And bring Sugar again. You can't leave her alone in the back yard on New Year's Eve. People shoot off guns and she could be hurt. And she would be frightened." New Years Eve in Phoenix always brought out the gun-toting cowboys, even though it was now illegal to shoot a weapon in the city. And New Year's along with the Fourth of July, was a night that many dogs ran away and were brought in to the County Dog Pound and the Humane Society.

"Okay, so the six of us. Wow, can't I ever get you alone, Jasmine?" Bill asked as he laughed and put his arm around her.

At nine o'clock on New Year's Eve, Jasmine heard the door bell ring. She went to answer it and there was Bill laden with packages of food, a bottle of wine, and a bag of presents, trying to hang onto Sugar.

"What's all of this?" Jasmine said as she let them in the door.

"Food and drink and New Year's presents for two lovely ladies."

"I didn't know that people gave out presents on New Year's," said Jasmine eying him suspiciously.

"We're starting a new trend." Bill put the presents under the tree as Jasmine took the food to the kitchen. Chinese takeout, her favorite for New Year's. She set the table with three places and opened a bottle of white wine, thinking that she would save the sparkling wine for later.

"Celeste, come and join us," Jasmine called. And Celeste, complaining about how uncomfortable she was, came out of her bedroom. They gathered around the table and helped themselves from the cartons of Chinese vegetables, Moo Shoo, shrimp and sticky white rice.

"When is your baby due, Celeste?" asked Bill.

"The end of the month. But I think it's going to be sooner rather than later. At least I hope so. I'm tired of carrying around this load."

"You're still going to have to carry it, sweetheart, only in a different way," Jasmine said as she spooned more Moo Shoo shrimp onto her plate.

They ate heartily and talked of the New Year to come, each hoping for better times.

"Okay, here's what's in your future," said Bill as he passed one fortune cookie Jasmine, one to Celeste and then took one for himself.

"Celeste, remember when your class toured the fortune-cookie factory in China Town in San Francisco?" Jasmine asked as she cracked open her cookie. "I was the room mother that year," she said, looking at Bill. And then to Celeste, "I think you were in the fourth grade."

"I do. I remember how we got lost and walked down a dark, narrow alley and went into this kitchen where dead ducks or chickens were hanging from the ceiling. It was disgusting."

Jasmine read from the little slip of paper that she pulled from her cookie. "'You will have great wealth within a year.' Oh, I am so glad. Now I don't have to worry. Celeste, read yours."

"'A stranger will soon come into your life.' Well, I guess that's true. My baby is a stranger. I don't know him yet."

"Bill, it's your turn, said Jasmine.

"'You will be traveling to far-away places.' How intuitive. I probably will—Seattle," said Bill. But then he said, "That's not far away—really."

And they all laughed together. Then Celeste excused herself, saying she was very tired and was going to bed. "I hope I can sleep. The baby keeps kicking and turning and it wakes me up and then I can't get back to sleep again."

"It'll be over soon, Celey. And then we'll have a crying baby to contend with every night. That'll keep you awake for sure," said Jasmine. "In fact that'll keep all of us awake," she added.

Celeste went back to her room and closed the door.

"Oh, I didn't give Celeste her present," said Bill. "Let me give you yours and you can give Celeste's to her in the morning."

And they went to the small living room and sank down onto the sofa. The three dogs followed and lay down at their feet. Jasmine had dialed to a classical station on the radio, and with the soft music of Chopin and lights of the Christmas tree, the room had a special, soft radiance about it. Bill handed Jasmine a small package, wrapped in shiny silver paper with a blue bow. Jasmine shook the package and then smelled it. "Its cologne, isn't it?" she guessed.

"You are just too smart, my lady."

Jasmine opened the package and, sure enough, it was a bottle of Trejor cologne. "Oh, my favorite. How did you know?" And Jasmine kissed Bill and Bill kissed her back.

"I just guessed. But I'm glad you like it."

They sat there holding one another for awhile taking in the magic of the moment, the lights of the tree, the soft music and the peacefulness of it all. .

"To be truthful, I saw a small bottle of Trejor in your bathroom on Christmas Day."

He's very observant, thought Jasmine, dismissing the fact that he'd told a small, white lie. I like that in a man.

"How is Celeste doing? Is she prepared for her big event?" asked Bill.

"I don't think so. But I don't think any woman is prepared for the first baby. I know I wasn't. Oh, I take that back. She's prepared with the baby clothes and diapers, but not for how her life is going to change after the baby gets here."

Bill kissed Jasmine on her head and caressed her hands.

"And then she wants to have this baby at home, which frankly, I think is a big mistake. But she's determined."

"If she's healthy, she should get through it okay. And it's not that far from your house to the hospital. Have the phone number and the car ready in case."

"No kidding," said Jasmine. And she thought about that for a few minutes. "And how is Chas doing these days?"

"He's doing much better. For awhile there he was just staying in his room all of the time, playing computer games. His friends would come over occasionally, but after awhile they didn't want to be around him. He was definitely depressed."

"Was he taking medication for it?"

"No. We hadn't gotten to that point yet." Bill now turned to look at Jasmine, pulling his arm away from her. "You see, his mother was his best friend. They were very close. She was his go-to person. I was seldom around, I regret to say. Always working, the bread winner, you know. Helen, who was a former teacher, worked part time as a tutor, so she was able to schedule her time to always be there when Chas got home from school."

"Somebody has to be there for the kids. I think that's one of our problems in this society is that kids, especially teens, are left to their own devices with two parents working these days. And then they get into trouble and we wonder why."

"Well then, when she was diagnosed with this aggressive breast cancer," Bill continued, "his world just fell apart. And I couldn't do anything about it."

"How long was she sick?" Jasmine asked, not really wanting to know the details. She didn't want to stir up sadness in Bill. In fact, she had avoided talking about this very subject whenever they were together. But Bill seemed to want to talk about it now.

"About three years. I knew as soon as the diagnosis came in that she was going to leave us. The cancer had already spread to her lungs and her liver, and that was not good," Bill said as a tear started rolling down his cheek. "It was a roller coaster ride from then on. Some days she was good and seemed to be getting better and then some days not so good. It was really hard on all of us."

"I'm so sorry for you and Chas. It must have been a horrible time in your lives."

"Yes, it was. I could never imagine Helen dying like that. She was always so healthy and vibrant, so full of life, and then to have her taken with this disease."

"So when you got Sugar, did that help Chas?" Jasmine asked trying to help Bill out of his melancholy.

"Oh yes, it did. The dog took to Chas right away. It was as if they'd always been together. Sugar slept with Chas and I would hear him talking to her before he went to sleep. And then for Chas to have the responsibility of feeding and caring for an animal was really good for him. It just took his mind off himself."

"I'm glad. Of course he'll never forget his mother, but maybe he can feel better about his life and his future. Time heals all, they say."

Bill looked at Jasmine and put his arm around her again. "Jasmine, I'm so glad that I met you." He kissed her. And then he hesitated for a minute or two. "I think I'm falling in love with you, but ...."

"But what?"

"I keep thinking it's too soon for that. Helen hasn't been gone that long."

"Again, I say, let's just take our time. I'm here for you, Bill. No hurry," said Jasmine as she kissed him again.

Bill cleared his throat. "I'd like to stay the night."

Jasmine sat up, not knowing how to answer him at first. She had strong feelings for Bill as well. What harm would it do? But if she slept with him, would that bond her to him, when she didn't know where her head was at as far as a relationship was concerned? And she certainly didn't want to build up his hopes and then reject him. He must be pretty fragile with just having lost his wife. But then, having his arms around her all night long sounded pretty wonderful. She thought for a few minutes and then said, "We'd have to be really quiet. I don't want Celeste to know."

Bill looked straight at her. "She's an adult. She's about to have a baby. She would understand."

"I know, but….," Jasmine stammered for another minute or so.

"I'll leave early and she'll never know. Come on, let's go to bed," Bill said with pleading eyes as he got up off the couch and started to pull Jasmine toward him.

"But it isn't even midnight yet and we haven't had our champagne."

"I'll get the bottle and we'll celebrate the New Year from bed," said Bill as he went into the kitchen to uncork the champagne and retrieve two glasses. He then led Jasmine into the bedroom.

"What about the dogs?"

"They'll have to find another place to sleep tonight."

"But it's not even midnight yet. And what about Chas? Shouldn't you be there when he gets home?"

"Chas is a big boy now. He can take care of himself. And he's pretty reliable; I can trust him."

Jasmine was running out of excuses.

"I'll take the dogs out. I usually do that just before I go to bed," said Jasmine. What am I doing? she thought. But I do love this man. At least I think I can love him. When she came back inside with the dogs trailing behind, Bill took her hand and led her off to the bedroom. He shooed the dogs out, closed the door, and led her over to the neatly made bed. Jasmine self-consciously took off her sweater and jeans and put on her flannel night gown and climbed into bed along-side Bill, who had taken off his pants and shirt. Bill reached for the two glasses and filled them with the sparkling wine.

"Here's to the best New Year ever," Bill said.

They clinked glasses and drank and then Bill put down his glass and pulled Jasmine closer and kissed her deeply.

"Do you need a condom?" asked Jasmine.

"Are you on birth control?" asked Bill

"I've had a tubal ligation awhile back."

Bill continued to kiss her neck, her ears and her shoulder.

"Aren't you a little overdressed?" he asked. "If you're afraid of AIDS, I haven't been with anyone but my wife since long before we were married."

Jasmine took off her nightgown and Bill tenderly held her in his arms and then slowly they came together. Jasmine melted into Bill, her face in his chest, her breasts against his warm body, taking in his smell, twirling her fingers in his hair. It had been a long time for Jasmine as well, and she was feeling all of the electricity, the indescribable mounting tension, that she had felt years ago.

When they were finished, Jasmine heard the sound of gun shots all over the neighborhood.

Very early in the morning, about four o'clock, she awoke to find that Bill had gone and Chance and Blondie were snuggled up to her, keeping her warm.

The next day, early in the morning, Jasmine dressed in her favorite sweats and took Blondie and Chance for a long walk on the canal near her home.

The canals in and around Phoenix were originally built 1400 years ago by the Hohokam, an indigenous group of people who had lived in the area from 600 AD. They were used to maintain extensive irrigation networks along the lower Salt and middle Gila Rivers that rivaled the complexity of those used in the ancient Near East, Egypt, and China. There were thought to be 50,000 people living in the area at that time, and then around 1459 they mysteriously disappeared. The current system of nine canals has been developed over the last 100 years and is still used for irrigation of crops and city lawns.

It was a cool day, fifty degrees, with an Arizona cloudless sky, and the mountains to the east were a verdant green from a recent rain. The ducks on the canal were pairing up again in preparation for spring mating season a month away. Chance pulled hard at his leash, wanting to chase them.

"No, Chance, you can't go after those birds. They're too big for you, anyway." Chance turned around and looked at Jasmine as if to say, "wanna bet?"

It had been over a year since Jasmine lost her job, and so far she had survived. She thought about all of the events that had happened over the year: finding Chance and Blondie, and then Blondie having puppies. Celeste coming back to live with her and about to become a mother, too; that would make Jasmine a grandmother. No, I'm not old enough, she thought. But yes, this would happen in a few weeks' time. And her new relationship with Bill.

She wondered what the New Year would bring. Would she get a job, and if not would she be able to support herself and help Celeste, too? But Ramon was on his way back from London. He should be here next week, in fact. Would he be able to take care of Celeste and the baby? There were so many unknowns, but that was the fundamental nature of life: one great big adventure, each day bringing new and exciting events. And Jasmine was hopeful. She thought about how fortunate she and Celeste were. They had a place to live, a very fine place. They had enough to eat. It was true that they were not living a lavish life, but they had the basics and more. And as Jasmine watched the dogs sprinting out in front of her, always pulling and wanting to go faster, she was grateful to have these wonderful, intelligent, beautiful dogs to share her life with. Was she missing anything in her life? She didn't think so. Not even a man.

Chapter 40
Chance

Just when I thought life around here was really boring, a couple of weeks ago, things started to get interesting. Mom brought this huge box into the living room and took out green plastic things that looked like tree branches and started putting them together. And when she was finished there was a tree standing in the middle of the room. I didn't know if I was allowed to pee on it or not, but since I did know that peeing in the house was forbidden, I thought better of it.

Celey came in and joined her. They brought in more boxes; I don't know where they came from. And they took out long strings, and balls, and other strange things and put them on the tree. I guess Blondie thought the balls were a different kind of tennis ball and that they were for us to play with and she kept trying to pull them off the tree, but Celeste told her no. They had food, cookies. I tried to eat one, but that wasn't allowed either.

And when they were finished, they put this pronged thing into the wall and turned a switch and the tree lit up. It was amazing. And kind of fun too.

Over the next few days, packages wrapped in paper appeared under the tree. I thought these were put there for us as well because a couple of them smelled suspiciously like rawhide, so I started to tear them apart and guess what, I got into trouble again.

And then the most exciting thing of all happened. Mom took this big, dead bird without any feathers on it out of the refrigerator and put stuff inside it and then put it in this hot place in the wall, I think she calls it an oven. Mom rarely uses this so I'm not sure.

The smells all afternoon were almost more than I could take. And Blondie was excited as well. She parked herself right under the oven where the bird was cooking and waited, and waited some more. I told her it would be a long time, but she said she didn't mind if she could grab a bite.

Later that afternoon Mom's new friend showed up with Sugar and another person. We were so happy to see her. It had been a long time and we had a lot of catching up to do. So we were put outside to play for awhile.

And then, it seemed like hours, Mom took the bird out of the oven and put it on a big plate. The aromas were divine. Blondie, Sugar and I sat right underneath, watching and waiting for a treat. We gave all the signals that we were ready for a bite: heads cocked to the side, ears forward, and tongues hanging out. But Mom just put us outside again, saying we were in the way. Can you believe it?

A little while later, as we were lying around on the patio, the door opened and Celey let us into the house. Mom and Celey were carrying dishes, plates of food and other stuff, and they put this all on the table. They told us to leave it alone but that was hard to do and I tried to take a bite again and I got into trouble again. Then they all sat at the table, Mom, Celey, Mom's new friend, and the other person, and they ate and ate. I sat under the table and waited for something to come my way, but it was futile. And then Mom told us to go and lie down, and we knew what that meant, that we were bugging them. And they kept eating and there was nothing for Blondie or Sugar or me. But then they finally finished eating, Mom got up from the table and patted me and Blondie on the head and said, "Now it's your turn. I'm going to fix the three of you a turkey dinner. Okay?" And I perked my ears and thought, oh boy here it comes, what we've been waiting for all day. I ate every last piece and I wanted some more. It was so delicious.

After we all ate we went into the living room and Celey passed out presents to everyone, even me, Blondie and Sugar. We ripped open the brightly colored packages that I had been trying to get to for a week now, and each of us had rawhide bones, and I had a rope toy, Blondie a furry squeak toy that she tore apart in record time, and Sugar, a rubber toy with food in it. It was so much fun.

I wish every day could be like this.

Chapter 41

Preparations

Celeste had been collecting baby clothes and accessories for months now. She used some of the money that her father had sent, looked for department store sales, and visited used clothing stores as well. With very little money she was able to provide a good assortment for her coming child.

Jasmine bought a cradle for the baby to sleep in for the first couple of months. She'd found it at a used furniture store in November. It was old, probably antique, and appeared to have been well used. With slatted sides, an ornamental headboard with the image of a lamb carved in the wood, it sat on turned legs attached to two rockers. It was sturdy, and, with some fixing up, it would be as good as new. Every day when Celeste was at school, Jasmine dragged it out of the shed and onto the patio. She stripped away the pealing paint and found that underneath three layers of turquoise, yellow and white was a quality hard cherry wood. She sanded and stained the wood and applied a sealer.

Jasmine then bought a new mattress and some soft flannel fabric in a baby-blue color with a rosebud design to make a mattress cover and a liner that tied to the sides with blue satin ribbons. The project took a month and a half, but, as the cradle began to come together, Jasmine beamed with pride at the little bed that would hold her first grandson. It was a very satisfying feeling.

"Mom, they gave me a baby shower at school. Can you believe that?" Celeste exclaimed as she came into the house one Thursday afternoon early in January, her arms loaded with bags and packages. "Look at all of the cute clothes, the baby blankets and bibs and bottles. I was so surprised. I have the nicest friends."

"Celeste, that's wonderful. Now all we need is a bed for the baby."

"He can sleep with me for awhile. I'll be nursing him in the middle of the night anyway."

"No way. He needs his own bed. I think I have something that might work," said Jasmine as she went out to the shed to bring in the cradle. She struggled to bring it into the house with Chance and Blondie trailing after. And once she pulled the sheet off of it, Celeste was awestruck.

"Mother, where did you get this? It's so beautiful! I love it," said Celeste as tears ran down her cheeks.

"I found it at an antique store, and I refurbished it for you and the baby. I'm glad you like it."

"It's perfect. I can keep it beside my bed at night and rock the baby when he cries." Celeste circled around the cradle with the dogs following close by. They were infinitely interested, sniffing the bedding. Blondie put her paws on the railing to get a better look, causing the cradle to tip to the side. "No, Blondie. This is for little Rafael. You can't do that," Celeste said with concern.

Then it occurred to Celeste that having the dogs around a newborn might be difficult. "Mom, what about the dogs?" she asked. "Will they be a problem with the baby?"

"I don't think so. But you can never leave the baby unattended when the dogs are around, until Rafael is old enough to handle himself around them. And that's probably at around age four or five."

"I'm going to be out of here before then. I hope."

"I hope so, too. I'm enjoying your company, honey, but it will be better for you to be in your own home. Have you heard from Ramon recently?"

"He called me last week and said he was leaving London on Wednesday. But I haven't heard anything since then. I'm worried. He has to get here for Rafael's birth. He just has to."

"I'm sure you'll hear soon, "said Jasmine, trying to calm Celeste. "I like the name you chose. Where did that come from?"

"I just liked it. Rafael Martinez Alvarez. It sounds like an important name, don't you think?"

"I do. I think it's beautiful. Does that mean you two are getting married?"

"Mom, I don't know at this point. All I know is that Ramon has proven to me that he is hard-working and that he is loyal and I think he loves me. I also think he's a pretty good guy."

"I think so too, Celey. You would have my blessing." Jasmine thought for a few minutes while petting Chance. "You do know, Celey, the most important decision in your life is choosing a mate. That one decision can make your life go smoothly or it can tear it apart."

"There you go again, Mom, giving advice," Celeste said with a smile. "I think you're right. But I worry that Ramon will not make enough money to take care of us,

although I still intend to have my own career," Celeste said as she looked at the little t-shirts and buntings that her co-workers had given her. "Mom, I need to get some diapers."

"Oh, we'll pick up some Huggies at the drugstore. That's not a problem."

"No, I want cloth diapers for Rafael."

"Why on earth for?"

"Because it's earth-friendly. I don't want to contribute to the landfills with more disposable diapers. And I think cloth diapers are softer and more comfortable for the baby."

"But then you have to clean them and wash them. It's kind of messy and you'll have your hands in the toilet for a couple of years."

"I know, but for Rafael I will do that." Celeste petted Blondie and then looked at her mom. "So did you make a bad choice in marrying Dad?"

"Not necessarily. When I was growing up and starting to date, my mother told me to find a man who would be successful. I think she grew up in such poverty and she didn't want that for me."

"But you did that. You married into a blue-blooded family from the East. How much more successful can you get? And Dad makes a lot of money."

"Yes, if you look at it that way. But your dad had some character flaws. His values were not the same as mine, and he didn't always tell the truth. Especially when it came to affairs with his secretaries," said Jasmine. She thought about those early days stuck at home with a little baby, not knowing whether her husband would be coming home at night. "You know, Celeste, if Ramon is honest and if he loves you, that's all that matters. He's young yet and he's smart enough to figure out a way to make a good living."

"Are you sorry that you left Dad?"

"No. I did the right thing. It was really difficult, especially being separated from you all those years. But I had to be true to myself."

"What about Dad? Do you think he has regrets?"

"I do. I've sensed that in talking with him lately. You know you are his little girl, his little angel, and always will be. Now that you're having this child, I think he wants to be more a part of it. I think he found out that he lost something very special when our family broke up."

Celeste thought about this and then said, "It's too late now. He should have thought about that years ago."

"You are becoming a wise woman, Celey."

"Maybe he'll show up for the birthing. I asked him to come, you know."

"No, I didn't know that. Don't count on it, though. Deborah keeps him on a short leash."

Bill called the day after New Year's, and they talked about everything except what happened on New Year's Eve: the weather, Celeste and her birthing, the dogs, Chas. Finally Bill asked Jasmine, "Are you sorry that we made love?"

"No. I'm glad we did. I just worry that we're rushing things. Especially for you. It hasn't been that long, you know."

"I do know. Let me be the judge of that. I have very deep feelings for you, Jasmine. And I hope it works out for us."

"But you have to think of Chas as well," said Jasmine. "To bring another woman into your life right now could be devastating for him."

"He likes you. He really does."

"He might not like me so much if he thinks I am replacing his mother."

Bill was silent for a time as he thought this over.

"Let's take it slow. We have time," said Jasmine.

And they decided to go on a hike with the dogs the next Sunday afternoon in the mountain preserve. And that's what they did. Chance loved hiking in the desert. There were so many little creatures running about, and the smells were captivating.

After the hike they came back to Jasmine's house and she prepared hamburgers with potato salad and baked beans for supper. Celeste was out with some of her friends for the evening, getting in her last days of freedom before the baby arrived.

After dinner Bill and Jasmine sat in the living room, drinking port wine and talking about the day's events. The dogs, exhausted from the hike, were lying at their feet.

"What are you hearing on the job front?" Jasmine asked. "Didn't you have an opportunity in Washington State?"

"It looks like it's coming together. I'm negotiating salary right now."

"That's wonderful, I guess. That means you'll be moving away from Arizona."

"Yes, and I have reservations about doing that. I've lived here most of my life and moving to Seattle is not going to be easy."

"And the weather. It's so different there, rain every day. I don't think I could take that."

"I think you'd get used to it. It's beautiful country—mountains and forests; great hiking and skiing. Why don't you come with me?"

"Bill, I can't imagine that right now. I can't leave Celeste. She's going to need me more than ever in the next year or so."

"Didn't you say that her boyfriend, the father of the child, is coming back to be with her? He's the one who has to take care of her and the baby. He's the one responsible."

"Yes, he is. And I'm sure he'll do that. But he isn't here yet, so until I actually see him and know that he'll be here for her, I am the one."

"You can think about it, anyway. I know Chas will be with me for a couple of more years until he goes to college."

"I really like Chas and we get along well. But I just don't know. That would be a drastic change for me."

Bill took a sip of his wine and then took Jasmine's hand in his. "I thought you liked adventure."

"I do like adventure. But right now I have to get my life in order here before I do anything. I need to get a job or have some kind of income coming in."

"You wouldn't have to worry about that if you came with me. I will make enough for both of us and you could do what you want, be that writing or painting or getting another job."

Jasmine thought about this for a few moments. Putting her life again in the hands of a man? That wasn't appealing to her. And then what if it didn't work out? What would she do then? She'd be even older than she was now, and it would be even harder for her to find work. She could never have that dependency again; she had to be her own person.

"No, Bill. That's kind of you, but I need my independence. I need to know that I can make my own way in this world. I've done it for many years now and I can do it again."

"Well, think about it anyway."

This man does not give up, thought Jasmine. That's a good quality to have, she thought. And she would think about it, but she had to concentrate on her own career. That was critical.

On Monday night Ramon finally called, and Celeste was so relieved.

"I'm sorry, honey, that I didn't call sooner, but I've been coordinating some things over here. I'll tell you about it when I get there. I'm leaving tomorrow morning and I should be there in the early afternoon. I can stay at a motel for a couple days."

"That's expensive. You can stay here. I know Mom won't mind."

"No, I would imagine that you need all of the space in your bed at this point. I can't wait to see you. You must look beautiful."

"Beautiful? Hardly. With a belly sticking out, and huge breasts, and swollen ankles. Can't get into any clothes. I don't think I look anywhere near beautiful."

"To me you will. I love you, Celeste, and I'll be by your side as long as you want me to be."

"I love you, too, Ramon."

And Celeste slept a little better that night knowing that Ramon was on his way.

Chapter 42
Full House

Celeste's due date was days away, and her energy level was off the charts. She started cleaning everything in the house, organizing her room and making sure that she would be ready for the big event. Blondie and Chance were full of energy as well, running around the house, tails wagging, ears forward, play-fighting and generally getting into mischief. They seemed to sense that something important was about to happen. They also kept a close watch on Celeste, staying by her when she sat and watched TV, or at the dinner table. But then Celeste had been spending a lot of time with then lately, taking them with her for her daily walks. She also had taken over the duties of feeding them and brushing their coats and their teeth at least once a week, in addition to picking up the yard twice a day. Jasmine had handed over these tasks to Celeste to prepare her for the time when she would have a little one depending on her for everything. It was good training, she said. But Celeste didn't mind. She loved Chance and Blondie.

It was Saturday evening, and Jasmine had been working on a project in her office. She decided to take a break and walked into the living room to find Celeste on the couch with Chance curled on one side of her and Blondie draped over Celeste's tummy, seeming to listen to the baby. Jasmine watched for a few minutes, taking in the tender scene before her. When the baby kicked, Blondie lifted her head with a surprised look on her face, then looked down at Celeste's belly and gave a little snort.

"She knows, Mom. She knows there's a baby in there."

"I think she does. These furry beings are aware of what's going on with their humans. In fact all animals have knowledge of life that we don't even understand."

"Oh, Mom I think you are totally right about that. Some have superior sight, and dogs can smell things that we can't. Humans are supposed to be so advanced, with a big brain. Problem is they don't use that brain half the time."

"I love you, Celeste. You are indeed my daughter."

Celeste's cell phone rang. "Hello. Oh, hi, Dad?" Celeste went to find her mother. "Dad's in town. He's going to be here for the birth. I'm so excited and happy." She went back to the phone. "Where are you? Where're you staying? I'm so glad you're here."

"Sweetheart, I wouldn't miss this for anything. I had some vacation time coming and I couldn't think of a better way to spend it. I'm at the Hilton not far from your mother's house. I'll be over in the morning."

Richard has finally figured out that family matters, Jasmine thought to herself. It only took him twenty-five years. "I'm glad he's going to be here, honey. He really does love you."

Celeste was not sleeping well these nights. Along with the discomfort from the baby, she couldn't turn off her thoughts at night. There were so many things to do, to plan for. Her due date was next Tuesday, but the baby could come any time now and she knew that. She had everything ready for the birth, the supplies that Michelle, her mid-wife, had told her to have ready: towels, a large bowl to receive the placenta, cord clamps, blue waterproof pads, sanitary pads, and oil and blankets for the baby. And she had been cleaning her room thoroughly every day in preparation for the birthing.

Michelle had come by two days ago to check on Celeste, and she said that the fetus was in position and ready to make his debut.

Michelle tried to prepare Celeste, knowing that labor for first-time moms is oftentimes lengthy and painful. "But once you hold your baby in your arms, it will be well worth all of the pain you've endured. Trust me," said Michelle.

Celeste believed that would be true. Now all she had to do was wait. She kept wondering what it was going to be like. But she would find out soon enough.

Ramon left Los Angeles driving through the Palm Springs area and onto the high desert heading east to Arizona. It was early morning, and the sun had yet to rise above the mountains to the east. Once that happened he would be driving into it until mid-morning.

What a journey he'd been on this last year. He'd lost his job, gone to Phoenix with Celeste, back to LA and then to London where he finally found work and was able to earn some money to keep himself in food and pay the rent. While in London, he and Dave had taken many side trips to Paris, Rome, Dublin, Madrid—places where centuries of wars were fought, religious and otherwise, where democracy was nurtured and kept alive. He felt that he had a much broader view of the world now and how he fit into it.

He kept thinking about Celeste and the son that would be born within days. He thought about the life he was going to have with his new family, and he was in the clouds. This was something that he had been fantasizing about ever since he had met Celeste, and it had seemed to be unattainable until recently. Celeste was the woman of his dreams. He thought about how intelligent and beautiful she was and yet playful and full of positive energy. This was the woman he wanted on his team. And now that he had a real plan for their future, he knew they would have a chance at a prosperous and happy life. It would take some work on his part, but he was up for it. Whatever it took to be a loving husband to Celeste and a caring father to his son. Wait a minute; Celeste hadn't agreed to marry him yet. But she would. She would see how much he loved her and their son and she would marry him. He was confident.

Celeste heard the doorbell ring from her bedroom where she was still lying in bed. She looked at the clock. It was ten AM. She'd been awake until three and she finally zonked off. Who could that be? Probably Dad, she thought. "Mom, someone's at the door. Can you get it?" No answer. She must be out with the dogs or something. Celeste grabbed her bathrobe and went to the front door and opened it and there he was: Ramon, standing there with a dozen red roses and a smile on his face from ear to ear.

"Well, aren't you going to let me in? The father of your child."

"Ramon! You got here. You finally got here," Celeste said as she opened the door and pulled him inside. They put their arms around each other and kissed.

"There's something in the way here," said Ramon as he was trying to hug Celeste. He put his hand on her belly. "Something very precious." He kissed her again and then kissed her belly. "Are you okay? Are you feeling well? How soon .....?"

"Yes, I'm fine. Any minute now. My due date is tomorrow, but they tell me that babies seldom come exactly on their due dates. So it could be tonight, or any time after that."

"Here, Celeste, come and sit down," Ramon said as he took her hand and led her to the couch. "You need to conserve your strength."

"Nonsense. I'm strong. I'd better be. I'll soon be taking part in the athletic event of my life." Celeste laughed as she said this, but deep down she was still terribly apprehensive.

"I know, I know, sweetheart. It'll be okay. I'm here with you now and I'll stay by your side forever."

Celeste got up from the couch, with much difficulty, to put the roses in a vase and then she put the vase on the coffee table. She held a rose to her nose and inhaled deeply of the fragrance and touched the petals. "They are so beautiful. Thank you, Ramon."

"You are the beautiful rose," said Ramon. 'Not even a camera could capture your beauty." And he kissed her again as she sat down beside him.

Jasmine walked in from the back yard. "Ramon. We're so glad you're here. We were getting worried."

"I know. I had a lot to take care of before I came over here." And then Ramon paused as he looked at Celeste. "I have some wonderful news for us. Dad wants me to start a restaurant in Phoenix. He's putting up the money and wants me to manage everything. I'll be paid a salary so we can have money to get an apartment or buy a little house. What do you think?"

"Ramon, that's great, but we're in a recession. It's a bad time to start a restaurant, don't you think?" said Celeste.

"No, it's a great time to start a restaurant. I'll be able to pick up a good lease in the best part of town."

Celeste hesitated. Too much was happening for her to take it all in. "That's wonderful. Is that what you want to do, Ramon? Manage a restaurant for your dad? And what about my career? I need to finish school and get a job as well."

"I'll just step out and take care of the dogs and let you two talk," said Jasmine as she walked out the back door. Well, at least he has a plan, she thought.

"You can do that, too. Celey, I want you to have a career as well. Or maybe you could help with our business in some way: marketing, graphics arts. You'll see. It'll be a good life for all of us. It'll be hard work, but it'll pay off eventually. You'll see."

"But how can we ever get ahead with you just being the manager? We need to have our own restaurant. And is this what you really want to do?"

"Celey, I forgot to tell you the most important part. If after five years the restaurant is successful and making a profit, it will be signed over to me, to us. And to answer your second question, yes, I love this business. I found that out when I was in London. And just think of the possibilities. We could get this one started in Phoenix and then if we wanted to go and live in, say, Vancouver, Canada, we could go there and start another restaurant. There's no limit. Isn't that exciting?"

Celeste thought about this for a few minutes. "I like that idea. I like it a lot," She said, warming to the plan that Ramon had proposed. "Forgive me. I'm just a little preoccupied right now with this baby coming. You do understand. The past few months have been difficult, to say the least."

"Honey I'm so sorry that I haven't been here with you. But I'll make it up to you, you'll see. Celeste, I want to marry you. I want you to be my partner in life. Will you marry me, Celeste?"

Celeste looked at Ramon with that same fear in her eyes. What was holding her back now? She didn't know. Here he was declaring his love for her and the baby, saying that he would take care of them forever, and she was still unsure. "Ramon, let's wait until the baby's born. I just can't deal with this right now."

"We can do that. I don't have a ring yet. I need to get you an engagement ring."

"It's not the ring. It's just that ….. so much is happening. I'm overwhelmed. I do love you, Ramon. Just give me some time to think this through. And we have so much to talk about if we're to marry."

"You're right. I'm being impetuous. I can wait."

And just then the door bell rang again. "Ramon, can you get that? I'm just too tired to get up right now," said Celeste.

Ramon went to the front door and opened it and there, standing on the other side of the door in all of his intimidating stature, was Celeste's father.

"Is this the house where my grandson is about to be born?"

"You must be Mr. Bailey, Celeste's father."

"Richard. Please call me Richard. And you must be Ramon, Celeste's fiancé," Celeste's father said as he entered the house carrying a large square box wrapped in tissue paper and a huge bouquet of flowers.

"Dad, you're here! I'm so glad to see you. I didn't think you would come," Celeste exclaimed as she rose from the couch with difficulty. "Thank you for the flowers. And who is the present for?"

"Who do you think? For my new grandson," Richard said matter-of-factly.

At that moment Jasmine came back into the house with the dogs. Chance and Blondie went from one person to another, sniffing, trying to jump up on Ramon and Richard. "Down, Chance, Blondie. Go lie down, both of you." But they continued to jump and lick faces and hands.

Richard handed Celeste the present and told her to open it. She tore off the paper and there was a box with an official NSL match soccer ball limited edition. "Dad, it's going to be a few years before Rafael will be using this."

"Get them started young, I always say," Richard said as he beamed at his daughter. And then a frown came over his face. "When are you two getting married? Aren't you putting the cart before the horse, as they say, having a baby and then…?"

"Dad, that's for us to decide." She paused, not knowing quite what to say. "We need to get this baby born first and then we'll decide what we're doing after that."

Richard started to open his mouth, but Jasmine gave him the "don't say a word" look.

"And what's this that I hear? You're having your baby at home, not in the hospital?" said Richard as he settled his large frame into one of the side chairs next to the couch.

"Yes, Dad, you heard right."

"Oh baby, don't you know that having a baby is a very dangerous thing. Women die having babies when they don't have proper care."

There was a deafening silence in the room. Jasmine looked at her daughter as if to say, see, I told you so, and went into the kitchen carrying the bouquet to find another vase. It's beginning to look like a florist shop around here, she thought. And Ramon grabbed the soccer ball and examined it, not looking at the others.

"Dad, my mind's made up. I'm an adult now and I know what I'm doing. I have the best mid-wife in town...."

"What if something goes terribly wrong? Do you have a back-up plan?" asked Richard. "Are you just trying to save money?" he continued. "Because if that's the case, I will pay your hospital bill."

"No, Dad. It's not about money. I can get assistance with the hospital bill. I have decided that I don't want to be in the cold, uncaring hospital when my son comes into this world. I want for him and me to be surrounded by a loving family in my own bedroom. That's it."

"Richard, I've tried to tell her," said Jasmine. Jasmine's head went down as if in defeat, and after a minute or two she said, "Your daughter won't listen to me. She won't listen to anyone. I guess she's afraid of hospitals."

"Oh, now she's *my* daughter. I thought she was *your* daughter, too," Richard shot back.

"Stop. Stop right now!" Celeste looked angrily from her mother to her father. "I know what I'm doing. If there are complications, I'll go to the hospital. I've already made arrangements."

"How far is the hospital from here?" asked Richard.

"It's three miles. We can be there in five minutes," said Celeste.

Chance and Blondie had settled on the floor near Celeste, and they looked up at her with sympathetic eyes as she talked.

Celeste got up off the couch and stormed out of the room. She went to her bedroom and slammed the door. Jasmine, Richard, and Ramon sat in the living room, too stunned to say anything. After a few minutes, Jasmine went to Celeste's door and knocked. "Honey. let me in. I want to talk to you. I don't want to see you upset like this."

"No. You are all against me. Except Ramon."

"We aren't against you. We only mean to keep you safe. That's all. Please let me in. I'm your mother. I understand."

"No you don't. Nobody understands what I am going through."

"Look, honey. I had you, didn't I? I do understand. Just let me in to talk with you. We all love you."

By this time Chance and Blondie were standing at Celeste's door with Jasmine, wagging their tails.

Slowly, Celeste opened her door and Jasmine, along with Chance and Blondie spilled into her room. Celeste fell into her mother's arms crying.

"I'm so scared. And then Dad talks about how women can die giving birth," she sobbed on her mother's shoulder. "Is he trying to scare me even more?"

"No, honey. He just cares about you." Jasmine put her arms around Celeste and hugged her. "We love you. We don't want anything to happen to you. That's all."

"Nothing's going to happen. I just know that."

"You know Celey, when you're young you think that nothing can happen. You're invincible. Nothing can touch you. But let's hope you're right. I see that we're not going to change your mind."

"Thanks, Mom." Celeste pulled away from Jasmine and sat on the bed. Chance and Blondie jumped up on the bed and started to lie down next to Celeste.

"No, Blondie, No, Chance. You have to get down. This bed is all ready for the baby, and I don't want any dog germs on it."

Chance and Blondie reluctantly crawled down on the floor, looking up at Celeste as if to say, "but you always let us be on your bed. Why not now?"

Chapter 43
Bill's Dilemma

"**D**ad, I'm not going with you. I can't. My whole life is here in Phoenix."

"I can't let you stay here by yourself, Chas. You have to come with me."

"I'll get a fulltime job. I can get my own apartment. and Grandma is here. She can look in on me once in a while." Chas had worked part time bussing tables and washing dishes at Mary Coyle's ice cream shop for a year now, and he was saving for a car. Although at the kind of money he was making, it would be years before that would happen.

"Chas, you do understand what's happening, don't you? I'd stay here if I could find a job, but I've been without work for a year now. We can't survive here. And I have a good job in Seattle. I need to go there. We need to go there."

Chas looked at his dad as they were sitting at the kitchen table having breakfast on this chilly January morning. It was early, and the sun was just beginning to creep over Piestewa Peak in the East, melting the frost on the lawns. The bushes and plants around the homes were covered with tarps and old sheets to keep them from freezing, looking like a picture out of a Dr. Seus book.

"Dad, I've lost my mother, and now you're asking that I move with you and lose my friends, too? To a place where it rains all the time!"

Chas's mother had been gone now for over a year. The memory of her death was permanently etched in his mind. He had been so close to her; she had been his best friend, confidante. And to watch her, in her illness, waste away to nothing was more than he could bear. When he'd been told that his mother had breast cancer four years ago, he had thought at the time that wasn't the end of the world. Many women have this disease and survive and go on to live long lives. So he wasn't that concerned. But as he watched her lose weight over the next couple of years, becoming very ill from the chemo therapy, he began to realize that she was losing the battle and was soon going to leave him. And that made him angry. How dare she do that when he needed her the most?

Eventually she was spending more time in the hospital, to try to build her body up again so she could fight the cancer. But Chas was told that the cancer had spread to her vital organs, and it would only be a matter of time before she would be gone.

When she was brought home from the hospital the last time, he thought, maybe she's getting better. But, no, Hospice started coming to their home every day to try to help his mother be comfortable and free from pain. And for the last two weeks, he saw her writhing in pain. Then she slept. And there was more pain. After several weeks of this she stopped eating, and that was when he knew that the end was near.

He would come home from school every day and sit beside her and give her ice chips and sips of water, put lotion on her hands and lip balm on her lips.

"Chas, I'm not going to be with you much longer…" She took a breath and then continued. "And you have to be very brave and go on and live your life."

"No, Mother. You can't do this. You can't leave us." Tears were streaming down his cheeks, dropping onto her soft green blanket.

"We've had a good run together, Chas, you know. Many happy days. I want you to remember those times." She paused to take another labored breath. "I remember when you were born. When we brought you home from the hospital…" Another pause…. "we put you in a basinet next to our bed." She took a deeper breath. "I went into the bedroom every five minutes just to look at you sleeping." Another breath. "You were so beautiful and so perfect." Another breath. "Your little nose peeked out from the receiving blanket that we wrapped you in. And your hands with five pink little perfectly formed...." His mother coughed. "perfectly formed fingers on each hand. I thought then, those hands have talent and will do something wonderful," she continued with difficulty. "But I'm sure every new mother thinks like that."

Chas blushed. They talked that day about the ski trips they had taken, about the wonderful hikes they had done in the mountains. They reminisced about the time they baked cookies together when he was little and how he had eaten half the cookie dough while she was on the phone talking to a friend, before she could bake the cookies.

His mother was feeling especially strong that day, and Chas again thought, hope against hope, that she might get better. But then a week later, he came home from school and his father and grandmother were there, and he knew. He went to his mother's bedside and held her hand. Her breathing was shallow and raspy and she no longer had the strength to speak. He spread some lip balm on her lips and said, "I love you, Mom. I'll always love you." Her eyes flickered as if she'd heard him. She faded in and out for a couple of hours. And then she let out one last breath, as if to say, here I go, and she was gone.

He watched as they carried her body out of the house. She was cremated, and weeks later they were given her ashes. His father and the family arranged a memorial service for her many friends to say goodbye. And then in October, when the aspen were turning on Mount Humphries, they took her ashes and scattered them to the wind on the mountain where she loved to hike and ski.

And now, here he was, having to choose between his friends and his father. Why did he always have these terrible choices to make? He wasn't up to it. He wasn't strong enough yet to decide.

"I know, Dad; I can stay in the house with Sugar. I'll pay you rent and maybe get a roommate to make more money and that way you won't have to sell the house in a down market. And I can finish out school here and then maybe come up to join you. By then the housing market should be better and you can sell this house for a profit." Sugar looked up at Chas and moved even closer to him as if to say, yes, we will be buddies together.

"And then I would be in Seattle, trying to work, worrying whether you were okay back here in Phoenix. I don't think so."

"Look Dad, have I gotten into trouble lately? I'm getting good grades, almost straight A's. I have good friends, we don't do drugs, and I'm not having sex." Chas neglected to tell his dad that he had tried some marijuana recently and he did have a new girl friend. Her name was Mia. But they weren't having sex yet. "I'll be fine, and you won't have to worry. If you want, you can have some of your friends spy on me."

"It's not that I don't trust you. I do. I just know that you're being bombarded with all kinds of temptations these days. And it must be really difficult refusing to take part. You want to be a part of a group, and they are doing certain things, and if you don't do them too, they call you names like nerdy, sissy…. I don't know what the terms are these days. You tell me."

"My friends are more into science projects and getting good grades so they can get into college. Their big thing and mine is getting high SAT scores. And doing drugs won't get me there."

"But how would you get around? You can't live in Phoenix without a car."

"I can take the bus everywhere. And maybe I could buy a clunker to get me to the grocery store and back."

"Chas, if what you're telling me is true, you are mature beyond your years. I'll think about it."

Chas put a leash on Sugar to take her for a walk. He thought he had made a good case for his cause. Maybe he should be a lawyer, he thought. No, he didn't like most lawyers. And he wanted to be an engineer and design stuff like bridges and tall buildings. He opened the door and took Sugar down the front walk, her tail wagging with happiness. Dogs are so easy to please, Chas thought.

Chapter 44
Celeste's Time Is Here

Celeste was in the kitchen the next morning feeding the dogs. As they were milling about her, eager for their morning meal, she felt a tug in her abdomen. Not thinking too much about it, she cleaned up the kitchen, putting the breakfast dishes in the twenty-year-old dishwasher. *This thing is probably not going to last all that long. That's all Mom needs, to have the dishwasher go out.* But then, she thought, *you can survive without a dishwasher.* She went into her bedroom to straighten up and make the bed and felt another tug. She couldn't explain it but it felt like something was happening in there.

"Celeste, I have to go to the grocery store and the drug store this morning. Is there anything you need?"

"Mom, I don't think you should go. I think my labor is starting."

"What's happening? Are you having pains?"

"No. Not really. Just a pulling, or tugging. I can't describe it."

"Has your water broken?"

"No. Nothing like that. I think I'll call Michelle. She'll know what to do."

"I think that's a good idea. You're probably just starting labor and it'll be awhile before this little guy makes his debut. I'll be back in thirty minutes."

Celeste was nervous now. The time was here. Was she ready for this marathon, she wondered to herself? She'd better be. There was no going back. She was about to become a mother very soon. She punched in Michelle's number on her cell phone and Michelle answered immediately. "Michelle, I'm having these funny pains, like twinges. Does this mean the baby's coming?" Celeste asked in a higher pitched voice than normal.

"It most likely does. How far apart are these twinges?"

"I'd say twenty minutes apart. And they hardly hurt."

"Are you ready? Is your room ready?"

"I am and it is. Let's get this over with."

"No, don't think that way," said Michelle over the phone. "This is the most wonderful moment of your life. You'll see."

"I'll believe that once I'm holding little Rafael in my arms, but getting there is gonna be a trip."

"It won't be that bad. Now, keep timing your contractions and when they're fifteen minutes apart, I'll come over to your house. That may take a while, by the way. But if your water breaks, call me right away. That would mean that the baby is due any minute. Got that?'

"Yeah, I think so. I'll be fine. But maybe you should be here now."

"You will be fine. You're going to sail right through this. I know you are," said Michelle. "And I live only a couple of blocks away, so I can be there in minutes. Don't worry." As Celeste closed her phone, she felt another twinge. She checked the clock and made note of the time. I had better call Ramon and Dad and alert them that the baby is on his way. What a happy event, she thought.

As Jasmine was driving down Glendale Road to the grocery store, her cell phone rang. Her thoughts had been on Celeste and the baby. She checked the number on the phone and saw that it was Bill calling. Well, she would just have to call him back later. She never talked on her cell phone while she was driving, and she had more important things on her mind right now.

She went into the grocery store and got a cart and started putting in the items on her list: milk, butter, whole-wheat bread, deli ham slices and cheese, vegetables, lettuce, broccoli. Oh, she had better get some orange juice, and did she have enough coffee? With the baby vigil starting they would probably need lots of that. And then it dawned on her: she was going to be a grandmother. How exciting, on the one hand. But that meant that she was really getting older. What would the baby call her when he started to talk? "Grandma"? No, she really hated that moniker. "Nanna"? She didn't like that one either. When she was a child, she only really knew her father's mother who lived in the same town, and she called her "Grandmama." Her maternal grandmother lived in Mexico, and Jasmine had never met her. Maybe she should change that now. Go to Mexico and find her. If she was still alive. What was the word for "grandmother" in Spanish? she wondered. And why didn't her mother tell Jasmine to use the Spanish name for her grandmother when she was little? I guess she was trying to be so American. She would look it up when she got home. She saw some Champagne, sparkling wine, on sale for four ninety-nine a bottle. This is perfect; we can toast the new arrival, she thought.

She pushed the grocery cart to her car and, unlocking the back, started putting the groceries in. She then took the cart back to the designated area and walked back to her car. As she sat in the front seat, she thought she had better call Bill. Everything would be a little chaotic back at the house. It would be better to talk to him now.

His cell phone rang several times before he picked up. "Hi, Bill. I just came out of the grocery store. How are you?" she asked after he answered the phone. "You called?"

"Yes, I did. I haven't talked with you in quite a while. Is everything all right with you? How's Celeste? Any signs of the baby coming?"

"As a matter of fact, the baby's on his way. Celeste started labor this morning. Although both you and I know first babies usually take a long time to show their heads to the world."

"That's true. Two days almost for Chas. I thought she was never going to deliver our baby. But then I spent most of the time in the waiting room with the other expectant fathers. These days dads are in the delivery room helping out, and that's as it should be. I sure am glad I've never have to go through child-birth."

"Sh. Don't tell that to Celeste. She's pretty nervous about this. And it looks like we'll all be helping out."

"Look, Jasmine, I want to get together with you in the next couple of days. I have some things that I want to talk to you about. I know you're busy with Celeste and the baby and I guess you have a houseful these days. But if we could steal away for a cup of coffee...."

"Sure. I'd say day after tomorrow. She'll be in labor all day today, and the baby is likely to be born tomorrow. I'll give you a call. What a happy thought. I'm going to be a grandma."

The contractions were fifteen minutes apart now. Celeste had called Ramon and he was on his way, as was her father. Where is Mom? she wondered. She's taking a long time at the market. But just then Jasmine's car pulled into the driveway. Jasmine got out of the car and grabbed several bags from the back. "Mom what took you so long? The contractions are coming faster; oh, there's another one, oh ...ow ....and that one hurt."

"Is Michelle coming? Honey you'd better go and lie down."

"No, I don't want to lie down. It feels better to be walking around. And yes, Michelle is on her way." Celeste had called her mid-wife again and told her that she wanted her here with her. This baby was coming, and she couldn't do it alone. She went to the back door to let Blondie and Chance inside, and they started following Celeste as she paced back and forth.

"And what about Ramon and your father?"

"Yes, they're coming, too," Celeste said as she walked into the living room with the two dogs following, looking up at her expectantly.

"Maybe we'd better keep the dogs outside. They're likely to get in the way," Jasmine said as she started putting the groceries away.

"No, I want them here. They calm me down." Celeste was reclining on the living room couch with the dogs, one on either side. "We can put them out when the time is near. Ohhh, … Mom it's really starting to hurt."

"That just means that your cervix is opening up for the baby to pass through," said Jasmine as she walked into the living room with a concerned look on her face.

Michelle's car pulled up in front. She got out carrying a black bag and came up the walkway to the front door. Celeste saw her coming through the front window and opened the door before she could ring the bell.

"I'm so glad you're here. I was getting worried."

"Not to worry," said Michelle. "I want you to go into your bedroom. We need to check to see how far you've dilated."

"Hi Michelle. Looks like we might have a baby soon. Yes?" said Jasmine.

"Hi Jasmine. Well, we'll see," said Michelle as the dogs were circling her, sniffing and greeting her. "Jasmine, we need to put these dogs outside."

"That's what I thought," said Jasmine. And just as she had herded Blondie and Chance out the back door, she heard the doorbell ring. She went to the front door and Ramon was standing there fidgeting, waiting to come in.

"How is she? Is she really in labor?" asked Ramon.

"Yes, come on in. She's in her bedroom. Michelle is checking her progress."

"Can I go back there?"

"I don't know why not. You're the father."

Celeste's father arrived shortly after Ramon and Jasmine sat him down in the kitchen with a cup of coffee, He then got up and paced the floor as the screams from Celeste's room grew louder. Towards evening, he could hardly stand it. Jasmine told him to take the dogs for a walk after she fed them their evening meal. She prepared sandwiches for everyone. Later that evening, close to midnight, Michelle came out of the room and said that the baby's head was crowning and would they like to see the birth of a beautiful baby boy?

After scrubbing thoroughly and putting on hospital gowns, Richard and Jasmine walked into Celeste's bedroom. Ramon was sitting beside Celeste, holding her hand. As another contraction came, he told her to breathe, breathe hard and push. Jasmine could see the baby's head beginning to emerge from between Celeste's legs. Jasmine turned to Richard and exclaimed, "What a miracle this is." And just as the words came out of her mouth, Richard fell to the floor in a dead faint.

"Here, give him this and take him into the living room," said Michelle as she handed Jasmine smelling salts.

"You're prepared for everything, aren't you, Michelle?"

"It's pretty common for the men to faint, so yes, I'm prepared."

Jasmine revived Richard and led him into the living room, giving him a cold cloth for his forehead and settling him on the couch. "I guess you're not up to this tonight. Just stay here and relax. I'll come and get you when we have a baby."

As Jasmine walked back into the birthing room, she saw Rafael come sliding into the world, all slippery with a white fluid covering his little body. Michelle clamped and cut the cord and laid the baby on Celeste's chest for her to look at.

"Oh my god, here he is. Ramon, he's beautiful. Look at him," said Celeste as she held Rafael for the first time. Rafael then let out a whopping scream that startled everyone.

"He has lungs," said Ramon. "We know that for sure."

Richard, hearing the baby scream, came back into the room and observed the tableau before him; his daughter Celeste, new mother, holding her newborn infant, smiling like he had never seen her smile before. "I guess I'm a granddad," he finally said very quietly. And his face broke out in a wide smile.

An hour later, after mother and baby were settled in and asleep, Richard and Jasmine, exhausted, sat in the living room. Michelle was gone, her job finished with another successful home birth. Ramon had decided he was staying the night to be close to Celeste in case she might need him. He put some blankets and a pillow on the floor beside her bed and was soon fast asleep.

"We have some Champagne, I almost forgot. Let's open it and have a toast," said Jasmine.

She went to the kitchen, and took two of her best crystal glasses from her china cabinet, and went to the refrigerator to get the bubbly.

"Here, Richard, you open it. I hate opening these bottles."

Richard, using a napkin, pulled and twisted the cork and it flew off and landed on the other side of the room. "This isn't really Champagne, you know," he said as he poured the two glasses. "It's sparkling wine."

"I do know that, Richard," murmured Jasmine as she raised her glass in a toast. "Here's to parenthood. The toughest job in the world. But it looks like we've been successful."

"Yes, he's a beautiful baby. And Celeste is so happy. I have never seen her glow like she did tonight." Richard took another drink of his wine.

They sat in silence for awhile, each contemplating the past and wondering what the future would bring.

"I wouldn't have missed this for anything. I'm so glad I came. And I think Celeste will make a great mom. She had a wonderful role model."

"You're giving me credit for something. I can't believe it," said Jasmine somewhat sarcastically.

"Look, Jasmine. I am truly sorry about what happened with us. It was more about my parents than anything. I truly loved you."

"Let's talk about the future and let the past go into oblivion. It's done and we can't change it now. We both made mistakes. And so here we are in the present."

"Are you happy, Jasmine?"

Jasmine finished her glass of sparkling wine, poured herself a second glass, and asked Richard if he wanted more. "Am I happy? Well, it sounds ridiculous, being that I don't have a job and some days don't know where the money is coming from to pay the bills, but yes, I am happy. I think more accurately, I'm hopeful."

"I am glad for you. And I think you're right about the future. Especially when we have beautiful babies like Rafael." Richard raised his glass for another toast. "Here's to Rafael."

And they both drank to that.

Chapter 45
Chance

I knew something was up when I saw Celeste pacing back and forth like a she- wolf in distress. So I decided that I would stay as close to her as I could and help her. That's what the pack is for. But then other people started coming into our den and this one woman, I didn't know her, said that we should be banished to the back yard. I couldn't believe it. After all these months, waiting for the newborn to come, we weren't even going to be allowed to watch and be a part of it. You are asking how I knew there was a newborn on the way. I could smell it. My nose tells me everything.

As it grew dark, I heard Celeste screaming and I couldn't help her. I felt so bad. I paced back and forth with Blondie at my heels. And the screaming got worse. I went to the door and scratched. I know I'm not supposed to do that but I couldn't help it. And then I did something I have never done before: I howled. I don't know where that came from but I say again, I couldn't help it. The screams were piercing my ears and I was hurting. There was just some primal part of me that said I had to howl. And then Blondie joined me and we were both howling like a pack of wolves in the forest. I guess we must have been pretty loud, because somebody shouted out the back door to knock it off. I don't know if it came from my house or the one that is really close by in back of us.

I decided there was nothing to be done, so I crawled into my dog house and Blondie came in with me and we huddled together to wait it out. I guess I must have finally fallen asleep, because when I awoke, it was quiet but still dark. I walked out into the yard to relieve myself on my favorite Palo Verde tree and then went back to the dog house. It was cold, very cold and dark. No moon that night, and you can't even see the stars in the city on a dark night for some reason.

Early in the morning Jasmine opened the door and came out to give us both hugs. She brought us into the house, and we wagged our tails and licked her face. Dogs never carry a grudge. What happened last night is in the past. We have to move on.

Jasmine fed us. We heard Celeste calling from her bedroom, and then Jasmine put leashes on both of us and took us into Celeste's room. We looked around and didn't see anything at first. Celeste was sitting up in her bed, looking pleased with herself. But then I heard a noise from the basket next to her bed and it started crying loudly and then Celeste reached in and pulled out a puppy. No, a human puppy—I guess humans call them "babies." She held the baby to her breast and the baby started to suckle, just like Blondie's puppies used to do. I wanted to get up closer, but Jasmine held me back.

Oh well, I guess our star is falling. Nobody will pay attention to us anymore with the new baby in the house. It was like that when Blondie had puppies. Nobody wanted to play with me anymore. When people came to the house they only wanted to see Blondie's puppies. But I have to remember one thing. Within a few weeks, people came and took those puppies away, except Sugar. And I was king again. I can't wait for someone to come and take this crying machine away so that we can get the attention again that we deserve.

Chapter 46
Baby in the House

It is true, dog is man's best friend. However, a dog is as much an animal as man still is; albeit man's brain is more developed, humans lose control in times of passion, and humans are one of the most violent animals on earth. Dogs have emotions, too, and can and will act on them with the same impunity as humans with less control. That being said, watch your children around dogs at all times. Especially very young children. Young children can be rude, poking at a dog's eye and pulling on its ears. The dog may be tolerant for a time, but when it reaches its boiling point, it can and will bite, can even kill a baby. A dog also feels displacement when a new baby comes into the household. The dog has gotten all of the attention to this point, was treated like a child in the household, and now it may be banished to the back yard, with all of the attention going to the new baby. Simply put, a dog can be jealous.

The key is never to leave your small children unattended with your dog. And as the child matures, teach him or her how to respect the family pet. The child should know not to take the dog's toy away from it. The child should not play with the dog's food while it is eating. And the child should learn respect for the dog's space and not follow the dog wherever it goes. The dog needs to have a private place where it can get away from the child or children where it will not be pestered, where the dog can rest and eat without little hands poking at it constantly.

As children mature, they can be of assistance in training the dog. In that way the children will learn how to care for their pets humanely and will carry that forward into the future with their own families.

Jasmine didn't get to bed that night until three in the morning, but in spite of the lack of sleep she awoke at eight, with the dogs lying beside her. Oh, what a night, she thought as she petted Blondie, who was snuggled up close to her side. Chance was at the bottom of the bed, seeming to be out of sorts for some reason.

"Chance, Blondie, we have a new little being in our midst. A new baby boy. What a joy for all of us."

Chance looked at her as if he was saying, speak for yourself; just another distraction.

Jasmine got out of bed and put on her robe and called the dogs. "Come on, you two. Time to go out, both of you."

She then went into the kitchen to prepare the dogs' morning breakfast. She listened for any sounds coming from Celeste's room. Better not disturb them. And she remembered that Ramon had spent the night. Surely he was still in there. Could they still be sleeping? It was close to nine o'clock. She would have some breakfast and, if she didn't hear anything, she would knock on the door to see if everything was all right.

After a quick bowl of cereal, she couldn't stand it any longer. She tiptoed to Celeste's room and knocked on the door. Celeste answered, "Come in. We're all here, the three of us."

Jasmine opened the door and saw Celeste getting up and getting dressed. Ramon was holding the baby, rocking him back and forth.

"Isn't he the most beautiful baby you have ever seen?" Ramon asked as he looked at Jasmine.

"Yes, I would agree with that," said Jasmine as she walked in and peered over Ramon's shoulder. "Are you all right, Celeste? Are you feeling okay?"

"I feel wonderful. I feel strong. I'm a little sore but I'm not tired at all, even though I was up most of the night."

"Take it easy. You can have a nap this afternoon. What can I fix you for breakfast? How about some scrambled eggs and toast. Does that sound good to you?"

"Yes, I am so hungry."

"It's important for you to eat good healthy meals when you're nursing. And drink lots of fluids."

"Yes, Mother. I know all about it.

"I'll fix some for you too, Ramon."

"No, that's all right. I have to go back to the hotel. I found an apartment for us yesterday, and I have to sign the papers today. And then I'm going to have to scare up some furniture."

"Ramon, that's wonderful! You didn't say anything about it yesterday," said Celeste.

"I think you were a little preoccupied yesterday, honey. It's a two-bedroom, one being for the nursery. I'll take you shopping for baby furniture as soon as you feel up to it. We can move in next week if you like."

She's leaving me, thought Jasmine. I've only had her here for a few months and off she goes. But I guess that's as it should be. "How far away is the apartment, Ramon?"

"It's close. About a mile, I would say. It's a really nice apartment with a fireplace and a beautiful kitchen. You'll approve, I know you will, Mom."

He's calling me Mom. So what is that? But I guess Ramon is soon to become my son-in-law. The next event in this household will be a wedding. Oh, my. It's hard keeping up with all of this.

Later in the day, while Celeste and the baby were sleeping, Jasmine thought about Bill and decided to give him a call. He answered on the first ring.

"So do you have a new member of your family?" he asked.

"Yes. You should see him. He's just gorgeous. Dark hair and lots of it, pink skin, tiny fingers and toes and a little rosebud of a mouth that is constantly looking for food when he isn't wailing. Oh, yes, and he has great lungs. You can hear him a block away—well, almost."

"Sounds like the perfect baby," said Bill. "When would you like to meet? I'm trying to wrap things up here, but I could get away this afternoon. I would like to see you. It's been so long."

"Only a week. That would be fine. There's this new coffee shop down on Glendale and seventh. Want to meet me there at one?"

Bill said yes, and Jasmine thought she had better shower and change clothes. It was 11:30, and she was still in her pajamas. After her shower she put on her favorite jeans and a pretty mauve knit top. As she was putting on her makeup, of which she wore little these days, just some eyeliner and lip color, she wondered what Bill wanted to talk with her about. But then she probably knew. He was moving to Seattle, and he most likely wanted her to go with him. Did she want to do that? She still wasn't sure. But having the new baby was swaying her to stay in Phoenix.

When Jasmine walked into the coffee shop, she saw Bill sitting at a corner table in the back. He was dressed in jeans and a forest-green Oxford shirt and looked even more handsome than ever. "Are you meeting someone?" Jasmine said with a wink. "I'd like to be that someone if you are."

"Hey, there you are. Have a seat. I've just ordered coffee, but they have sandwiches if you're hungry."

"I'm always hungry. Especially after last night. You should see the baby. Well, here, I have pictures." And she took out her small camera and paged through to photos of the baby wrapped in a soft receiving blanket, taken soon after his birth. He was sucking his thumb in one, and the other photo he had gone to sleep and looked so peaceful. "He looks like Ramon, don't you think? Oh, that's right you haven't met Ramon. Well, he's a handsome guy and he and Celeste are a great couple together. They'll be a great team."

"Speaking of a team. That's why I wanted to meet with you. I'm leaving next week for Seattle. I guess you knew that. It's not ideal. If I had a choice I would stay here, but I just haven't found any work here and I'm running out of money."

"This job market sucks. I'm in the same boat, you know. Every job that I apply for there are a hundred applicants, and they choose the one with the lowest salary demands and sometimes the least experience."

"Exactly. Well, so this job in Seattle is a good opportunity for me. I will be in management and I'll be able to move up in the company. I think they appreciate my experience, and they are paying me handsomely."

"That's great, Bill. So how's Chas handling this?"

"Not well, as you can imagine. He's refusing to go with me."

"But he has to go. He can't stay here by himself."

"Well, we talked about that, and he convinced me that he could stay here in the house, with Sugar, and finish out his senior year in high school. He's seventeen, and he seems to have a good head on his shoulders."

"But Bill, won't you worry? How can you leave him alone?"

"Yeah, I'll worry. But his grandma, is here and she'll look in on him."

"And I can too, Bill. I would be happy to do that. I'll have him over for dinner often and check to see that he's doing okay."

"That's really sweet of you. But what I would really like you to do is come with me to Seattle."

Jasmine knew that was coming. She had grown to love Bill, but move with him to a new city? But then she didn't have a job here, either. Maybe she could find something in Seattle as well.

"Bill, I don't know what to say."

"Just say yes. I love you, Jasmine. I know we haven't had much time together, but I think we have similar ideas, and our politics are the same. That's a big one," Bill chuckled. "And you like the outdoors and hiking and skiing like I do. We could have a wonderful life together adventuring in the mountains of the Northwest. The world, in fact. We could go to Europe, climb in the Alps, and the Andes in South America. There is so much to see and do."

"What you're offering is difficult to pass up. But Bill I have my life here. I'm a grandmother now, and I need to stay here with Celeste and help out with the baby. I want to be part of his life, too." Jasmine looked into her coffee cup and then took a drink. "You know, I never knew my maternal grandmother. She lives in Mexico, if she's still alive. My father's mother was somewhat aloof, never approving of her son's marriage to the daughter of a Hispanic field worker. She never forgave him." Jasmine paused for a moment, sipping her coffee, and then she looked straight into Bill's eyes. "I want those strong family ties with my daughter and her family. I've never realized until now how important that is. Celeste and I have formed a bond that I didn't know was possible. And I have to say this all came about because of the calamity of the recession. If we hadn't lost our jobs, Celeste would be in Hollywood, pursuing an acting career, working part-time jobs, and I would be still tied to my fifty-hour work week."

"What about this. I'll go up there and work. I'll find an apartment and work as hard as I can. Then you can stay here for awhile, and come and visit, especially this summer when it's beastly hot here."

"That might work," said Jasmine. Her sandwich had been brought by the waiter and she couldn't wait to dig into it.

After Jasmine put the sandwich down, Bill took her hand. "Look, I know how it must be with a new grandbaby. I would expect you to want to stay close to Celeste right now. But what would happen if Celeste moved away? Would you be following her and her husband to a new city?"

Jasmine had never thought about that. She told Bill about Ramon and how he was starting a new restaurant in Phoenix. They could possibly move away. Ramon even said that after the first restaurant gets off the ground and is successful, they could start a second one in another city.

"You have a point. I hadn't thought that through yet. But this grandmother thing is pretty new to me. Give me a break."

"Yes, I know. When can I come over to see the new baby?"

"How about tomorrow? I'll have to ask Celeste, of course."

"That'll be great. Think about all that we talked about. You don't have to give me an answer today. I know this is a big decision."

"Bill, I love you, too. But I don't know you that well yet to make this kind of decision. If my heart were to decide, and I wasn't a new grandmom, I would say yes. But we still have a lot to work out. One problem that you haven't faced yet, is how Chas would take to this idea."

"He loves you."

"He can say that now, but if he thought I was taking the place of his mother, that might be an entirely different story."

"I see what you mean. It's all still too raw for him," said Bill. He took a sip of his coffee and thought for a few minutes. "If he gets to know you better over time that would be best."

And they left it at that. Jasmine went home, getting there at about three o'clock. Celeste was sitting on the couch nursing Rafael with the dogs sitting on either side, as happy as can be.

"Looks like family time. Be careful of the dogs. They can become jealous and even though you wouldn't think so, could attack the baby."

"I know Mom, I read up on it on the Internet."

"Bill's coming over tomorrow to see the baby. Is that okay with you?

"I would love that."

Epilogue

asmine lay in bed, propped on three soft pillows, reading her favorite mystery novel, with Chance and Blondie snoozing beside her in complete happiness. Every night now, after a day of writing, she would call the dogs into the house to the reading room, as she called it. She would climb on the bed first to secure enough room for herself and then call the dogs to jump up and lie down next to her. If the weather was warm they would keep their distance from her, but when it was colder they would snuggle as close as they could.

It was early May, and the weather was warming up again as expected for this time of year in Phoenix. Jasmine had turned on the ceiling fan to cool the room. It silently rotated above them as they settled in.

So much had happened since baby Rafael had been born. Celeste moved out of the extra bedroom that had been the birthing room for her first grandchild and into an apartment with her partner and soon-to-be husband Ramon. They came over often as they lived close by. And Jasmine was asked to baby-sit Rafael often, which she didn't mind at all. It gave her a chance to be with her grandson and provided a parenting break for Celeste and Ramon. Yes, much to Jasmine's delight, Ramon took fatherhood very seriously and had an active part in taking care of his son. He even changed dirty diapers.

The wedding was being planned for June, of course, and many family members on all sides would be in attendance along with their many friends. The list was at 150 at this point, and Jasmine and Celeste were just figuring out how they were going to pay for it. Hopefully Richard, as the father of the bride, would come through for them.

Ramon had started his new restaurant, Ramon's Tropical Sizzle, featuring native foods from the Dominican Republic, and it was already a huge success. The restaurant was full every evening, and the lunch crowd was large as well. It was located near the new light rail station at Central and Indian School. Ramon was trying to get Celeste as well as Jasmine involved in the business. They had already designed and created the web site, and Celeste was working on some promotional ideas.

Jasmine heard from Bill often and even took a trip to Seattle to visit and do some skiing. She liked Seattle, but the weather was a bit damp and cold for her. She decided for now that she did not want to live there with Bill. But that could change. She had to admit that she missed him very much, and they talked almost every day.

For the time being Jasmine was the happiest she had been in years and she didn't know why. She had no job and lived in her austere little house in the middle of Phoenix having to make a little bit of money stretch a long way. But she often counted the pluses in her life, thinking of all of the people who were without homes, as well as jobs. People whose children were deployed in the wars. She felt so fortunate.

She put her book aside for a few minutes, petting the dogs. They looked up at her with those big, endearing eyes, and Chance put his paw on her arm. She felt so safe here, like nothing was going to harm her or the dogs. She looked at the expanse of the bed and how it was taken up by the dogs. There was really no room for anyone else in that bed. But then this was the way she liked it. She would rather sleep with dogs.

Note from the Author:

I started writing this novel in 2008, the beginning of the recession, when I was laid off from my job as a computer programmer. As I was completing the manuscript I was diagnosed with a very aggressive breast cancer, causing me to put the book aside for a couple of years. Instead I wrote a diary and a cancer blog, www.alittlerain.com. After six months of chemo, removal of my right breast, and another month of radiation, I was cancer free, as I am today. At that point, not knowing what I was going to do with the unfinished manuscript *She Sleeps with Dogs*, I let it sit for several more months. I wanted to publish this book in the traditional way, the soft-cover hard copy, but I knew how difficult that would be; getting an agent and a publisher these days is a long haul. So then I realized that many books these days are being e-published. Why not do that with this book? So that is what I am doing. It is unfortunate that it will not be in paper format for those who do not have electronic devices. Also, my only other regret is that I will not be having book signings in book stores, which I love to do.

zSome of this story, as I mentioned, is true. I did have a big red Doberman. As an unemployed person I did experience difficulties with storms and sewers backing up and many other obstacles. However, unlike Jasmine, I do not have a daughter. I have a son who lives in the San Francisco Bay Area and is the light of my life.

I want to thank my editor, Judith Humbert, for polishing this manuscript and righting all of the wrongs. I couldn't have done this without her. I also want to thank two writing friends, Pat Klemme and Jill Wingell, who took the time out of their busy lives to read *She Sleeps with Dogs* and give me the positive feed-back that I needed to bring this book to publication.

Phoenix, Arizona 2013

Post Script 2015

My dream has come true. This wonderful story will be in print form.

Made in the USA
San Bernardino, CA
16 April 2017